EDUCATING THE CONSUMER-CITIZEN

A History of the Marriage of Schools, Advertising, and Media

Sociocultural, Political, and Historical Studies in Education
Joel Spring, Editor

EDUCATING THE CONSUMER-CITIZEN

A History of the Marriage of Schools, Advertising, and Media

Joel Spring
New School University

LEA LAWRENCE ERLBAUM ASSOCIATES, PUBLISHERS

2003   Mahwah, New Jersey   London

Lawrence Erlbaum Associates, Inc., Publishers
10 Industrial Avenue
Mahwah, New Jersey 07430

Cover design by Kathryn Houghtaling Lacey

Library of Congress Cataloging-in-Publication Data

Spring, Joel H.
  Educating the consumer-citizen : a history of the marriage of schools, advertising,
and media /   Joel Spring
    p.   cm. — (Sociocultural, political, and historical studies in education)
  ISBN 0-8058-4273-X (c : alk. paper) — ISBN 0-8058-4274-8 (pbk. : alk. paper)
  1. Consumer behavior—United States—History.   2. Consumer education—United
States—History.   5. Advertising—United States—History.   4. Mass media—United
States—History.   I. Title.   II. Series.

HF5415.33.U6 S67   2002
306.3—dc21
                                                                2002192790
                                                                      CIP

Printed in the United States of America
10   9   8   7   6   5   4   3   2   1

Contents

Preface

Consumerism is the dominant American ideology of the 21st century. "Shop 'til you drop" is the clarion call of our age. The triumph of consumerism was made possible by the related actions of schools, advertising, and media. This book illustrates the history of that joint endeavor to create a consumerist ideology and ensure its central place in American life. Like any history, this story is not a straight line from one time period to another. There was no master plan or conspiracy. However, through the twists, turns, and contradictions of life, consumerism now rules the American economic system and society.

I begin this history in chapter 1 by defining *consumerist ideology* and *consumer-citizen* and discussing their 19th-century origins in schools, children's literature, commercialization of American cities, advertising, newspapers, and development of department stores. In chapter 2, I examine the development of the home economics profession and its impact on the education of women as consumers and the creation of an American cuisine typified by Jell-O and Wonder Bread in home economics courses, school cafeterias, hospitals, and the food industry. The new professions of advertising and home economics created public images of the new woman as a consumer. In chapter 3, I discuss the crisis in White male identity in the late 19th and early 20th centuries and its resolution in male identification with professional sports, high school sports, cowboy images, and advertising images of the clean-shaven businessman. In this chapter, I also trace how a teenage consumer market was created when the high school became a mass institution and attempted to control male sexuality through sports, sex education courses, and ritualized dating practices.

Inherent in consumerist ideology is the dictate that commercial leisure, such as movies, radio, and TV, should spur people to consume more, work harder, and live moral lives. In chapter 4, I explore the interrelationship and conflicts that arose between educators and movie executives with the simultaneous growth of the movie industry and the high school in the early 20th century. Movies competed with school instruction and contributed to the sexual revolution among youth as movie houses became centers of ritualized teenage dating and movie stars provided lavish consumer images. By the 1930s, this tension was complicated when radio revolutionized consumerism by integrating advertising and entertainment. In the 1930s, educators worried that commercial radio would decrease their control over national culture, use advertising to manipulate student minds, and teach violence.

An important advance in consumerist ideology was the attempt to create a spontaneous association in the public mind among consumption, democracy, free enterprise, and Americanism. In chapter 5, I discuss the effort by business groups, patriotic organizations, advertisers, and educators to create these associations through public relations methods, censorship of textbooks and comic books, and the purging of so-called *radical teachers*. In the 1950s, schools, TV, and the advertising profession played leading roles in creating an image of the ideal American home and housewife based on the consumption of endless new products. This consumer image became central to America's anticommunist ideology of the 1950s.

The consumer image of the early 1950s was primarily of White Americans. In chapter 6, I discuss how the civil rights movement endeavored to integrate previously excluded groups into the consumer society. Targeting textbooks, school curricula, media, and advertising companies, civil rights groups attempted to erase negative images of cultural minorities and replace them with positive images. The result was the racial integration of the consumer market. Also women's groups demanded image changes in textbooks, school curricula, media, and advertising. The result was a changed image of women in the consumer market. In the 1960s, *Sesame Street* revolutionized children's TV by combining education and entertainment with efforts to teach racial tolerance and prepare children for school. *Sesame Street* also taught consumerism to preschool children by marketing product spinoffs in the form of dolls, games, videos, and books. *Sesame Street* epitomizes the marriage of schools, advertising, and media in creating an integrated consumer market.

In chapter 7, I conclude the book by demonstrating how the evolution of the marriage of schools, advertising, and media has resulted in the 21st-century consumer society. Advertising is now present in schools, and schools specifically teach consumerism in Family and Consumer Science courses. Global teenage culture is unified by consumerism. Teenage identity centers on brand names and icons. The combination of education, advertising, and entertainment in textbooks, media, and theme parks educates children into consumerist ideology. Symbolic of this marriage is the involvement of fast-food franchises such as McDonald's, Pizza Hut, KFC, Taco Bell, and Burger King in education and entertainment. Fast-food education represents the fruition of American cuisine as initiated by 19th- and 20th-century home economists, integration of schools into the consumer market, and the advertising dream of combining education, entertainment, and shopping.

ACKNOWLEDGMENTS

My daughter, Dawn Spring, drew my attention to consumerism while she was writing a film script on the appearance of middle-class female shoplifters after the first department stores opened in the 19th century. The film script was her master's degree project in Media Studies at the New School. Our conversations led me to examine the burgeoning literature on the history, impact, and ideology of consumerism in contemporary society. I explored the topic by examining the history of advertising, the economic justifications for consumerism, and the role of media in my New School courses on The History and Dissemination of Ideas and Culture and Transnationalism. In these classes, we concluded that America's contribution to world culture was consumerism, advertising, Hollywood movies, mass media, and processed, packaged, and fast foods.

During these investigations, I found a close relationship between schools and the development of consumerism in U.S. society that paralleled the work I did in a previous book, *Images of American Life: A History of Ideological Management in Schools, Movies, Radio, and Television*. Here I explored the mutually influential relationships among professional educators, school officials, and the development of the movie and broadcasting industries. *Images of American Life* is now out of print, and I have used some of the material on educators and media, as well as textbooks from that book, in this current work on consumerism.

Again I would like to thank my daughter, Dawn, for her suggestion to explore the history of consumerism and our many conversations on the topic. I would also like to thank Lawrence Erlbaum Associates' external reviewers, Debra Merskin, University of Oregon, and William Pinar, Louisiana State University, for their helpful comments and suggestions. I would like to thank my wife and editor, Naomi Silverman, for teaching me how to write and for her editorial insights. Also I would like to thank Naomi for all the fun times we have had shopping.

Chapter 1

Horace Mann Meets the Wizard of Oz

**PART ONE: INTRODUCTION
AND OVERVIEW OF THE BOOK**

"A survey of American school children finds that 96 percent could identify Ronald McDonald. The only fictional character with a higher degree of recognition was Santa Claus. . . . The Golden Arches are now more widely recognized than the Christian cross," Eric Schlooser reported in *Fast Food Nation.*[1] On arriving in the United States from Bangladesh at the age of 8, Dewan Kazi knew two English words: *hello* and *Coca-Cola.*[2] The Golden Arches, Ronald McDonald, and Coca-Cola symbolize the worldwide spread of the icons of consumerism.

The prelude to a mass consumer society began in the early 19th-century society when schools, newspapers, national postal service, and advertising created a common culture among Americans mainly of European descent. Before discussing these origins of mass consumer society, I would like to explain the basic premises of this book and outline the historical argument that is presented about how the marriage of schools, advertising, and media contributed to the development of a consumer society. I also explain the ideology of *consumerism* and the meaning of *consumer-citizen.*

A premise of this book is that consumerism is the dominant ideology of the United States and the driving force of the global economy. Mass-consumer culture integrates consumerism into all aspects of life from birth to death, including, but not limited to, education, leisure time activities, the popular arts, the home, travel, and personal imagination. Mass-consumer culture captures the fantasy world of people with brand names and fashions

1

that promise personal transformation, the vicarious thrill of imagining the glamorous lives of media celebrities, the promise of escape from hard work through packaged travel and cruises to an envisioned paradise, and the idea that in America everyone has an equal opportunity to consume. When I ask current American college students how they would introduce an immigrant to American culture, the response without exception is, "I would take them to the mall!"

The most important aspect of mass-consumer culture is the ideology of *consumerism*. This ideology was articulated in the late 19th and early 20th centuries with the appearance of industrial and agricultural abundance. As articulated by the turn-of-the-century economist Simon Patten, consumerism reconciled the Puritan virtue of hard work with the abundance of consumer goods. From the Puritan standpoint, the danger of abundant goods was more leisure time and possible moral decay. This fear was expressed in the folk saying, "Idle hands . . . [are the] devil's tools."[3] In Simon Patten's 1907 book, *The New Basis of Civilization*, he argued that the consumption of new products and leisure-time activities would spur people to work harder. In Patten's words, "The new morality does not consist in saving, but in expanding consumption."[4] Patten explained, "In the course of consumption . . . the new wants become complex . . . [as a result the] worker steadily and cheerfully chooses the deprivations of this week . . . they advance onto a period of restraint and morality, Puritan in essence. . . . Their investment in to-morrow's goods enables society to increase its output and to broaden its productive areas."[5]

The professionalization and expansion of advertising in the late 19th and early 20th centuries was a key contribution of the United States to the creation of a mass-consumer culture. Advertising prompted desires for new products; it convinced consumers that existing products were unfashionable and, therefore, obsolete; it made brand names into playthings in personal fantasies. The advertising profession transformed the capitalist model of buyers making rational choices in a free market into a consumerist model where the buyer was driven by irrational emotions associated with particular brand names and/or products.

In chapter 2, I explore one major theme of this book: While advertising professionalized, home economists were advocating reforms of American diets and families by introducing home economics courses in schools, starting school cafeterias, and linking greater freedom for women from household drudgery through processed and packaged foods. Jell-O epitomized the new American cuisine as it became a staple in school cafeterias, hospital kitchens, and family cooking. I pick up this thread of the story in chapter 7, when I discuss how, by the 1950s, McDonald's, Burger King, Taco Bell, and other fast-food franchises had joined with prepared and processed food manufacturers to define American cuisine and provide the American family with a quick meal. Today these fast-food franchises have not only entered school cafeterias, but also sponsor their own educational programs. (Burger King Academies) and (Pizza Hut's BOOKIT!) reading program typify what I call fast-food education and the marriage of schools, advertising, and media.

A second major theme is how, in the first half of the 20th century, schools and advertising joined radio and TV in educating workers and consumers. This theme is discussed in chapter 4. Movies were an important form of commodified leisure that captured the fantasy world of workers and helped them escape the drudgery of the office and shop floor. Simon Patten had predicted that people would work harder to consume leisure products. "Their [workers'] zest for amusement," Simon wrote, "urges them to submit to the discipline of work, and the habits formed for the sake of gratifying their tastes make the regular life necessary in industry easier and more pleasant."[6]

Educators worried about the potential threat of movies to the school's efforts to regulate national morality and culture. In the 1920s, a major concern existed about the effect of movies on the morality of youth. The development of radio resulted in a public debate in the 1930s about whether schools or media should control national culture. Commercial media eventually gave advertisers a new means of shaping a consumer society. By the late 1960s, with the development of *Sesame Street,* media were fully recognized by school people as the third educator. *Sesame Street* and other children's TV programs taught children the art of consumption through the marketing of program-related dolls, toys, and games.

A third major theme of this book is the importance of the emergence of a teenage market that served to prepare future consumers. This is addressed in chapter 5, where I show how this teen market was a result of the high school becoming a mass institution in the 1930s and 1940s. The term *teenager* was coined in the 1940s to identify the high school cohort group as a particular consumer market. The founding of *Seventeen* magazine in the 1940s played a major role in defining the teenage market for advertisers. By the 21st century, marketers were referring to a *global teen market.* This market developed in the same period of the 1940s and 1950s when the advertising and public relations industries were creating a popular image of the American way of life symbolized by a suburban family with a stay-at-home housewife who consumed vast amounts of new products. In the 1950s, this consumer model of the American way of life was used as propaganda against the Soviet Union.

A fourth major theme in this book, which I focus on in chapters 2, 3, and 6, is how the marriage of education, advertising, and media was affected by issues of gender identity and racism. In chapter 2, I discuss the interplay between late 19th- and early 20th-century concerns about female identity, home economics, packaged and process foods, schools, and advertising.

The changes in this interplay—particularly among female identity, schools, and advertising—is continued in later chapters. In chapter 3, I discuss the interrelations among male identity, school sports, and advertising. I continue the discussion of these interconnections through later chapters. In chapter 6, I focus on efforts by civil rights leaders in the 1950s and 1960s to provide positive images of all Americans in school textbooks, advertising, and media. These changes transformed earlier textbook and advertising images that are discussed in earlier chapters of the book. In part, I argue, the civil rights movement attempted to achieve equal participation in the consumer market for all Americans.

In the concluding chapter 7, I pull together the various themes to show how the historical evolution of schools, advertising, and media is now manifested in commercial advertising in schools; in the transformation of home economics into Family and Consumer Sciences; in the development of themed environments, such as Disneyland, that function as educators; and in the marriage of schools, advertising, and media in the fast-food industry.

Consumer-Citizen and Ideology

Before examining the early 19th-century roots of a mass-consumer society, it is necessary to provide some brief definitions of what I mean by *consumer-citizen* and *consumer ideology*. These brief definitions take on more meaning in the context of the total book. By *consumer-citizen*, I mean a person who accepts any political situation as long as there is an abundance of consumer goods. I refer to this as "Sonya's choice." As I discuss in chapter 2, Sonya Vrunsky, a character in Anzia Yezierska's 1923 novel, *Salome of the Tenements,* exclaims, "Talk about democracy. . . . All I want is to be able to wear silk stockings and Paris hats the same as Mrs. Astorbilt, and then it wouldn't bother me if we have Bolshevism or Capitalism, or if the democrats or the republicans win."[7] In the 1950s, a consumer-citizen is a person who supports the American way of life against Soviet communism and is a *responsible* consumer. In this context, responsible consumers buy what they can afford within their limits of credit card debt. In contrast to the 19th-century Protestant ethic, with its emphasis on saving, avoiding debt, and simple living, the consumer-citizen's goal is spending, maximizing their use of credit, and consuming as much as possible. Shopping becomes a patriotic act that demonstrates the superiority of the American way of life over other political and economic systems. The anthem of the consumer-citizen is "Shop 'til you drop." Seemingly apolitical, the consumer-citizen is wedded to the ideology of consumerism.

Sonya's choice does embrace consumerist ideology. Understanding of an ideology requires a knowledge of how its various individual ideas were assembled. No ideology appears fully formed on the world's stage. Consumerist ideology emerges in the 20th century as a mixture of earlier ideas about the value of work, the accumulation of wealth, and equality as equality of opportunity. In addition, there is an acceptance of progress as economic growth, the development of new products, and consumer spending.

Consumerism is strikingly different from other ideologies that place an emphasis on either social harmony or an abandonment of worldly concerns. Many religions value the denial of materialistic desires. Different branches of Islam, Hinduism, Buddhism, and Christianity reject the way of life represented by the consumer seeking personal transformation through the buying of goods. Confucianism emphasizes the importance of social harmony over individual pursuit of wealth. Today fundamentalist Islamic governments, such as in Iran and Afghanistan, are attempting to protect their populations from what they consider to be degenerate Western consumerism.[8]

The following is a list of the basic ideas that form the ideology of consumerism. When I use the term *consumerism* throughout this book, I refer to this ideology. This book explains how these ideas become mutually supporting and influence human actions. For example, three essential ideas of consumerism—work ethic, equality of opportunity, and savings—are present in the early 19th century. In the 20th century, these three ideas take on new meaning within the context of consumerism. The utilization of the work ethic provides the means to purchase goods that promise personal transformation. Equality of opportunity takes on a slightly added meaning to that of just having an equal chance to get ahead in society. It comes to mean an equality of opportunity to consume. The 19th-century emphasis on the virtue of saving is in the 20th century used to justify consumer credit plans as forced savings. As a form of forced savings, people have immediate access to new products while still being required to pay their credit bills.

Consumer purchases and credit motivate and discipline the workforce. Consider the interrelationship among the work ethic, equality of opportunity, and consumer credit. Equality of opportunity gives everyone an equal chance to work hard to purchase goods. Consumer credit allows immediate use of goods by providing a forced savings plan to cover the cost of the goods. Purchasers must then work hard to pay off the debt accrued through consumer credit. Both the desire to purchase goods and the necessity of paying off consumer debt causes the purchaser to work harder.

Basic Ideas of Consumerist Ideology

1. Work is a virtue and it keeps people from an indolent life that could result in vice and crime.
2. Equality means equality of opportunity to pursue wealth and consume.
3. Accumulation of material goods is evidence of personal merit.
4. The rich are rich because of good character and the poor are poor because they lack virtue.

5. The major financial goal of society should be economic growth and the continual production of new goods.

6. Consumers and producers should be united in efforts to maximize the production and consumption of goods.

7. People will want to work hard so they can consume an endless stream of new products and new forms of commodified leisure.

8. Differences in ability to consume (or income) is a social virtue because it motivates people to work harder.

9. Advertising is good because it motivates people to work harder to consume products.

10. The consumer is irrational and can be manipulated in his or her purchases.

11. The consumption of products will transform one's life.

12. Consumer credit is forced savings allowing for the immediate consumption of products.

Early American Puritanism provides many of the consumerist ideas that turned the United States into a nation driven by work and consumption. However, it is not within the scope of this book to detail the history of Puritan thought. It should be noted, however, that scholars such as Jackson Lears link the history of advertising with early Puritan fear that in the Americas the abundance of goods and opportunities for pleasure would destroy the work ethic. In reference to the effect of Puritan thought on recent industrial development, Lears wrote, "The process of accumulation [of property] had to be kept moving forward, energized by the restless desire for purchase rather than the pleasures of possession. In the modern culture of abundance . . . desire . . . is curiously dematerialized."9

I think that Lears and other scholars are correct in emphasizing the Puritan quality of American thought. Later in this chapter, I discuss how Puritanism was contained in 19th-century textbooks and Sunday School literature. Puritanism is a continuing influence on U.S. culture. Throughout this book, I refer to its impact on the development of schools, advertising, and media. Having introduced the book's basic structure and providing a brief definition of consumerism and consumer-citizen, I expand on the meaning of mass consumer society by examining its early roots in the 19th century.

PART TWO: PRELUDE TO A CONSUMER SOCIETY

There were certain developments in post-Revolutionary society that set the stage for the mass-consumer society that developed in the 20th century. First, the interaction with Native Americans made White Americans conscious of the differences between societies based on manufacturing and consumption and those based on minimal wants and needs. Second, the origins of a mass society can be found in the shared experience of advertising, newspapers, telegraph, postal service, and schools. These provided a shared body of experience, knowledge, and icons that created common bonds among people, mostly those of European descent, across the nation. Third, early 20th-century leaders of school reform, home economics, advertising, and advocates of censorship of the early movie industry were mainly White Anglo-Saxon Protestants who were exposed to the same or similar texts in public schools and in Sunday schools creating a certain unity of values.

The early interactions between the U.S. government and Native Americans exemplified the use of consumer desires as a prod to hard work and reactions against consumerism. The example was important because anti-consumerism groups in the 20th and 21st centuries romanticized Native American values in their searches for alternative economic and social organizations. In the early years of the new Republic, the U.S. government attempted to integrate Native Americans into Anglo-Saxon culture through exposure to manufactured products. Foreshadowing later arguments that consumerism motivated people to work hard, President Thomas Jefferson, after assuming office in 1801, argued that government trading posts selling manufactured goods would attract Native Americans to a cash economy. Wanting to buy manufactured goods, Jefferson reasoned, Native Americans would sell their lands and use the money to buy manufactured goods from trading posts. The acceptance of a cash economy, Jefferson reasoned, would cause Native Americans to abandon hunting for farming. "When a man has enclosed and improved his farm," Jefferson wrote in reference to the trading post policy, "builds a good house on it and raised plentiful stocks of animals, he will wish when he dies that these things shall go to his wife and children, who he loves more than he does his other relations, and for whom *he will work with pleasure during his life*" (italics added).[10]

Many Euro-Americans believed that the major flaw in Native American cultures was the lack of value placed on hard work and the accumulation of material goods. Missionary work among Native Americans was often direct at instilling a work ethic. Typical of most White settlers and missionaries, the Moravians believed that a major problem was the lack of a work ethic among Native Americans. Before teaching reading and writing, the Moravians organized model farms where Indian students were put to work from sunrise to sunset. Moravian missionary John Gambold wrote, "that where the Indians are not cured from their idleness, which is admired in their nations and deeply ingrained in their nature, things must remain precarious for Christianity."[11]

The failure of the trading post system to change Native American values prompted the U.S. Congress to pass the Civilization Act of 1819. This legislation sent missionaries into Indian lands to convert tribes to Christianity, farming, and hard work. Although many members of Southern tribes were converted and took up farming, this did not result in large-scale land sales. Consequently, President Andrew Jackson in his first annual message to Congress in December 1829 declared the Civilization Act of 1819 a failure and called for the forced removal of the Southern tribes from their lands to Indian Territory (later Oklahoma).[12]

While Euro-Americans struggled to convert Native Americans to Christianity and hard work, the great Shawnee leader Tecumseh attempted to unite Western and Southern tribes against the U.S. government. Given the size of these tribes, tribal unification might have resulted in the defeat of the U.S. government and a major change in the course of American history. Tecumseh's failure in 1811 to persuade Southern tribes to join his confederacy and the destruction of his army at the Battle of Tippecanoe doomed efforts to create a united front against U.S. aggression.[13]

Tecumseh hoped to keep the materialistic White culture from infecting Native American cultures. His brother, Tenskwatwa, also known as the Prophet, served as the movement's ideological leader. Echoes of Tenskwatwa's message later appeared in the 20th and 21st centuries as anti-consumerist groups sentimentalized Native American values. The Prophet argued that the White cash economy and desire to accumulate material goods had resulted in the destruction of forest animals and, consequently, Native American's traditional hunting cultures. As recorded by one of his disciples, the Prophet delivered the Great Spirit's message: "My children, you complain that the animals of the forest are few and scattered: How shall it be otherwise? You destroy them yourselves for their skins only [to be sold to Whites]. . . . You must kill no more animals than are necessary to feed and clothe you. . . ."[14]

Preparing a Consumer Public: Schools and Equality of Opportunity

In the 1830s, while President Jackson was removing Southern Indians because of unwillingness to relinquish their lands, a spreading common school system was inculcating children with the values of hard work, amassing wealth, and equality of opportunity. The concept of equality of opportunity resolved the contradiction that faced early White American leaders between the existence of inequality and the claim that America was the land of equality. The idea of equality of opportunity emerged from the equalitarian rhetoric of the U.S. Declaration of Independence and the pronouncements of Revolutionary leaders. In *The Pursuit of Equality in American History*, historian J. R. Pole wrote, "The Declaration of Independence proclaimed a universalist egalitarian rhetoric as the standard of a highly differentiated social order."[15] In fact, Revolutionary society was socially and legally unequal by gender, race, and wealth. As Pole indicated, it "was almost believed, women were by *nature* different from men."[16] Most, if not all, slave holders did not believe Blacks were equal to Whites, and most Whites did not accept equality with Native Americans. In addition, full citizenship rights were only given to men with property. As Pole pointed out, the resolution of the contradiction between rhetoric of equality and existence of inequality was to define equality as equality of opportunity.

After the American Revolution, equality of opportunity meant that every free White man had an equal chance to work hard to accumulate property. In the late 18th century, ownership of property was required to exercise full citizenship rights through the right to vote. Noah Webster, the so-called Schoolmaster of America, creator of the American language, and author of spelling books used in schools throughout the 19th century, argued in 1793 that equality in the United States meant, "here every man finds employment, and the road is open for the poorest citizen to amass wealth by labor and economy, and by his talent and virtue to raise himself to the highest offices of the State."[17] Webster hoped that his version of the American language and ideology as represented in his spelling books would create a unified American culture.

Webster's influence in creating a common culture and popularizing the idea of equality of opportunity is difficult to measure. We do know that his textbooks were a success. Both his salesmanship and the content of his textbooks proved successful. One and a half million copies of the speller had been sold by 1801, 20 million by 1829, and 75 million by 1875. The speller became a model used by other spelling book authors. Its extreme popularity was demonstrated by the publication in 1863 of a Civil War edition in the South that was adapted "to the youth of the Southern Confederacy."[18]

The work ethic also played a role in the acceptance of the doctrine of equality of opportunity. As J. R. Pole indicated, there was a general acceptance in the early 19th century among American leaders that "God intended indolence to lead to poverty and want."[19] Poverty indicated a failure of character. This meant that character could be measured by the willingness of people to work hard to accumulate wealth. From this perspective, those who achieved wealth had good character and those in poverty had poor character.

Therefore, the doctrine of equality of opportunity gave a chance to everyone to gain wealth and prove, through work, that they were moral and of good character. In the late 19th century, a Massachusetts speaker declared to a society of mechanics, "Every man stands on his own merits. . . . The fact that he may become a capitalist, is a spur to exertion to the very newsboy in our streets."[20]

Common school advocates, particularly Horace Mann, the so-called *father of the public school system*, declared that schools should be the central social institution for ensuring equality of opportunity. In *Pillars of the Republic*, one of the best discussions of the foundations of U.S. public schools, Carl Kaestle argued that public school advocates wanted to protect and ensure the domination of Anglo-Saxon Protestant culture. The virtue of property and the availability of economic opportunity in the United States, according to Kaestle, were to be taught in public schools. Kaestle wrote, "property was to be respected because it taught virtue. Everyone should be taught to desire property and to respect property."[21]

Eventually the schoolhouse became a public icon symbolizing equality of opportunity. In this context, public schools helped establish the foundations of a mass-consumer culture. School attendance promised everyone an equal chance to consume property, and it linked school success with good character and good character with accumulation of property. Failure in school supposedly limited the possibility of economic success. Linking school failure with poverty and low income, the school could perpetuate the idea that poverty was often a sign of failed character. The formula for schooling was this: If you worked hard in school and worked hard after graduation (a sign of good character), you would be blessed with high income and the ability to consume vast quantities of material goods.

Children Read About Wealth and Its Uses

Most late 19th-century Protestant White children were exposed to similar textbooks and children's literature distributed by Sunday Schools. Considered together, textbooks and Sunday school literature taught similar values regarding work, wealth, and salvation. Later in the early 20th century, these values were frequently reflected in professional work employing primarily Anglo-Saxon Protestants, such as advertising, social work, and education. In *Advertising the American Dream*, Roland Marchand analyzed the backgrounds of the architects of American advertising. He found that the overwhelming majority were White, Northern European, Protestant, male, and Ivy League graduates.[22] Also it was primarily those of Protestant background who restructured public schools to meet what they perceived to be the needs of the urban-industrial society that blossomed at the end of the 19th century.[23] It was mainly Protestant religious groups and Protestant social reformers who led the campaigns to close urban taverns, dance halls, and movie theaters.[24] It was also the influence of these values on rising industrial abundance that helped form a consumerist ideology.

Textbooks and Sunday School literature dealt with themes that shaped the direction of American consumer society. Important themes in this literature were differences in wealth and the temptations of urban life. Worries about the evil of urban life directly affected the expansion of the school as a social welfare institution and the efforts to impose censorship on movies. The reading material also dealt with shopping and the ostentatious display of wealth. Finally, this children's literature reflected the tension between Christian pastoralism and industrial destruction of the environment.

An examination of the most popular textbooks of the mid- and late 19th century, the *McGuffey Readers*, will provide insight into the shared information and ideas of those (primarily White Protestant children) who attended public schools. Children's literature in the 19th century came mainly from religious societies, and it was distributed through Sunday Schools to Protestant children. The *McGuffey Readers*, first published between 1836 and 1838, contained a primer, a speller, and four readers. Sales figures for the series indicate their popularity. Between 1836 and 1920, approximately 122 million copies were sold.[25] By the 1830s, the American Sunday School Union and the American Tract Society were publishing over 12 million children's books, tracts, pamphlets, hymn books, devotional books, journals, magazines, and newspapers. In 1832, 75% of Sunday Schools had children's libraries. The Sunday School Union's book approval committee was composed of representatives from the following Protestant dominations: Baptist, Methodist, Congregationalist, Episcopal, Presbyterian, Lutheran, and Reformed Dutch. Surrounded by public school textbooks and Sunday School books, Protestant children were receiving similar ideas and information.[26]

The issue of economic inequality appeared frequently in *McGuffey Readers* and Sunday School books. The existence of economic inequality was presented as a blessing that allowed people to gain salvation. Wealth was presented as both a blessing from God and a sign of a virtuous character, and as a burden that could lead to moral failure. Similarly, poverty could be a sign of failed character and an ungodly life, but it could also provide the suffering needed to achieve salvation. It was religious faith that determined the ultimate value of wealth or poverty. Wealth was a sign of industrious character, but not necessarily a sign of salvation. Without salvation, the rich could quickly become indolent and sink into a life of luxurious dissipations. Without salvation, the poor could become criminals or succumb to alcoholism. Despite these similar possibilities, the poor were presented as better off because their sufferings helped them achieve salvation.

In *Making the American Mind: Social and Moral Ideas in the McGuffey Readers*, Richard Mosier argued that the economic philosophy of the Readers was premised on the Calvinistic concept that wealth is an outward sign of inner salvation. In other words, the accumulation of material goods is a sign of a virtuous character. This economic argument allowed for an acceptance of a society divided by wealth. Wealth was a sign of God's blessing, and poverty was a sign of God's disapproval. Within this economic argument, for the

poor to gain wealth they had to be godly and industrious, and for the rich to continue receiving the blessings of God they had to use their wealth in a godly fashion. Mosier argued that the *McGuffey Readers* taught that, "Those who are wealthy are reminded that they are so by the grace of God, and that this grace and concession implies a responsibility toward the poor. . . . Many are the lessons that praise the charitable activities of the merchant, and many are those that show the kindness of the rich to the poor."[27]

The conflicting attitudes about the rich and poor were highlighted in two successive stories in the 1843 edition of McGuffey's *Newly Revised Eclectic Second Reader*: "The Rich Boy" and "The Poor Boy." In the first story, the rich boy learned "that God gives a great deal of money to some persons, in order that they may assist those who are poor." The rich boy was also presented as a model of virtue who cared for the poor. He proclaimed, "If I were a man, and had plenty of money, I think no person who lived near me should be very poor."[28] The poor boy was also presented as virtuous. He was industrious, helpful, moral, and eager to learn. However, the story makes a clear distinction between poor boys who were good and those who were bad. In the story, the poor boy hurried home from his lessons to help his parents. On the way, the reader was told, "he often sees naughty boys in the streets, who fight, and steal, and do many bad things; and he hears them swear, and call names, and tell lies; but he does not like to be with them, for fear they should make him as bad as they are; and lest anybody who sees him with them, should think that he too is naughty." Unlike the rich boy wanting to help the poor, the poor boy dreamt of earning his own living. The poor boy liked his food of bread and bacon and did not envy the rich little boys and girls "riding on pretty horses, or in coaches." At the end of the story, the poor boy stated his acceptance of his social position: "I have often been told, and I have read, that it is God who makes some poor, and others rich;—that the rich have many troubles which we know nothing of; and that the poor, if they are but good, may be very happy: indeed, I think that when I am good, nobody can be happier than I am."[29]

Although virtue was often associated with gaining of wealth, it was poverty and suffering that provided the easiest route to salvation. This idea was clearly presented in two Sunday School books, *The Factory Boy, or, the Child of Providence* and *I Wish I Was Poor*. In *The Factory Boy*, the main character's father is described as "industrious, frugal, and prudent. His industry enabled him to make money; his frugality prevented him from wasting it in unnecessary indulgences. . . . A merciful Providence blessed his business, so that he was able not only to meet his necessary expenses, but gradually to accumulate money."[30]

Yet the problem for the father, and later the son, Alfred Stitson, was the absence of religious conversion despite the presence of virtue and regular church attendance. After the father's death, the mother lost the family's property to swindlers and they sunk into dire poverty. The mother fell ill and Alfred experienced a world of suffering. On the brink of starvation, the author commented, "we shall soon see that God does not err in his ways and that our greatest trials are designed for our good."[31]

The family's suffering provides an opportunity to gain something the father had lacked, which was religious salvation. Alfred's salvation saved the family from poverty. The lesson was that poverty was a blessing because it provided the opportunity for the virtuous to find God. After Alfred's salvation experience, the author declared, "Again he [Alfred] thought of his early afflictions, and of all the temporal circumstances in the history of his family. He now felt most grateful for them, as the means which finally led them to the knowledge and experience of religion."[32]

A similar scenario was presented in the Sunday School tract, *I Wish I Was Poor*. The story opens with Lucy Lee, who was confined to her home because of illness. Lucy complained, "Yes, I do wish I was poor; then Christians would talk to me about dying; they always do talk to poor people."[33] She felt neglected because, from her perspective, evangelical efforts were primarily directed at saving the poor. Then Aunt Lawrence arrived, who was described by a household servant as "so rich." On hearing of the visit, Lucy moaned, "I'm so tired of seeing rich people."[34] Yet Aunt Lawrence turns out to be a different type of rich person—she was a saved Christian. Aunt Lawrence provided a grateful Lucy with religious instruction that led to Lucy's salvation.

As the story closed, Lucy and Aunt Lawrence discussed the relationship between economic status and religious salvation. Lucy, of course, wanted to know why it is easier to be saved if you were poor. Quoting the Biblical statement, "It is easier for a camel to go through the eye of a needle than for a rich man to enter into the kingdom of heaven." Lucy wondered, "How can any rich people be saved? It does seem as if I should be a great deal more certain that I and all our family would go to heaven, if we were poor."[35]

In response, Aunt Lawrence asked, "Are all poor people good?" and "Are all rich people wicked?"[36] After Lucy admitted that good and evil exist in all economic groups, Aunt Lawrence explained the problem, "the minds of wealthy men and women are so taken up with the things of this world, that they neglect the greater good. And their children often have [more] temptations than the children of the poor."[37] As for the poor, their advantage was suffering, which helped bring about salvation. Lucy was saved because her illness opened her heart to religion. Aunt Lawrence explained, "God sent upon me, as he has upon you, a long sickness; he compelled me to take the time to think; and when my humbled heart sought him, I trust for Jesus's sake he freely forgave all my former pride and ingratitude. Was he not kind to afflict me?"[38]

Similar to the rich boy in the *McGuffey Reader*, Lucy learned that wealth was a blessing if used to help others. Aunt Lawrence justified the concentration of wealth with this argument:

> Wealth, rightly enjoyed and rightly used, is a great blessing to its possessor and to the world. The poor cannot be relieved, benevolent institutions of different kinds cannot be carried on, even the gospel cannot be preached in our own and foreign lands, without money. So you see, if God keeps the heart from loving it, money is of great worth.[39]

This justification of wealth eventually has to be adapted to a consumerist ideology that glorifies the purchase of goods. In the framework of these stories, wealth was a blessing when it was used to benefit the needy. Wealth was not a blessing when it led to the ostentatious display of goods. In a Sunday School Union publication, *Common Sights in Town & Country*, Farmer Jones accumulated wealth because "Industry and economy, under the blessing of God, will secure for the farmer an abundance of the good things of this life."[40] Once a year, he traveled to the city to purchase goods not available in a country store. In the city, Farmer Jones acted in a fashion quite contrary to later consumerism: "What he buys, however, he buys for use and not for show. He looks upon money as one of God's gifts, and tries to use it in a way that will be pleasing to the Giver."[41]

In summary, these stories provided a justification for inequality and equality of opportunity within the framework of 19th-century Protestantism. Inequality of wealth was not only inevitable, but provided opportunities for religious awakening and benevolence. The suffering of the poor opened the door to possible religious conversion. Religion combined with industry and virtuous actions provided the poor with the opportunity to climb the economic ladder. The suffering of the poor also provided the rich with an opportunity to use their wealth in a benevolent and Godly manner. Without the poor, the rich would have no one to save. Yet the failure to practice virtuous behaviors and achieve religious conversion led the poor down the path of drink and crime. Without religion, the rich were tempted by their wealth to squander their time and money on the purchase of ostentatious goods.

19th-Century Protestantism and the Environment

One later criticism of mass-consumer society was the destruction of the environment and the depletion of natural resources. Nineteenth-century children's literature provided contrasting views that could be used to either support protection of the environment or justify its exploitation. Many children's stories spoke highly of the beauty of nature as a blessing from God.

In *The Factory Boy*, the narrator reflected on the importance of nature in making humans aware of God's glory: "Nature is the goodly work of God, and like a glass, reflects back the smiles of His countenance. When we can escape away from the noise and wickedness of men, to where God's works alone surround us, how serene do our thoughts become, and how pleasant is it then to feel that there is a God who made all things."[42] The narrator worried that the growth of the surrounding city "has injured much this lovely scenery; the hills about the basin have been much dug away."[43]

In contrast to this Christian pastoralism was the argument that the earth was created by God for humans to exploit. An example is the Sunday School story, "The Coal-Cart." The story opened with the Biblical statement, "All that is in the earth is thine."[44] This Biblical line was followed by the statement, "It is but a few years since Anthracite or Stone-Coal was used for fuel. Now hundreds or thousands of tons are taken from the bowels of the earth every year, and consumed in grates, furnaces, steamboats, factories, etc."[45] This exploitation of the earth was then given another religious twist in the final lines about the driver of the coal cart: "We hope he is kind to his hard-working horse, faithful to the interests of his employers, not given to strong drink, and above all, one who fears God and keeps his commandments."[46]

Throughout the 20th and 21st centuries, there would be a continuing tension between the exploitation of the earth and the desire to preserve nature. Many anticonsumerist movements, such as the Green Party, combined environmental with consumer concerns. This tension existed in the children's literature of the 19th century with exploitation of the environment and was justified by the belief that God created Earth for the use of humans and that the act of exploitation was all right if it was performed by Christians.

Protestantism and Urban Leisure

Important for later development of movies and other forms of commodified leisure were stories that illustrated the potentially degrading temptations of city life. As I describe later, Protestant social reformers in the late 19th and early 20th centuries worried that dance halls, movies, bars, amusement parks, and other forms of working-class and immigrant urban leisure might destroy the moral fiber of the nation. Among other things, these concerns shaped the course of movie history in the United States.

The 1847 Sunday School book, *Frank Harper; or, the Country-Boy in Town*, illustrated these early concerns with urban living. After graduating from elementary school, Frank Harper left his farm in New Jersey to work in a store in New York City. Frank exhibited the industrious virtues that could lead to financial success, but he lacked religious salvation. Knowing little about city life, Frank's father consulted with the local tavern keeper about lodging for the young boy. Consequently, Frank's city lodgings proved less than reputable. Two of his fellow roommates tempted him into going to the Bowery theater. At the theater, Frank discovered that "he was among bad men and bad women. He saw and heard things that night which made him sure that it was wicked place."[47] Frank's city life also surrounded him with the enticing sights of store windows and taverns.

The lengthy narrative about Frank's city adventures took him from temptation to salvation. He was befriended by a Christian man, joins a Sunday School, and receives religious salvation from a minister. His country virtues combined with conversion saved him from city sins and ensured his financial success. In contrast, his original theater companions succumbed to city vices and ended up in jail.

The childhoods of the pioneers of advertising, the educational leaders who adapted the school system to the labor needs of mass production, and the moral leaders who demanded censorship of movies and purity in other forms of commodified leisure were surrounded in their childhood by this public school and Sunday School literature. They had to ignore or adapt the information and ideas from this literature to conditions of a mainly urban-industrial society that appeared to be producing more than could be consumed. They also worried about the temptations of mass media. Also some of these future leaders were surrounded by city reading and read newspapers.

Creating a Consumer Public: Advertising and Newspapers

"To a significant extent," David M. Henkin argued in *City Reading*, a study of signs, newspapers, and money in early 19th-century New York City,

> city reading helped to lay the social foundations for what would emerge by the end of the century as a consumer society—a society in which the mere capacity to spend money secured membership, though often on glaringly unequal terms and under increasingly impersonal and potentially alienating conditions.[48]

By *city reading*, Henkin referred to the proliferation of shop signs, trade bills, sandwich boards, banners, and newspaper vendors that characterized America's urban spaces.

Henkin maintained that because of the lack of street signs, and in many cases uncertainty about street names, people tended to identify public space in early urban America by signs hanging on buildings. Indicating the difference between European and American cities, foreign visitors frequently commented on how their city walks and fulfillment of personal desires were guided by commercial signs. Urban dwellers thought about their spacial locations by the location of signs on commercial establishments. For instance, people often identified the location of their homes by nearby businesses rather than by street names.

Buildings were designed to display advertising and reproduce well in illustrated newspaper ads. This meant that an urban dweller's sense of public space was identified closely with commercial advertising. Henkin's book contains photos from the mid-19th century that illustrate the cacophony of signs that dominated the urban landscape. One 1865 photo of New York City's Lower Hudson Street showed 3 three-story buildings displaying 13 commercial signs and what appears to be two posted handbills and one sandwich board. The signs indicated businesses that provided printing services, drugs, carpentry, house and sign painting, "oil'd clothing," shirts, drawers, "over-alls, and horse, cart & truck covers."[49]

In addition to building signs, the city walker was confronted with a wide range of temporary and mobile signs. Posters advertising goods, services, and entertainment were plastered across the city landscape. These temporary signs would eventually be covered by other posters. Mobile advertising signs adorned horse-drawn trams. People wearing sandwich boards advertising goods and services crowded sidewalks. Trade bills and cards were shoved into pedestrian's hands.

Eventually advertisers competed with each other for public attention. Leading the way was America's premier impresario and advertising genius P. T. Barnum, who, after opening the American Museum in 1841, covered New York with handbills and posters advertising a dwarf named General Tom Thumb and 161-year-old Joice Heth. Also Barnum used advertising to create mass interest in the 1850 New York concerts of Swedish opera singer Jenny Lind. Barnum's success in promoting Lind as a celebrity foreshadowed the celebrity and media star promotions of the 20th and 21st centuries.

Barnum was credited with introducing an advertising style of "spectacular discourse . . . where every item of publicity worked to create new items."[50] A typical Barnum ad contained eye-catching titles in a variety of type sizes, such as "A Mammoth Fat Woman" or "Noah Orr, The American Giant." Under the bold titles was more information in smaller type, such as "Miss Rosina D. Richardson, Weighing 660 lbs" and "Eight Feet three inches in Height." In some cases, even smaller type was used to give more details about the attraction, such as "unequaled in stature."[51] After being captured by a spectacular title, the reader's eye had to adjust to absorb new bits of information in smaller type. In this manner, the reader's eye was tempted into reading each item of the ad. In his 1869 autobiography, Barnum explained his methods in selling museum attendance to the public. "I fell in with the world's way; and if my 'puffing' was more persistent, my advertising more audacious, my posters more glaring, my pictures more exaggerated . . . it was [because] . . . I had . . . more energy, far more ingenuity."[52]

Later professional advertisers called Barnum a charlatan and tried to distance themselves from his tradition. In his cultural history of advertising, Jackson Lears stated,

> Seeking to deny their [advertisers] origins, most protested too much. On the hundredth anniversary of Barnum's birth, 1910, *Printer's Ink* [an advertising journal] disavowed the prophet. To celebrate his "advertising ability," the magazine charged, would be like doctors celebrating a quack as their godfather.[53]

Despite the denial by later advertisers that they were following in Barnum's tradition, most current historians recognized the connection. In her history of advertising, Juliann Sivulka contended, "New York showman P.T. Barnum (1810–1891) set out to attract public attention and ended up as the first advertising genius."[54]

It seems clear that commercial signs, posters, sandwich boards, handbills, and trading cards set the stage for America's pioneering role in professional advertising. City reading created a sense of public connections based on commerce and consumption. Henkin demonstrated how city reading spilled over into the world of political culture as political announcements joined commercial signs. Consequently, Henkin's conclusion on the effect of city reading goes beyond the creation of a mass-consumer society. He wondered,

> How significantly this impersonal urban print public has contributed to the historical processes yielding a society dependent on mass consumption, a disengaged electorate, a largely nondeliberative political culture, or a narrow popular understanding of the public good is difficult to measure.[55]

Of course city reading required literacy, and public schools were increasing literacy rates by the reading of common textbooks that instilled the idea that virtue could be measured by the material gains of hard work. Surrounded by advertising signs, the urban school student learned the material rewards of a good education. Within this urban context, it was not hard to translate equality of opportunity and hard work into an equal chance to consume.

Newspapers, Post Office, Telegraph, and Advertising

The sharing of common news about local and world events was important in creating a mass culture. The advertising accompanying the news was an essential step in creating a mass-consumer culture. By the 20th and 21st centuries, consumer news—that is, information about new products and price trends—became an accepted part of local and world news. The line between advertising and political news, and between consumption and social news, was increasingly blurred from the 19th to the 21st centuries.

The development of the newspaper as a mass consumer product paralleled the expansion of public school systems. A major factor was the U.S. Post Office's goal of ensuring a wide geographical distribution of newspapers. The U.S. Post Office Act of 1792 created a national postal system. European postal systems primarily existed to send official messages and collect revenue. In contrast, the U.S. postal system, in the words of Benjamin Rush, existed to disseminate "knowledge of every kind . . . through every part of the United States."[56] The result was the rapid spread of post offices as local communities petitioned for postal services. Between 1790 and 1840, the number of post offices per person improved from 1 for every 43,084 to 1 for every 1,087.[57]

Similar to the later goal of the common school system, an objective of the 1792 Post Office was to create a common culture by setting low rates for newspapers to encourage their national distribution. This allowed newspaper publishers in remote areas to draw on news provided by other papers. The result was a rapid sharing of political information among literate and primarily White residents. Between the 1830s and 1840s, railroads increased the speed of mail delivery. The result, according to Headrick, was that "the numbers of newspapers sent through the mail increased from half a million in 1790 (one for every five inhabitants) to thirty-nine million in 1840, or 2.7 newspapers per capita. . . . *The postal system became largely a newspaper delivery service*" (italics added).[58]

A contributing factor to the rapid increase in newspapers was the advent of the penny newspaper in the 1830s while the common school system spread. Prior to the 1830s, newspapers were relatively expensive. In 1830, New York City's 11 newspapers had a circulation of about 25,000 a day at a price ranging around six cents. Then in 1833, penny newspapers were introduced, and newspaper circulation climbed dramatically with the three leading penny newspapers reaching a circulation of 44,000 a day in 1835. Aided by technological advances in printing, newspapers became a mass commodity.[59]

The development of the telegraph increased the sharing of information. The telegraph and the establishment of the Associated Press news service in 1848 resulted in similar news stories appearing around the country. As a news organization, the Associated Press distributed news over the telegraph to local newspapers so that the newspaper reader in a small town was reading the same news as the reader in an urban area. They all shared the same news articles. By the 1880s and 1890s, syndicated features and comics appeared in newspapers.[60]

The importance of the newspaper in creating a mass culture cannot be overemphasized. Richard Ohmann argued, "That was the first time Americans had available in the format of the newspaper a homogeneous national experience of the news, of opinion, of household advice, and of entertainment."[61] In part, this mass culture included an imagined community. Having greater information about the world, the newspaper reader could imagine and think about geographical places they would probably never visit. "The newspaper," Henkin wrote, "replaced spatial communities with imagined ones, unsettling geographical boundaries and nullifying physical distances."[62]

The celebrity was created by newspapers and advertising. P.T. Barnum's sponsorship of Jenny Lind's performances sent her name into every community in the country. When Hungarian nationalist Lajos Kossuth visited New York in 1851, newspapers were filled with his daily activities and speeches. His visit resulted in look-a-like commodities, such as Kossuth boots, cigars, and hats. As a celebrity created by newspapers, Kossuth, similar to media celebrities of the 21st century, became a national fashion statement.[63]

Newspapers contributed to the rise of nationalism in the 19th century through the creation of an imagined community and by playing on patriotic feelings in news stories. Cherokee leaders recognized the contribution of newspapers to nationalism by publishing the first bilingual Native American newspaper, *Cherokee Phoenix*, on February 21, 1828. The columns were written in English and a Cherokee character system invented by Sequoia. The newspaper helped unite the Cherokees against the encroachments of the U.S. government through the dissemination of news and Cherokee laws.[64]

With the advent of penny newspapers in the 1830s, news quickly became a commodity. Newspapers competed with each other by displaying the most dramatic headlines. In urban centers, newsboys cried out headlines to gain sales. News dealers became part of the urban scene with their stands displaying front pages designed to attract the eyes of potential buyers. The front-page layouts became advertisements for the newspapers. Headlines that screamed terror or lurid events tempted passing readers to buy them.

Newspapers not only sold news, but they also sold advertising. The more copies a newspaper sold, the more its publisher could charge advertisers. By the 1840s, newspapers depended on advertising revenue to earn profits. "We lose money on our circulation by itself considered," Horace Greeley wrote in an 1841 *Tribune* editorial, "but with 20,000 subscribers we can command such advertising and such prices for its as will render our enterprise a remunerating one."[65] Cheap newspapers could only be sustained through advertising revenues.

The sale of news was linked to the sale of advertising. News became a commodity to sell other commodities. Newspaper layouts had to achieve a balance between attracting readers and seducing them to examine the advertisements. Henkin argued that newspaper layouts blurred the distinction between advertising and news. He contended, "To begin with, the very juxtaposition of items on the same newspaper pages tended to deny (or at least suppress) their differences."[66]

Many of the early newspaper ads featured patent medicines. Professional advertising agencies and advertisers would later distance themselves from the patent medicine tradition. For instance, the *Ladies Home Journal*, which depended on advertising revenue for its existence, banned patent medicine ads from its pages in 1892. The editor of the magazine, Edward Bok, wrote, "There is no evil in America to-day so great as this accursed passion for self-doctoring."[67]

Despite this later reaction to patent medicine, many of these medicines were eventually sold for different purposes or as homeopathic cures. They also represent the influence of Native American medicine on the American homeopathic tradition. For instance, Coca-Cola and Pepsi-Cola were originally sold as patent medicines for the brain and stomach, respectively. An 1892 ad for Coca-Cola proclaimed, "The Ideal Brain Tonic . . . For Headache and Exhaustion." Featured in the ads were testimonials from druggists. In contrast, a 1900 Coca-Cola ad only stated, "Delicious and Refreshing—Drink Coca-Cola—At Soda Fountains and Carbonated Bottles 5¢." There were no testimonials from druggists in these later ads, but these were endorsements from celebrities such as a large illustration of actress Helda Clark holding a glass of Coca-Cola. This transition from patent medicine to soda was marked by the increasing importance of the celebrity and the link between celebrity life and the advertising of products.[68]

A striking feature of early patent medicine ads were their promises of personal transformation. Consider the promise of Dr. Townsend's Sarsaparilla, which was sold as the "Wonder and Blessing of the Age." The ad stated, "To those who have lost their muscular energy by the effects of medicine or indiscretion committed in youth, or excessive indulgence of the passions . . . [that have] brought on . . . want of ambition . . . premature decay and decline . . . can be entirely restored by this pleasant remedy."[69] When I first read this ad, I thought of recent ads for sports utility vehicles that displayed the car on top of a mountain surrounded by wilderness. The promise of these recent ads is that the buyers' environment will be magically transformed from the drab cement of the city or blandness of suburbia into pristine beauty of the wilds with the purchase of the vehicle.

While the ad for Dr. Townsend's Sarsaparilla promised personal renewal, ads for Dr. Swayne's Compound Syrup of Wild Cherry and Morse's Compound syrup of Yellow Dock Root identified specific maladies. In addition, these patent medicines reflect the influence of Native American medical treatments. The claims of these 1850s' ads parallel those in John Lust's *The Herb Book* published in 1974 and reprinted 20 times by 1987.

The 1850s' ad for Wild Cherry states it would cure "coughs, colds, asthma, influenza, bronchitis. . . ."[70] Lust's book claimed, "Its [wild cherry] effectiveness was attributed to a sedative action on the respiratory nerves."[71] Lust listed uses by Native Americans including treatment for diarrhea and lung problems. The 1850s' ad for yellow dock root stated that it was a blood purifier and helped with skin problems. Lust's book also listed yellow dock root as a blood purifier and aid in curing skin problems. Lust wrote, "American Indians applied crushed yellow dock leaves to boils and pulverized roots to cuts."[72]

With the commitment of the postal service to the spread of newspapers, patent medicine ads appeared around the country. For those reading newspapers, there was a sharing of product information. Regardless of whether it was believed, this shared information included a claim that the purchase of products could result in personal transformation. This became an important advertising claim in the 20th and 21st centuries. Newspapers, while blurring the distinction between news and ads, turned news into a product to be sold like any other product. In addition, news became a form of entertainment used to sell other products through its ads. These trends would be important as consumerism took shape at the end of the 19th century.

The Wizard of Oz and the Architecture of Desiring

Another important 19th-century development that set a trend that later produced Disneyland and other themed consumer architecture was the department store. The department store turned urban strolling into window shopping. A pioneer designer of department store show windows was L. Frank Baum, who was also an author of children's books including *The Wonderful Wizard of Oz*. Both show windows and *The Wonderful Wizard of Oz* captured the consumer's fantasy world as both shopping and leisure time activities. Born in 1856, Baum grew up in a wealthy family in upstate New York, and during his youth he worked in theater and as a traveling salesman. With his experience in theater and merchandising, Baum eventually became an advisor on store displays to Chicago businesses. In 1898, he founded the National Association of Window Trimmers, and in 1899, he published a monthly journal called *The Show Window*.[73] In Baum's words, *The Show Window* taught window designers to "arouse in the observer the cupidity and longing to possess the goods."[74]

The use of the department store windows to arouse consumer desires should be understood in the context of architectural history.[75] Eventually the trend in designing buildings to attract consumers would lead to the distinctive architectural designs embodied in fast-food restaurants, shopping malls, and Disneyland-like theme parks. Traditionally, architectural designs were used to attract people and represent the building's functions. For instance, churches and temples were designed to attract worshipers and represent religious activity. When seeing a themed religious structure, most people understand the nature of the activity that took place within its confines. The same thing was true of schoolhouses. Of course some architectural designs were more powerful than others in attracting people. The beauty of European medieval cathedrals attracted and invited attendance of both the worshiper and nonworshiper as represented today by their popularity as tourist sites.

The architectural goal of themed consumption palaces was to attract consumers—this means the transformation of public space into planned consumer spaces. Open-air markets and enclosed arcades were traditional forms of consumer environments. In modern times, the first consumption palaces were department stores, with the first being Paris' Bon Marche, which opened in 1869. Department store buildings were designed to entice shoppers into their interiors. They were designed to stimulate consumer desires through the display of goods in exterior windows. Referring to the show windows that lined the exterior ground floors of his department store buildings in New York and Philadelphia, John Wanamaker wrote in 1916, "Our minds are full of windows. . . . Show windows are eyes to meet eyes."[76] Through the eyes of store windows, people were to be pulled into the interior space of consumer goods.

In the early stages, window shopping was encouraged by professional window gazers hired by department stores. People were taught to linger before store windows and energize their consumer desires. The use of plate glass allowed a clear view into the interior. In *The Show Window*, Baum, like the Wizard of Oz, recommended the use of a variety of theatrical methods to attract window shoppers, including revolving electrical displays. He was not interested in the quality of the goods, but how they looked in a display arrangement. If goods were properly displayed, he argued, "the show window will sell them like hot cakes, even though [they] are old enough to have gray whiskers."[77] As show window expert Frederick Kiesler stated, the goal was to "break down the barriers separating customers and merchandise."[78]

Mannequins enhanced the seductive qualities of window displays. Traditionally, only headless mannequins—without head, arms, or feet—were used as dress forms. According to historian William Leach, mannequins as complete human forms appeared around 1912 in displays of ready-to-wear clothes.[79] Eventually mannequins were built with movable parts so they could be made to assume different poses. According to one retailer, mannequins made it possible to "create an atmosphere of reality that aroused enthusiasm and acted in an autosuggestive manner."[80]

Female mannequins wearing only underwear stimulated sexual desires. Even the novelist John Dos Passos referred to the sexual arousing effect of "girls' underwear in store windows" in his novel, *1919*. Some underwear displays caused crowds to gather in front of store windows. In Spokane, Washington, police had to disperse a crowd gathered in front of a shop that displayed women's underwear. One man was arrested for refusing to leave the display window.[81]

The interiors of department stores were turned into palaces of consumption and made shopping a leisure time activity. Goods were displayed in plate glass counters that allowed consumers to be entertained as they strolled up and down aisles gazing at the cornucopia of merchandise. Prior to department stores, goods were sold in stores specializing in one area of merchandising. In these earlier stores, little effort was made to provoke consumer desires. Goods were kept behind counters, and shoppers asked clerks to put merchandise on the counter for examination.

In department stores, quick-selling items were kept far from entrance doors so that shoppers would be forced to reach them by walking through displays of luxury items. Each floor and department was organized in the same manner. Escalators were introduced in the early 20th century, which allowed the easy movement of shoppers to upper floors. Prior to escalators, many shoppers avoided the upper floors because of the crowding and perceived inconvenience of elevators. One merchandiser in 1912 claimed that its store's five escalators allowed for placing "the staple, year-round 'sellers' on the second and third floors, relieving the congestion of departments on the main floor."[82]

Departments stores made shopping a social activity. Cafeterias, lunch rooms, fountains, and coffee bars added to the social quality of department store shopping. Friends, particularly women, arranged to meet in department stores for lunch, and after eating they would continue to socialize as they wandered through the store's aisles gazing at the array of goods. They could attend the store's fashion show or demonstrations of housewares. Holidays, which by the end of the 20th century became another excuse for shopping, were celebrated with lavish displays designed to entertain and stimulate a desire to buy a holiday present.

Themed store interiors added to the grandeur of the shopping experience. Mirrors placed on elevator doors, walls, and pillars reflected merchandise back and forth across the expanses of each floor. Stopping to look at their images, shoppers found themselves starring at mirrors that combined their images with that of surrounding merchandise. Looking at their reflections, consumers could imagine themselves wearing or using the merchandise. Walking around the store, shoppers' images were constantly merged into images of consumer goods. Some department stores went to extreme lengths to entertain the shopper with the beauty of their interiors. The most renowned design was the iridescent glass-mosaic dome completed by Louis Tiffany for Chicago's Marshall Field department store. Supposedly the dome with its illusion of reaching up into a heavenly domain was to cast a mystical aura over the goods below.[83] Under this dome shopping was like going to church.

As department stores were themed to attract buyers, amusement parks were themed to attract consumers of commodified leisure. In fact, Fred Thompson, the pioneer builder of Coney Island theme parks and New York's theatrical extravaganza, the Hippodrome, linked his designs to the new department stores. Thompson's Luna Park, which opened in Coney Island in 1903, was the first theme park.[84] His biographer, Woody Register, argued that Thompson wanted to liberate theatrical entertainment from traditional concepts in the same manner that department stores liberated retailing from small stores. Register wrote, "The concept of the department store provided Thompson with an organizational model as well as a class setting and democratic vocabulary of public service to his theater."[85] While department stores turned shopping into a combination of social event and leisure time activity, Thompson wanted theme parks to be a commodified form of play that was social and fun. He proclaimed, "The trouble with this present age is too much work and too little play."[86] His Coney Island extravaganza, Luna Park, set the pattern for all future theme parks. Calling Luna Park "the Biggest Playground on Earth," Thompson's completed project included human cannonballs, marriage ceremonies in hot-air balloons, a floor show with 800 dancers, and a trip to the moon complete with moving scenery and a moon landing surrounded by midgets.[87]

Thompson believed that commodified fun was the answer to the drudgery and boredom of industrial and corporate work. As Register stated, "Thompson ultimately exploited it [the desire for fun] by applying his industrial patrimony to produce a marketable and fantastic form of rebellion against the diminishing rewards of work in an industrializing corporate society."[88] The very forms of Thompson's architecture provided an avenue of escape into a world of fantasy. Visitors to Luna Park paid their 10-cent entrance fee at five hand-carved Roman chariots posted at the entrance. The spectacular use of 200,000 incandescent lights caused it to be called "Electric City by the Sea." Inside the park, there were constructed illusions, similar to later ones created by Disney, of famous places. The spatial dimensions at Thompson's New York City Hippodrome were designed to impart a sense of awe and wonderment to the audience while they waited for performances enhanced by mechanical stage sets and lights.[89]

The difference between Thompson and Walt Disney's later vision of theme park entertainment was the audience. Thompson's world was geared for adults, with Luna Park offering child-care services so parents would be free to roam. Disney's parks were created for families and projected images of domestic morality. The closest to Disney's later moral world was Coney Island's Dreamland amusement center. Dreamland provided customers with educational exhibits of the Fall of Pompeii and exhibits claiming to show real life in Japan, Switzerland, and Venice. Moralizing themes were included in the biggest exhibit, which was "The Creation and the End of the Earth." The "End of the Earth" extravaganza showed people being thrown into hell for vanity, kissing before marriage, stealing, and drinking. The End of the Earth represented a Protestant vision of the future if urban America did not change its behavior.[90]

Conclusion: Development of a Consumer Society

The information and ideas disseminated in the 19th century through schools, textbooks, children's literature, city reading, and newspapers set the stage for the development of a consumer-oriented society. Department stores established a pattern of architecture intended to stimulate consumer desires. The public school became an icon for equality of opportunity and provided a resolution for the contradiction between the rhetoric of equality and the reality of existing inequalities. In America, equality was most often associated with an equal chance to accumulate property. Textbooks and children's literature presented inequality in wealth as an opportunity for the rich to gain salvation by serving the poor and for the poor to gain salvation through personal suffering. Inequality provided a test of individual character in the land of opportunity. In other words, equality of opportunity to gain wealth provided a chance for testing personal virtue and character.

The work ethic as a sign of virtuous character was represented in textbooks, schools, and children's literature. In the late 19th and early 20th centuries, fears that industrial advances would create too much leisure time resulted in arguments that the work ethic could be sustained by increasing desires to consume. Belief in the importance of the work ethic remained a strong fixture in American life. By the 21st century, Americans held the honor of working more hours than any other industrial nation. In fact, the number of hours worked increased from the 20th to the 21st centuries. According to Jeff Johnson, economist for the International Labor Organization, "The average American worked 1,978 hours in 2000, compared with 1,942 hours in 1990."[91] Americans worked almost an additional 40-hour week. Johnson emphasized, "The increase in the number of hours worked within the United States runs counter to the trend in other industrialized nations where we see declining annual hours worked."[92] Also the "compassionate conservativism" of President George W. Bush emphasized the work ethic along with the value of inequality for the promotion of morality among the rich and poor.[93]

There were other tensions resulting from industrial and economic abundance. Some Protestants felt threatened by the cultural values of Catholic and Jewish immigrants in pursuit of wealth that entered the United States in the late 19th and early 20th centuries. Although these newer immigrants embraced the products of industrial abundance, some traditional Protestants felt torn between the values of simple living and the necessity of buying new industrial products to maintain the economy. Also Protestant values of thrift and saving conflicted with the increasing use of consumer credit. The exploitation of natural resources as a result of industrial expansion created a tension between the belief that nature was an expression of the beauty of God and that God intended humans to exploit nature.

Finally, by the end of the 19th century, advertising signs, handbills, posters, department store windows, and other forms of city reading presented the urban dweller with a steady display of manufactured goods. As newspapers turned news into a commodity, the distinction between news and advertising was blurred. The public that shared the values embedded in schools, children's literature, city reading, and newspapers was ripe for a world where virtue and work were tied to consumption.

Liberation With Jell-O
and Wonder Bread:
Educating the New Woman

At the turn of the 19th and 20th centuries, new public images of women and consumerism were introduced by advertisers and home economists working in schools, the food industry, and other public institutions. Home economists envisioned the education of a new woman who, skilled in scientific household management, would be freed from domestic drudgery to participate in the general improvement of society. As part of this goal, home economists developed a distinctive American cuisine through instruction in public schools, setting standards and training cooks for school cafeterias and hospitals, and in their advocacy of using prepared and packaged foods in the home. Professional advertisers considered themselves engaged in mass education and central to the success of an economy dependent on consumer purchases. Home economists and advertisers had differing concepts of the public. The home economist imagined a rational and scientifically thinking public, whereas the advertiser thought of the masses as being driven by irrational desires. There were also important racial divisions as African Americans developed their own consumer markets and advertised using themes of racial pride. In contrast, Euro-American advertising agencies used African-American images to portray servitude to Whites.

THE CONSUMER WOMAN AND BRAND NAMES

In the late 19th and early 20th centuries, industrialization sharpened division of labor between men and women. The public image of domestic relations became that of the wage-earning husband as producer and the housewife as consumer.[1] As Susan Strasser argued, consumer wives took on more of the household tasks as husbands defined their work roles in industrial and corporate organizations. In the primarily rural settings of the past, husbands actively participated in household work by engaging in such tasks as carrying water, chopping and carrying wood for the stove, and cleaning poultry, wild game, and livestock while wives worked as producers maintaining vegetable gardens, storing food, and making clothes.[2] Discussions of masculinity resulting from increasing urbanization and employment in bureaucratic organizations centered on the loss of what Theodore Roosevelt called the *strenuous life*. In this framework, men were to recapture their masculinity by participating in sports, weekend and vacation hiking and camping, and fishing and hunting. Although fishing and hunting were no longer required to maintain the household food supply, they were considered necessary for retaining masculine attributes.[3]

The focus of this chapter is on the public discussion of the domestic and consumer role of women as household tasks shifted from production to consumption. During this period, women's roles as producers of household goods were being replaced by the availability of ready-to-wear clothing, factory-made bread, packaged and canned foods, and processed foods. Leading the discussion about the new domestic role of women as consumers were home economics experts. Schools played an important part in attempts to redefine the role of women. In addition, producers of food and household goods, advertisers, and the burgeoning cosmetics and ready-to-wear industries tried to shape the image and consumer patterns of housewives and wage-earning women.

Underlying all the forces shaping women's roles were tensions between the increasing abundance of goods, traditional Protestant culture, and new immigrants arriving from Southern and Eastern Europe. These cultural tensions were sometimes reduced by claims that democracy was being enhanced by a new consumer society that allowed equal opportunities to buy new products and fashions. Ready-to-wear clothing made it possible for the average person to engage in rapid fashion changes that, in the past, had only been available to those who could afford to buy tailored clothing. Home economists, as I discuss, believed they were promoting a democratic household by teaching a single standard of cooking and domestic management to all students.

The new consumer woman emerged as brand names flooded the market. After the passage of the 1870 federal trademark law, manufacturers were able to protect their trademarks by registering them with the federal government. One of the first registered was the "Underwood devil," a product image used on canned meats manufactured by the William Underwood and Company. This was followed by noted brand images such as Quaker Oats Man (1877), Michelin Man (1895), Aunt Jemima (1905),

Morton Salt Girl (1911), Betty Crocker (1921), Jolly Green Giant (1926), and Ronald McDonald (1966).[4] By 1917, a study in the *Journal of Applied Psychology* reported that 1 in 300 men could name one brand of pen, watch, and soap. By the 1920s, Susan Strasser reported that Chicago grocers said that more than three quarters of their customers asked for baked beans by brand name and that Campbell's soups were the best sellers.[5] By the 1920s, America was well on the road to a world dominated by brand- and designer-named clothing, appliances, cars, foods, restaurants, leisure-time activities, toys, recreational commodities, cosmetics, and health care products. Brand and designer names promised a predictable world of uniform goods.

Brand names established new ways to cook and think about food. What eventually distinguished the American way of eating were foods from cans, boxes, packages wrapped in wax paper, and, eventually, plastic containers and frozen food. Branding and packaging invaded the restaurant trade with the 1921 opening of the White Castle chain, which was later replaced in popularity by McDonald's. Like the manufacturers of processed foods, White Castle promised a predictable eating experience. An early advertisement claimed, "When you sit in a White Castle remember that you are one of thousands; you are sitting on the same kind of stool; you are being served on the same kind of counter; the coffee you drink is made in accordance with a certain formula."[6]

The transformation of American eating habits was an important factor in the growth of the advertising industry. Many of the early ad agencies depended on accounts from food manufacturers along with producers of soap, soft drinks, and new technologies. Few, if any, of the early food ads stressed the pleasure of taste. Ads sounded like the advice that home economists would give school children as they posted nutrition charts in classrooms without any suggestion that eating could be fun. Early advertising neglected pleasure in the same way that home economists neglected enjoyment as they planned meals for school cafeterias and hospitals.

Exemplifying the issue of food tastes was the discovery that Italian immigrants in Chicago were staying away from hospitals because of hospital food. Horrified, home economists tried to adjust their menus by making a few harmless concessions to immigrant tastes during the initial parts of the hospital stay. Later it was hoped by food planners that the immigrant could be weaned from their traditional foods to the solid and healthy fare of the hospital kitchen. It was suggested that, "Perhaps the treatment of an Italian during this period of change should be studied much as the treatment of an inebriate being won from his strong drink is studied."[7] A similar attempt to change the eating habits of immigrant children occurred in school cafeterias.

TEACHING CONSUMER IDEOLOGY: HOME ECONOMICS

Home economists supported consumerism because it promised to liberate women from the drudgery of household tasks, particularly cooking. Through the purchase of prepared foods and new cleaning technologies, housewives, home economists hoped, would have more time available to further their education and engage in efforts to improve society. Home economists imagined the new woman as highly educated and dedicated to social improvement projects. Early home economists were career scientists who, unable to find employment in existing scientific fields, created departments of domestic science in universities.

After its professional birth in the 1890s, the spread of home economics courses to public schools and colleges was ensured by the 1917 Smith–Hughes Act of 1917. This federal legislation provided support for home economics teachers in public schools to prepare girls for the occupation of homemaker. In turn, this required the hiring of home economic instructors on college campuses to train teachers. These college and university instructors also trained cooks for hospitals, school cafeterias, and other institutional settings. Home economists also expanded their careers by becoming researchers in food technology at private companies and universities and consultants to private industry for product development and sales. The vocational emphasis of the Smith–Hughes Act tended to compromise the role of home economists as scientists. Historian Rima Apple concluded, "In the early twentieth century, women who wanted to pursue careers in scientific research were frequently counseled to study home economics. . . . As home economics units became increasingly involved with teacher training for public school instruction . . . [this] lessened the perceived significance of the scientific aspects of home economics."[8]

In *Perfection Salad: Women and Cooking at the Turn of the Century,* Laura Shapiro credited home economists with the development of a distinctive American cuisine. She argued that, during the latter part of the 19th century, home economists "made American cooking American, transforming a nation of honest appetites into an obedient market for instant mashed potatoes."[9] Reflecting on the Puritanical quality of the teachings and writings of early home economists, Shapiro wrote, "But to enjoy food, to develop a sense for flavors, or to acknowledge that eating could be a pleasure in itself had virtually no part in any course, lecture, or magazine article."[10]

Home economists helped develop and sell the new American diet of prepackaged foods. In public school and college classes, they taught how to prepare the new American diet, how to handle fashion trends and consumer credit, and how to manage household budgets. As researchers, they did pioneer work in food technology that resulted in the development of new food products and made possible the proliferation of fast-food chains. They helped manufacturers develop and sell new gadgetry for the home, such as refrigerators, vacuum cleaners, and washing machines.[11] They helped make school and hospital cafeteria food healthy, inexpensive, and bland.[12] Through the school cafeteria, they hoped to persuade immigrant children to abandon the diet of their parents for the new American cuisine.

Home economists hoped that domestic science would protect the family unit against the worst aspects of urbanization and industrialization. As a profession, it focused on the adaptation of home life to new developments in science and technology. The 1909 announcement of the founding of the American Home Economics Association gave as its goal "the improvement of living conditions in the home, the institutional household, and the community."[13]

As a profession, home economics evolved from an annual series of conferences held at Lake Placid, New York, beginning in 1899 under the leadership of Ellen Richards. Richards, the founder of the American Home Economics Association and the first woman to receive a degree from the Massachusetts Institute of Technology (MIT), brought together a faith in the ability of science to improve human existence, a desire to improve women's education, and a belief that the home was the central institution for reforming society. Reflecting these concerns, after graduating from MIT in 1873, Richards convinced the institution to establish a Woman's Laboratory in 1876. In 1883, Ellen Richards became the first female instructor at MIT as the separate women's laboratory was torn down and women joined men as students at the institution. Richards taught courses on sanitary and household chemistry that focused on cooking and cleaning.[14] In 1887, Richards conducted a study of municipal sewage treatment systems and developed the first water purity standards.[15]

The new American diet resulted, in part, from Richards' research at MIT and her work with the New England Kitchen and the Boston School of Housekeeping. Richards and others at the New England Kitchen and the Boston School of Housekeeping believed that improper diet and household management were undermining society. "Is it not pitiful, this army of incompetent wives," declared domestic scientist M. V. Shailer in an 1898 issue of *New England Kitchen Magazine*, "whose lack of all knowledge of domestic science is directly and indirectly the means of filling our prisons, asylums, reformatories and saloons."[16] This feeling echoed earlier claims by Juliet Corson, the superintendent of the New York Cooking School. Written In 1877, Corson's booklet, *Fifteen Cent Dinners for Workingmen's Families*, claimed, "The laborer who leaves home in the early morning, after an ill-cooked breakfast, and carries in his basket soggy bread and tough meat for his luncheon, is apt to return at night tired and cross, not unfrequently he tries, *en route*, to cure his discomfort at a neighboring saloon."[17]

Placing society's ills at the doorstep of the home, domestic scientists saw a cure through nutritional food, sanitary cooking, budgeting, and household cleanliness. Nutritionally balanced food, it was believed, would provide the energy for hard work and resistance to the temptations of the tavern. Wholesome food served in the home and school cafeteria would stimulate the student to study and protect them from illness. Hospital patients would recover more quickly as a result of scientifically planned menus and food. Sanitary cooking and household cleanliness would protect everyone from sickness. Protected from illness and energized by nutritional foods, it was believed, workers would be less likely to miss work and more likely to retain their jobs. According to the calculations of home economists, these circumstances would reduce unemployment, crime, and alcoholism. For the same reasons, students would be able to complete their studies and find good jobs. Also proper management of the household budget would keep families from falling into poverty. Workers would be less likely to strike if their wives could make existing wages satisfactory through proper budgeting. This belief in the ability of home economics to reform society was summed up in 1902 by Marion Talbot at the fourth annual meeting of the Lake Placid Conference on Home Economics. These conferences foreshadowed the establishment of the American Home Economics Association. Talbot stated, "the obligations of home life are not by any means limited to its own four walls, that home economics must always be regarded in light of its relation to the general social system, that men and women are alike concerned in understanding the processes, activities, obligations and opportunities which make the home and family effective parts of the social fabric."[18]

Along with saving society, home economics was to liberate women from household drudgery and make them active participants in shaping society. Ellen Richards worried that "the industrial world is ruled by science that all the things with which we surround ourselves are now manufactured upon scientific principles, and, alas! women are ignorant of those principles."[19] The study of science and home economics would, Richards hoped, make housekeeping into a profession. A 1890 editorial in the *New England Kitchen Magazine* proclaimed, "We need to exalt the profession of home making to see that it is as dignified and requires as much intelligence as other professions."[20] Science and technology would be the key to eliminating household drudgery. As Ellen Richards explained, "The woman who boils potatoes year after year, with no thought of the how or why, is a drudge, but the cook who can compute the calories of heat which a potato of given weight will yield, is no drudge."[21]

Portending the future marketing of packaged and frozen dinners, Ellen Richards helped found the New England Kitchen in 1890. The founders hoped to improve the lives of working and poor people by providing already prepared sanitary and economical food that would have consistent flavor and texture. Richards envisioned a neighborhood establishment that would prepare and sell food. The establishment would be educational because buyers could observe the sanitary conditions and cooking methods. Also, cooked under scientific conditions, buyers would learn to expect the food to always taste the same.

Richards' dream of standardizing American eating habits was made possible by the work of Fannie Farmer and the Boston Cooking School. The Boston Cooking School opened in 1879; by the 1890s, it was training cooks for public school cafeterias using a curriculum that included Psychology, Physiology and Hygiene, Bacteriology, Foods, Laundry Work, the Chemistry of Soap, Bluing, and Starch, and Cookery Applied to Public School Work. Fannie Farmer joined the Boston Cooking School in 1888. Legend has it that standardized measurements were born when Marcia Shaw asked Fannie Farmer what it meant to measure out "butter the size of an egg" and "a pinch of salt."[22] In 1896, Fannie Farmer's *The Boston Cooking-School Cook Book* was published and quickly became a national best seller. A major innovation in Farmer's book was the use of leveled measurements, which gained her the epithet of the "Mother of Level Measurements." Embodying American approaches to scientific cooking, Fannie Farmer wrote, "A cupful is measured level. A tablespoonful is measured level. A teaspoonful is measured level."[23]

Ellen Richards' dreams of prepackaged and standardized meals spread across the country. Jane Addams sent a settlement worker from Chicago to learn Richard's methods and created a similar kitchen at Hull House. Another kitchen opened in Providence, and Richards was invited to create a New England Kitchen at the 1893 Chicago World's Fair. The exhibit was lined with food charts, menus, diagrams, and consumerist mottoes such as, "Wherefore do you spend money for that which is not bread, and your labor for that which satisfieth not?"[24]

After the World's Fair, the New England Kitchen focused its efforts on selling prepared foods to Boston's nine public high schools and office workers. In 1895, Richards helped create a model program in Boston's public school cafeterias. Prior to 1895, janitors in Boston schools were responsible for the lunch program. Using new theories on nutrition, sanitation, and food preparation, Richards and her cooking colleagues introduced the new American diet to Boston school children.[25] These efforts set the stage for trained domestic scientists to take over school cafeterias to ensure that students received healthy and sanitary foods. The other focus was on hospital food. Richards declared that "no better school of diet could be found than an intelligently managed hospital."[26]

In both schools and hospitals, cafeterias served the double function of supplying nutritional food and changing people's diets. Of primary concern were changing the diets of immigrants from Southern and Eastern Europe. Home economists believed that immigrants were harmed by foods that required long periods of digestion. American scientific cooks were guided by a 1820s' timetable created by an American army surgeon who studied a young man with a hole in his stomach caused by a hunting accident. The surgeon suspended food on a string in the man's stomach to determine the speed of digestion. According to this experiment, pork turned out to be the most difficult to digest, whereas clear broth and rice were the easiest.[27]

Concern about rates of digestion had a limiting effect on the role of spices in cooking. Fears about the overuse of spices reinforced already negative attitudes of home economists regarding immigrant food. In *The Chemistry of Cooking and Cleaning*, Ellen Richards argued that spices did have a role in stimulating digestive juices, but warned against heavy seasonings because they might wear out the digestive tract. In her words, spices should be, "Just enough to accomplish the purpose. . . ."[28] Based on concerns about digestion, menus were created that balanced the digestive aspects of one food against another. For instance, it was proposed that the first serving should include easily digestible items such as oysters and white fish, which would prepare the gastric juices for the more difficult meat dishes. The result were recipes and menus noted for their blandness and lack of sensitivity to taste.

The development of this new American diet was directly linked to an image of the new woman. As home economists invaded school and hospital cafeterias with their gospel of scientific cookery, they saw the possibility of freeing the American woman from home cooking and making it possible for her to extend her education. Ellen Richards believed that prepared foods, like those served by the New England Kitchen, would increase women's freedom.

In addition, the new American diet was associated with the so-called *democratization of domesticity*. Home economist believed the school cafeteria and home economics courses would unite students from differing social class backgrounds under a single standard of domesticity. In both the school cafeteria and food preparation classes, students were to develop similar tastes. Girls from lower class backgrounds were to be brought up to the same standard of cooking and cleaning as upper class girls, whereas upper class girls were to learn the arts normally practiced by their household help. The belief in democratic leveling was exemplified by a statement of a New York public school's supervisor of cooking's comment—that the female student "is wonderfully interested in the bacteria of the dishcloth, and the ice box, and the garbage pail, and when she becomes mistress of a home these things will receive her attention as well as the parlor, library, and music room."[29] Home economists hoped that standardized cooking and shared attitudes about housework and sanitation would open the door to a more democratic society.

PREPARED FOOD AND WOMEN'S EDUCATION

By freeing women from cooking chores, home economists believed, the new woman would have more time for education and civic reform. Also as a result of the social involvement and education of the new woman, the quality of civic life would improve, and the cultural level of homes and husbands would be elevated. In fact, the 1897 meeting of the Woman's Suffrage Association featured a keynote speech on the value of domestic science to the women's movement.[30] As educated women, home economists wanted other women to receive the benefits of an extended schooling. Prepared food, it was believed, would mean freedom from cooking and liberation of women along with supplying the family with a sanitary, nutritious, and balanced diet. In choosing the path of prepared food, the housewife shifted her emphasis from producer to consumer.

Ellen Richards projected this liberating role for prepared food in a 1900 article entitled, "Housekeeping in the Twentieth Century." In her dream home where the purchase of cheap mass-produced furniture allowed more money for intellectual pleasures, the pantry was filled with a large stock of prepared foods—mainly canned foods and bakery products. Richards' dream pantry was based on the reality of a growing industry for canned foods. As early as the 1820s, William Underwood sold meats packed in bottles, and in 1856 Gail Borden patented a method for condensing milk and preserving it with sugar. By the 1870s, the technology for canning meats was perfected. In the 1870s, H. J. Heinz sold crocked pickles, horseradish, and sauerkraut, and a decade later the company expanded its product list to include cooked macaroni products and vegetables. In the 1880s, the Franco-American Company began to distribute canned meals. In 1897, Campbell's introduced canned soups after the development of a method for condensing the product. According to Ruth Cowan, "By the turn of the century [19th to 20th], canned goods were a standard feature of the American diet . . . [including] processed foods of all kinds—packed dry cereals, pancake mixes, crackers and cookies machine-wrapped in paper containers, canned hams, and bottled corned beef."[31]

In Richards' ideal home, a pneumatic tube connected to the pantry speeded canned and packaged food to the kitchen where the wife simply heated up the meal. In addition, the meal would be accompanied by store-bought bread. Besides being unsanitary, home economists believed that home-made bread and other bakery goods required an inordinate amount of preparation time and therefore housewives should rely on factory-pro-duced bread products. Richards dismissed the issue of taste with the com-ment, "I grant that each family has a weakness for the flavor produced by its own kitchen bacteria, but that is a prejudice due to lack of education."[32] People would stop worrying about taste, she argued, when they fully real-ized the benefits of the superior cleanliness and consistency of factory kitchens and bakeries. In a 1900 book, *The Cost of Living as Modified by Sani-tary Science*, Richards provided another version of her vision of the com-modified housework. "Housekeeping," she explained, "no longer means washing dishes, scrubbing floors, making soap and candles; it means spend-ing a given amount of money for a great variety of ready-prepared articles and so using commodities as to produce the greatest satisfaction and the best possible mental, moral, and physical results."[33]

The so-called philosopher of home economics, Caroline Hunt delin-eated the role of women as consumers. Her interest in science and social reform paralleled those of Ellen Richards. Born in Chicago in 1865, Hunt entered Northwestern University in 1881 and, after interrupting her stud-ies to teach high school, graduated in 1888. Teaching high school for sev-eral more years, she again returned to Northwestern University to study chemistry. While at Northwestern, she lived with Jane Addams at Hull House and engaged in studies of newly arrived immigrants, including *The Italians in Chicago: A Social and Economic Study* (1897) and *Dietary Studies in Chicago* (1898). In 1896, she was hired to teach Domestic Economy and operate the cafeteria at Chicago's Lewis Institute. Then in 1903, she was hired by the University of Wisconsin to organize and head the School of Domestic Science.[34]

While at Lewis Institute, Hunt equated women's freedom with a change in household roles from producer to consumer. Women would have more free time for education, she argued, if they bought factory-made products rather than producing them in the home. For instance, a housewife could be a producer of soap or a consumer of factory-made soap. "The woman who today makes her own soap instead of taking advantage of machinery for its production," she wrote, "enslaves herself to ignorance by limiting her time for study. The woman who shall insist upon carrying the home-making methods of today into the tomorrow will fail to lay hold of the possible quota of freedom which the future has in store for her."[35]

Throughout her writings, she highlighted the importance of the transi-tion of the household tasks from that of production to consumption. For Hunt, this transition was part of the larger process of industrialization and job specialization. Comparing the past to existing conditions in a paper she read at the 1904 Lake Placid Conference on Home Economics, Hunt ar-gued, "The home has delegated to the school not only the technical but also

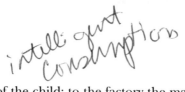

the general education of the child; to the factory the manufacture of clothing, of furniture, and of house furnishings."[36] Although the responsibilities of the household were changing, she contended, they still played an important role in society. Households were still responsible for raising the child to school age and teaching morality. Plus, Hunt added, homes were responsible for education about beauty and what she called "rational sociability."

According to Hunt, rational sociability was an important aspect of the consumer's education. From her perspective, the consumer had a social responsibility to influence producers regarding their treatment of workers and the sanitary production of food products. In her discussion of higher education at the 1906 Lake Placid Conference, she argued that "home economics, if considered as primarily a training for intelligent consumption, should be introduced into the college education."[37] She defined *intelligent consumption* as demonstrating a concern for the general welfare of society. "The wise consumer," she told the Conference, "has in mind not only his own advantage, but the welfare of those who make, transport and care for the commodities he uses."[38] From this perspective, the consumer must be educated into an awareness of workers' conditions. This added a social reform aspect to the role of consumption. "He [the wise consumer] thinks of himself as responsible, not only for the happiness and well being, but also for the continued efficiency and social usefulness of the producer. He hopes that by his own use of wealth he may so direct human energy as to educate the worker and to increase the world's resources."[39]

Arguing that home economics should be introduced into the college curriculum "primarily [as] a training for intelligent consumption," Hunt listed the need for food, shelter, clothing, cleanliness, and beauty as the focus of this study.[40] Although food courses were well defined, she argued, instruction on the satisfaction of the other needs had to be expanded. In a telling statement of her vision of the future role of women, Hunt argued, "There is . . . an important way, other than thru [sic] purchase of food, in which women control a large amount of human energy, and that is thru [sic] buying and using what may be called art products including clothing and house furnishing. We feel, I am sure, that the college should give students an intelligent attitude with reference to the responsibilities arising from their consumption of these products."[41]

Hunt envisioned college-educated women finding time to engage in social reform movements by consuming rather than producing household goods. In other words, women would be freed to engage in *municipal housekeeping*. Released from household chores, women could apply their education, particularly from home economics, to protecting the household from deleterious industrial and social practices. She called this "Woman's Public Work For the Home."[42] At the 1907 Lake Placid Conference, she argued that when women forced by their responsibility for the family welfare into a fight for a public milk supply of assured purity, and are unsuccessful in the fight, we may take this as an indication that young women now in college should be taught to seek and to overcome the difficulties which lie in the way of the present accomplishment of this much needed reform.[43]

Hunt related freedom from food preparation to the rise of democratic thought and an emphasis on freedom for the individual. Under democracy, she contended, individual freedom meant enhanced opportunities for women rather than absence of restraints. Freedom for women, Hunt argued, required passing "over to public enterprise the work of food preparation and the responsibility for the care of houses, thus releasing in woman's life energy for individualization."[44]

Richards and Hunt's hopes seemed to be realized with the rapid spread of home economics courses in public schools and colleges. According to Barbara Ehrenreich and Deirdre English, 20% of high schools offered courses by 1916–1917, and the number of college students enrolled in courses increased from 213 in 1905 to 17,778 in 1916. Most of those enrolled in college courses were preparing to be home economics teachers.[45]

Richards wanted training in home economics to begin in elementary school. Along with Alice Norton, she prepared a widely used curriculum, which began:

Ideals and Standards of Living

13. Historic Development of the Family
    a. The darkest ages of history
    b. The beginnings of human society
    c. The psychology of races—expression of the home ideal in races other than the Anglo-Saxon
    d. Early social life of the Anglo-Saxon people
       i. The home life of the Anglo-Saxon vs. the communistic family system.[46]

Besides teaching domestic science, this curriculum was designed to Americanize immigrant children to Anglo-Saxon standards. In this context, domestic science leaders saw their efforts as an evolution in Anglo-Saxon culture. In the first grade, children were to compare their homes "with that of lower animals and primitive peoples." By the third grade, they were to build and decorate model homes.[47] The impact of these courses on non-Anglo-Saxon cultures continued after World War II. Elinor Polansky, a second-generation Russian–Jewish immigrant, reported about her 1949 home economics classes in a Bronx junior high school:

What came across was this idea that your home environment was no good and you had to make it different. For example, we learned that the only right way to cook was to make everything separately . . . that was the good, wholesome way. Things all mixed together, like stews, that was considered peasant food. I would never have admitted to my teacher that my family ate its food mixed together. There was something repulsive about food touching. The string beans weren't supposed to touch the mashed potatoes and so forth. . . . Only later did I realize that I hate that kind of cooking. But then I can remember even asking my mother to buy plates with separations in them.[48]

WONDER BREAD AND JELL-O: HOME ECONOMICS, THE NEW WOMAN, AND SOCIAL REFORM

The evolution from home-made to factory-made bread exemplifies the variety of forces shaping the new consumerism. From the perspective of home economist, the purchase of factory-made bread freed the housewife from the time required to mix, knead, and bake bread at home. Also factory-made bread prepared under proper supervision ensured sanitary conditions and standardization. Following this line of reasoning, the consumption of factory-made bread contributed to a healthy diet while freeing the homemaker to engage in municipal housekeeping. In turn, municipal housekeeping ensured that the bread factory would provide adequate wages and working conditions for its employees, maintained sanitary conditions for bread production, and baked a uniform and nutritional product.

Caroline Hunt preached the gospel of factory bread and social reform at the Ninth Annual Lake Placid Conference. She argued that women wasted a great deal of energy on home-made bread. 'If they spent half that time in the effort," she contended,

> to agree upon a standard for good bread and in the insistence that the baker's product must come up to that standard, they would not now . . . depend on the use of a kind of bread which in no way comes up to their ideals as to quality, and which is frequently sold and delivered without proper protection from dirty hands, from dust and from flies.[49]

The separate packaging of each loaf of bread ensured the sanitary condition of the product. Following the same line of reasoning, the prepackaging of all food products would make food distribution even more sanitary.

What happens if the husband does not like prepackaged factory-made bread? According to Hunt, the husband was compensated by having an educated wife. Using an example of a wife taking a course on Dante's writings rather than staying home and baking, Hunt claimed, "if he [the] husband considers the advantages of eating . . . his baker's bread flavored with drip-

Led to Fem. Mystique, not liberation

pings of information concerning the great poet and his times, he may conclude that baker's bread with Dante sauce is more to him than homemade bread."[50]

Although home economists believed these prepared products liberated women for political and social action, advertisements often conveyed a different message. This was particularly true of ads in women's magazines, such as the *Ladies Home Journal, The Delineator,* and *Good Housekeeping,* which, according to historian Ellen Garvey, had "a special and often more self-conscious role in the construction of the woman reader as consumer."[51] Similar to newspapers, advertisements became the largest source of revenue for magazines. Edward Bok, editor of the *Ladies Home Journal* from 1889 to 1919, tried to develop the image of women as stay-at-home consumers as opposed to the home economics' image of the consumer woman fighting for social improvement. Garvey argued that, although Bok and other male editors of women's magazines tried to play down the idea of the politically and socially active women in their columns and stories, the advertisements appearing in the magazines often stressed the new woman. However, these magazine ads, Garvey contended, used

> feminist and quasi-feminist catch phrases and slogans [that] patronizingly trivialized a serious quest for political power into a choice of trimmings and appliances, and suggested, along with anti-suffrage propaganda, that a woman's effect on the home sphere was so powerful that it exceeded and made unnecessary any power she sought in the larger world.[52]

The difference between the vision of home economists and what was often conveyed by ads was exemplified by a 1930s cartoon-style ad for Wonder Bread that showed in the top panel the face of a distressed wife looking up into the eyes of a stern-faced husband with the couple surrounded by the headline "People Whispered." In the next smaller panel, the wife was shown on the phone saying, "But, Dick, you're *always* eating in town! Please come home!" Near her was a woman whispering to another woman, "I *told* you so." In the next panel, the wife announces the husband is coming home and invites both of the other women to stay. One woman excuses herself and the other agrees to stay. In the next panel, the wife complains that her bread was stale, and her guest responds by offering to buy bread that never got stale. In the following panels, the guest presents the wife with a loaf of Wonder Bread, the husband returns home and loves the Wonder Bread. In the next to last panel marked "Next Day," the husband turns down an office invitation for lunch with the statement, "Can't . . . I'm reporting home for a real meal."[53]

In the ad, the home economist vision of female liberation was replaced by a servile wife struggling to maintain her marriage by serving the best pre-

packaged food. However, the ad did support the home economists contention that good food would keep husbands from straying from family life.
The final panel illustrated the gulf between the feminist and advertising images of the housewife. Across the top of the final panel was written, "Hurry
Your Husband Home!" Below this headline was, "Smart women know that
meals are an important part of *every* husband's life! That's why wives by thousands serve Wonder Bread. It's made of the *finest* ingredients. Slo-baked.
Makes *every* meal *worth* hurrying home for!"[54]

Wonder Bread and Jell-O became signature dishes of the new American
cuisine. Wonder Bread, with its soft, white, and mushy texture, and supposedly easy-to-digest contents, quickly replaced the hard-crusted breads of European tradition. Invented in 1897, Jell-O transformed an aristocratic European dish, as declared in an ad featuring George Washington, into
"America's Most Famous Dessert."[55] Jell-O signaled the beginning of American instant foods, which only required adding water and stirring. In her history of Jell-O, Carolyn Wyman opened the introductory chapter:

COCA-COLA MAY SELL BETTER.
APPLE PIE MAY SEEM MORE TRADITIONAL.
BUT THE TRUE TWENTIETH-CENTURY AMERICAN
FOOD WAS CERTAINLY
JELL-O GELATIN.[56]

Wyman continued, "Jell-O more closely resembles such high-tech marvels
of the '50s and '60s as Cool Whip and Cheez Whiz . . . Jell-O was, in fact,
one of America's first processed foods. As such it was a model for all the
bland, sweet, cheap convenient foods we now eat."[57]

Although home economists loved Jell-O, immigrants arriving at Ellis Island in the early 20th century refused to eat it. One Ellis Island detainee
stated, "because they didn't like the . . . wobbly texture." Aboard a ship
bound for the United States, one German immigrant was frightened by her
introduction to American cuisine. Served as the first dinner course, she
wrote, "It was a square piece of Jell-O and as the ship was moving the Jell-O
was wiggling. And they told us we could eat this Jell-O. I was really frightened by this piece of orange Jell-O."[58]

In contrast, home economists hailed Jell-O as an essential dish in the
new American cuisine and made it a frequently served dish in school and
hospital cafeterias. Domestic scientists loved Jell-O because it democra-
tized the American diet while providing a digestible dish. Originally, gelatin foods were primarily served at the tables of the wealthy because of the
difficulty of preparation. It required the laborious efforts of servants to
produce a good gelatin dish. Preparation required the cleaning of calves'
feet and extraction of fat between the claws. The calves' feet were then

boiled and, after cooling, residual fat was skimmed off. The feet were boiled again with the addition of egg whites and shells to pick up the impurities. After straining through a cloth, spices and sugar were added, and the mixture was placed in a mold and packed in ice. Similar to Jell-O molds of the 20th and 21st centuries, the original gelatin molds came in elaborate shapes and designs.[59]

Democratization of gelatin dishes occurred in 1893 after home economist Sarah Tyson Rorer of the Philadelphia Cooking School asked the Knox Company to develop an instant gelatin. Responding to the request, Knox introduced an instant gelatin with the descriptive label, "Sparkling Granulated Calves Foot Gelatine."[60] Almost immediately, home economists jumped on the gelatin bandwagon as a vehicle for making salads along with desserts. They recommended blending granulated gelatin with whipped cream, grated cheese, or mayonnaise and to harden dishes such as chicken salad. Gelatin was proclaimed an ideal mold for layers of fruit. The crowning touch to the American gelatin salad appeared shortly after the beginning of the 20th century. Perfection Salad, as it has been called, used gelatin to hold together a mixture of finely chopped raw cabbage, celery, and red peppers. Making gelatin dishes became a common part of the public school home economics courses.[61]

Jell-O, and later Crisco, opened corporate doors for domestic scientists to work as recipe writers and publicity agents for process foods. As publicity agents, they promised that the new processed foods would liberate women. As a preflavored gelatin, Jell-O further reduced the skills and time required for cooking. Domestic scientist Marion Harland helped advertise Jell-O with assurance that, "Even the woman who cannot cook need have no difficulty in devising a new desert every day if she is supplied with Jell-O and common sense."[62] As an example, Harland suggested mixing prunes into lemon Jell-O. A Jell-O ad featured a statement by the principal of Fanny Farmer's School of Cookery, "Jell-O is an up-to-minute food designed to meet the needs of the modern housekeeper whose problem is to save time, energy, and money in doing her daily tasks."[63] Philadelphia Cooking School instructor Sarah Tyson Rorer offered her opinion of the healthfulness of Jell-O in the advertising booklet, *What Six Famous Cooks Say of Jell-O*: "Elaborate desserts, such as boiled and baked puddings and dyspepsia-producing pies, have given place to the more attractive and healthful desserts made from Jell-O." In the tradition of domestic scientists, Rorer also proclaimed the liberating effects of Jell-O: "Why should any woman stand for hours over a hot fire mixing compounds to make people ill, when in two minutes, with an expense of ten cents, she can produce such attractive, delicious desserts."[64]

Procter & Gamble used the same method to market Crisco. A vegetable shortening, Crisco was a product of 5 years of secret experimentation prior to its marketing in 1911. One of the reasons for its development was to ensure Procter & Gamble's domination of the cotton seed oil market, which it also used in its soap products. Its rivals for control of this market were Armour and Company and the N. K. Fairbank Company, which sold cooking fats mixed with lard. Procter & Gamble's goal was an all vegetable solid fat. Crisco was an entirely new product that required changing the traditional use of animal fats, particularly lard and butter, in cooking.[65]

The company hired the editor of the Boston Cooking School Magazine, Janet McKenzie Hill, to write the first Crisco cookbook. She invented another signature dish of the new American cuisine—the Crisco white sauce composed of two melted tablespoons of Crisco, two tablespoons of flour, and one cup of milk. About this invention, food historian Laura Shapiro wrote, "With the Crisco white sauce, scientific cookery arrived at a food substance from which virtually everything had been stripped except a certain number of nutrients and the color white. Only a cuisine molded by technology could prosper on such developments, and it prospered."[66]

Besides establishing a market for processed foods, Crisco helped sell the idea of packaged goods. Traditionally, lard and butter were sold in bulk from containers. Following the pattern of home economists, Crisco ads stressed the sanitary and scientific qualities of the product. One of the first full-page ads appearing in a 1912 issue of the *Ladies Home Journal* proclaimed, "Crisco is never sold in bulk, but is put up in immaculate packages, perfectly protected from dust and store odors. No hands touch it. . . ."[67] The ad contained photos of fried fish, a cake, cookies, and a large pile of Crisco shortening on a plate. The headline declared, "An Absolutely New Product," followed by the subtitles, "A Scientific Discovery Which Will Affect Every Kitchen in America" and "Crisco—Better than butter for cooking."[68]

MAKING UP THE MODERN WOMAN

As domestic scientists were attempting to achieve their vision of the modern woman, the cosmetics industry was creating another image of the modern woman. Cosmetic ads provided models for how to look and act like a so-called *new woman*. This new woman was envisioned as independent, outspoken, and sexually assertive. The female leaders of the cosmetic industry were independent business women defining their roles in the new corporate world. However, their model of the sexually assertive and independent woman was often in conflict with the sanitized model of independent reformer presented by home economists.

As chronicled by Kathy Peiss in her wonderfully titled book, *Hope in a Jar: The Making of America's Beauty Culture*, cosmetic ads were the most blatant sellers of sexuality and promises of personal transformation.[69] Prior to the

20th century, Peiss argued, cosmetic products were primarily sold to keep the skin free of blemishes and maintain a clear and clean appearance. The face was considered a reflection of inward purity. Heavy use of paintlike cosmetics was associated with prostitution. In the early 20th century, the use of cosmetics changed with the marketing of make-up products by Estee Lauder, C. J. Walker, Helena Rubinstein, Elizabeth Arden, and Max Factor.

The leading women in the cosmetic industry—Max Factor got his start as a make-up artist for Hollywood films—promoted cosmetics as an industry open to women that would result in increasing women's power by enhancing their independence and sexuality. "The cosmetic business is interesting among modern industries in its opportunities for women," Helena Rubinstein argued. "Here they have found a field that is their own province—working for women with women, and giving that which only women can give—intimate understanding of feminine needs and feminine desires."[70] By 1930, beauty writer Nell Vinick was able to declare that cosmetics were "merely symbols of the social revolution that has gone on; the spiritual and mental forces that women have used to break away from conventions and to forward the cause of women's freedom."[71]

Although Elizabeth Arden did support women's suffrage, her political activity did not match that of Helena Rubinstein and C. J. Walker. Helena Rubinstein was a life-long supporter of women's equal rights, and C. J Walker, a pioneer developer of African-American cosmetics, supported equal rights for both women and African Americans. Walker promoted the use of cosmetics as a matter of racial pride. African-American women, she felt, should look good and project a positive social image. Using saleswomen, Walker hoped to create a new career route for African-American women. One of her salespeople claimed that she had enabled "hundreds of colored women to make an honest and profitable living."[72] Walker gave financial support and time to industrial education, recreational programs, and charitable giving to African Americans. She was active in the National Equal Rights League and the International League of Darker Peoples.[73]

The image of independent and politically active women sometimes appeared in advertisements. Leading women in advertising sometimes went out of their way to include their own political views in ads for cosmetics. The 20th century's largest advertising firm, J. Walter Thompson, had a separate Women's Editorial Department. In the early 1920s, members of the department cheered when they heard that Alva Belmont, a wealthy suffragist and feminist, agreed to endorse Pond's Cold Cream for a $1,000 donation to a feminist cause.[74] The resulting 1924 ad showed a small picture of her library at the top and a small picture of two bottles of Pond's creams at the bottom. The ad was entitled, "An Interview with Mrs. O.H.P. Belmont on the care of the skin." The opening quote from Mrs. Belmont quickly established that using Pond's creams increases a woman's chance for influence and success. "A woman who neglects her personal appearance loses half her influence. The wise care of one's body constructs the frame encircling our mentality, the ability of which ensures the success of one's life. I advise a daily use of Pond's Two Creams."[75] In the ad, Mrs. Belmont commented to the interviewer, "I suppose you want me to tell you what I think is the relation between a woman's success and her personal appearance. . . . It is vital. That is just as true for the woman at home or in business as for those who are socially prominent. . . . Don't you know how often the woman with an unattractive face fails in the most reasonable undertaking."[76]

A 1928 advertisement for Armand face powder portrayed eight different versions of the modern woman from sexual powerhouse to energetic club type:

1. Cleopatra Type—Masculine hearts pound when she goes by
2. Godiva Type—Anglo-Saxon, blond, winsome, and how!
3. Sonya Type—Dark and mysterious, she has a way with her
4. Cherie Type—She brings the boulevards of Paris to America
5. Sheba Type—Dark-brown and a queenly air
6. Lorelei Type—Blond and aggressive, she "gets her man"
7. Mona Lisa Type—Light-brown hair and a devastating smile
8. Collen Type—She has more pep than a jazz band.[77]

The modern political woman was emphasized in Listerine tooth paste ads in the 1920s. One ad showed a sultry-looking woman standing in a dimly lit room. Just below her in large type was: "When lovely women vote."[78] In smaller type, the ad claimed, "To thousands of women of this type—charming, educated, well-to-do, prominent in the social and civic life of her city, we put this question: What tooth paste do you use? To our delight, the majority answered Listerine Tooth Paste."[79]

Ads produced by African-American-owned companies emphasized the new African-American woman and enhancement of racial pride. A 1925 ad for C. J. Walker cosmetics showed a group of women attending an opera performance. Next to the drawing of the opera house interior was a photo of C. J. Walker. Below the photo and drawing was the declaration in large type, "Glorifying Our Womanhood." The text of the ad stated, "No greater force is working to glorify the womanhood of our Race than Madam C. J. Walker's Wonderful Hair and Skin Preparations. . . . We tell you, Madam C. J. Walker through her preparation, if for no other reason, remains yet, the greatest benefactress of our race."[80]

Advertisements directed at African-American consumers did provoke a great deal of criticism. Cosmetic ads were the richest source of revenue for magazines and newspapers published for the African-American community.[81] Some critics suggested that these ads promoted a White standard of beauty as exemplified by the following: "New 3-way Skin discovery Gives You WHITE SKIN OVERNIGHT"; "At last! The lighter complexion that increases beauty and . . . Makes Skin So Light Would Hardly Know She is Colored"; and "MAKE YOUR HAIR STRAIGHT AND BEAUTIFUL."[82] However, there were differences between the ads produced by White- and African-American-owned companies. White companies tended to portray the hair of African Americans as *ugly*, *kinky*, and *unruly*, whereas African-American companies simply marketed their hair products as promoting healthy hair and skin.[83]

The commodification of the woman's body created an advertising image of the new woman who was independent, aggressive, and sexually alive. In the 20th century, advertising portrayed make-up, soaps, underarm deodorants, mouthwashes, toilet paper, and body odor treatments as sources of social freedom. Although ads played on personal fears and anxieties, they also promised greater social freedom for women through the consumption of products. The purchase and use of products promised the new woman freedom from embarrassment and rejection. Through consumption of the right items, every woman was promised sexuality, independence, and assertiveness.

PLACING THE PRODUCT IN THE WOMAN'S MIND

Dominated by Protestants who grew up with the McGuffey readers and Sunday school literature, the advertising agencies that blossomed at the turn of the 20th century tried to distance themselves from earlier patent medicine ads, P.T. Barnum methods, and other forms of city reading.[84] Richard Ohmann argued that manufacturers poured money into these new advertising agencies to match industrial output with consumption. By the end of the 19th century, the crisis was no longer production, but consumption. People needed to buy more goods to keep the wheels of industry rolling. Not only did gross national product increase from $9.1 billion in 1873 to $29.6 billion in 1896 (figures in 1929 dollars), but, more important, output per person hour or productivity increased by 64% between 1869 and 1899. Increased productivity meant cheaper goods. Also new types of goods appeared on the market. In 1860, ready-to-wear men's clothing was practically nonexistent, but by 1890 ready-to-wear made up 90% of the market.[85]

Through advertising a new relationship was established between the owner and worker. In Ohmann's words, "They [manufacturers and advertisers] would urge workers—first those of the middle class, then all workers—to bring more and more commodities into homes, and to share in the vision of the good life conducted through the use and display of these products."[86] Between 1890 and 1904, advertising expenditures grew at the impressive rate of 128%.[87] In summary, the primary drive in building the advertising industry was the increased industrial output of old and new products.[88]

How did these early advertisers deal with abundance? After spending hours examining early advertisements, I was struck by the fact that few suggested the purchase of a product would result in some form of indulgent pleasure. An exception was Coca-Cola's claim to be "Delicious and Refreshing."[89] One of the earliest brand images was the Quaker Oats' man who first appeared in an 1888 ad to sell packaged oatmeal. Prior to packaging, people bought their oats directly from grocery store bins without any brand markings. There were few hints on packages or in ads that eating oatmeal was tasty and pleasing. The kindly figure of an elderly Quaker man appeared in the first ad with the promise that, "One pound of Quaker Oats makes as much bone and muscle as three pounds of beef . . . [they] supply what brains and bodies require."[90] Other food and beverage ads through the 1920s, as far as I can determine, emphasized the home economist's goals of purity, health, and good digestion. An early Schlitz beer ad compared "Poor Beer vs. Pure Beer" without any mention of taste or, heaven forbid, the pleasurable mental state caused by alcohol. The ad sold Schlitz beer as healthier than poor beer. The ad stated in making the comparison, "One is good, and good for you; the other is harmful." After comparing the differences in production, the ad asked, "Don't you prefer a pure beer, a good beer, a healthful beer, when it costs no more than the common?"[91] An early ad by the Quaker Oats Company for Puffed Wheat, Puffed Rice, and Corn Puffs mentioned one time that they had a "fascinating taste." Otherwise the emphasis was on digestion. The text might have been written by a professional home economist: "The purpose in Puffed Grains—Puffed Wheat or Puffed Rice—is to make digestion easy and complete. Digestion usually consumes much energy, because food cells are not broken." The ad continued with an explanation of how the puffing process made grains "wholly digestible without any tax on the stomach."[92] A famous 1925 Lucky Strike cigarettes' ad, which was designed to entice women into smoking, failed to mention anything about taste or the pleasure of nicotine racing through the nervous system. The ad proclaimed, "To Keep a slender figure, No one can deny, Reach for a Lucky instead of a sweet."[93]

The Lucky Strike ad highlighted another way consumption was separated from the pleasure of using a product. In *Fables of Abundance: A Cultural History of Advertising in America*, Jackson Lears argued that in "national advertisements . . . designed by . . . educated Anglo-Saxon professionals, pleasure was subordinated to a larger agenda of personal efficiency."[94] Food, tobacco, and beer ads promised health or slimness. Personal efficiency was linked to personal transformation. In the Lucky Strike ad, an attractive woman in a low-cut gown with puckered lips and half-closed eyes looks into an empty distance. The ad suggests that by smoking Lucky Strikes a woman will be transformed into the woman in the ad.

The goal of advertisers, according to Lears, was to awaken consumer desires while keeping them within the boundaries of Protestant propriety and market needs. Lears claimed, "advertisements did more than stir up desire, they also sought to manage it—to stabilize the sorcery of the marketplace by containing dreams of personal transformation within the broader rhetoric of control."[95] The combination of tapping into desire along with the stress on personal efficiency was exemplified by a 1916 Quaker Oats ad that read, "Mark the lovers of Quaker Oats. . . . They believe in keeping young. For oats create vitality. They feed the fires of youth. They are vim-producing, spirit-giving. . . . Lovers of life eat them liberally. Lovers of languor don't."[96] Throughout the ad were illusions of sexual desire through words such as *lovers* and *fires of youth*. The ad promised personal efficiency through greater *vitality* and *keeping young*.

SERVING WHITES: AFRICAN AMERICANS AND NATIVE AMERICANS

Advertising targeted at Euro-Americans used African-American images to give respectability to products. These images were in sharp contrast to advertisements directed at the African-American community. As mentioned previously, the ad for C. J. Walker cosmetics showed African-American women attending an opera. In contrast, ads for Euro-American audiences showed African Americans as smiling servants and cooks. The ads implied that a product was used by a family that could afford the use of African-American servants. Two of the most famous African-American icons were Aunt Jemima, who was used for a pancake mix, and Chef Rastus for Cream of Wheat Cereal. Besides being a pancake icon, Aunt Jemima, in the person of Nancy Greene, traveled around the country cooking pancakes at fairs with the advertising slogan: "I's in town, honey."[97] A 1897 ad for Cream of Wheat showed a poorly dressed and elderly African-American man staring at a billboard illustration of the smiling face of Chef Rastus. The billboard simply stated, "Cream of Wheat for Your Breakfast." The elderly African-American man proudly said, "AH RECKON AS HOW HE'S DE BES' KNOWN MAN IN DE WORL'."[98]

In contrast to African Americans, there were no ads directed to Native American consumers. While African Americans were forming a consumer market, Native Americans continued to be marginalized and considered outside the mainstream of Euro-American culture. In his study of the depiction of Native Americans in advertising, Jeffery Steele concluded, "African-Americans, wearing familiar [European-style] clothing are often depicted

indoors in domestic or vocational scenes, whereas American Indians are almost always shown outdoors in traditional, native attire (for example, moc-
casins, leggings, and headdresses)."[99] Images of exotically dressed Native
Americans were used to sell Hiawatha canned corn, Cherokee coal, Red
Warrior axes, and Savage rifles. Even to this day an Indian chief adorns cans
of Calumet baking powder, and packages of Land O'Lakes butter shows a
kneeling Indian maiden.

THE IRRATIONAL CONSUMER

Early advertising agencies dipped into psychological theory to design advertisements to direct human emotions to consumer purchases. Ads attempting to manipulate human emotions appeared around 1908 when Stanley
Resor was hired by J. Walter Thompson, the largest and most financially
successful advertising agency of the 20th century.[100] Originally, Resor was
hired to head the Cincinnati branch of J. Walter Thompson. In turn, he
hired as a copywriter his future wife, Helen Lansdowne, who became the
first major female advertising executive. Cincinnati was the location of
Procter & Gamble, which became one of the world's largest manufacturers.
Resor's branch was the first outside advertising agency to be hired by Procter & Gamble. Helen Lansdowne played the major role in the Procter &
Gamble ad campaigns, adding what she called "the feminine point of
view."[101] Her first Procter & Gamble ads were for the 1911 introduction of
Crisco and later Yuban coffee, Lux soap flakes, and Cutex nail polish. In
1916, Stanley Resor bought out J. Walter Thompson and assumed the presi-
dency of the firm. In 1917, he married Helen Lansdowne and they both became the driving forces in the firm.[102]

Resor believed that "Advertising, after all, is educational work, mass education."[103] While attending Yale, Resor said he was influenced by William
Graham Sumner's lectures on how the irrational desires of hunger, vanity,
fear, and sexuality determined human action. Whereas traditional economics posited a rational consumer making choices in a market of goods, Sumner's analysis of human motivation posited consumer choices as resulting
from basic instincts rather than rational choice.

In the early 20th century, both advertising and public relations operated
on the view that the public was primarily driven by irrational emotions. By
the 1920s, theories of irrational crowd behavior dominated advertising and
public relations views of the public. For instance, Ivy Lee, one of the founders of public relations, told a newspaper reporter in 1921 that, "Publicity is
essentially a matter of mass psychology. We must remember that people are
guided more by sentiment than by mind."[104] In the same year, he told an audience at Columbia's School of Journalism that, "You must study human

emotions and all the factors that move people, that persuade men in any line of human activity. Psychology, mob psychology, is one of the important factors that underlay this whole business."[105] In general, social psychologists who were influential in advertising and public relations emphasized the irrationality of the public mind. Historian Stuart Even wrote, "For publicists of the 1920s, however, irrationality had become the habitual filter through which human nature, in its most general terms, was understood."[106]

In playing on human emotions, advertising tended to accent social fears as opposed to pleasure as reflected in the work of famed child psychologist John Watson. In 1920, Resor hired John Watson and made him a vice president in the firm in 1924. Watson reinforced Resor's belief in the role of basic instincts in consumer decisions. The difference was that Watson believed that these instincts could be controlled. Referring to the human as an "organic machine," he explained to his advertising colleagues, "To get hold of your consumer or better, to make your consumer react, it is only necessary to confront him with either fundamental or conditioned emotional stimuli."[107] Besides controlling emotions to direct consumer choices, he believed that it could also be used to spur "the individual to reach a higher level of achievement."[108]

Watson exemplified how so-called *scientific methods* could be used to achieve traditional Protestant goals. He believed that emotional controls could stimulate the drive for achievement and the motivation to work. Watson translated the work ethic into the scientific jargon of psychology. He argued that the manipulation of emotions could cause a person to eliminate "his errors, work longer hours, and plan his work in a more systematic manner."[109] Watson's biographer concluded, "For Watson, then, the application of emotional controls could have the effect of increasing efficiency, order, and, of most importance for an industrial society, individual productivity."[110]

Fundamental to Watson's psychological theory of control were fear, rage, and love. Watson's actual experiments attempted behavioral control of infants' emotions. In his famous "Little Albert" experiments, he elicited fear from an infant by pounding a hammer on an iron bar while presenting the child with stuffed animals. The goal was to condition the infant to fear animals. It was these emotional controls that were to be translated into advertising copy.

At J. Walter Thompson, Watson dismissed the idea of advertising a product by its actual ingredients or components. For instance, cars, he argued, all contain the same basic components of engines, wheels, and other mechanical parts. Therefore, constantly changing designs and styles should be the basis for selling cars. This argument fit into an important part of the developing ideology of consumerism. Making a product obsolescent could be achieved by changing its style rather than through the deterioration or wearing out of the product. For Watson, it was important to create emotional conditioning for the design or style of a product.

Changes in design and style were planned to keep consumers in a state of dissatisfaction so they would continue to buy. Actual buyer satisfaction would defeat the purpose of consumerism, which was to keep factories busy and the economy rolling. The realization of happiness through the purchase of a product—something that many ads seemed to promise—would be destructive to the economy. In the 1920s, the director of research at General Motors said, "The whole object of research is to keep everyone reasonably dissatisfied with what he has in order to keep the factory busy making new things."[111]

Under Watson's guidance, and with the participation and approval of Stanley and Helen Resor, ads were consciously directed at emotions rather than at the content of the product. Cigarette ads presented smoking as sexual, contributing to enhanced attractiveness, independence, and self-fulfillment. Toothpaste ads emphasized sex appeal as opposed to personal hygiene. Many ads were erotic. These ads promised, as Lears noted, personal transformation.

Helen Lansdowne (later Helen Resor) used sex appeal in the 1911 Woodbury's Facial Soap ad. How much of this ad reflected discussions with her future husband and at the time agency head, Stanley Resor, would be difficult to determine. However, the ad certainly mirrored the lessons Stanley Resor had learned from William Graham Sumner that humans act from irrational desires connected with hunger, vanity, fear, and sexuality. The ad depicted a couple with the woman clutching a bouquet of flowers while the man ardently kissed her hand. In large type, the ad proclaimed, "A skin you love to touch" and in smaller type warned, "A skin of this kind is as rare because so few people understand the skin and its needs. They neglect it, and then use some powerful remedy. . . . Woodbury's Facial Soap re-supplies what is exhausted from the Skin. . . . Use it [Woodbury] regularly, not sporadically, and gradually the texture of your skin changes. . . ."[112] Here was sexual allure combined with the promise of personal transformation. Cleaning, the essential purpose of soap, is not mentioned. The ad portrays the objective of purchasing the soap to be creating skin that men will love to kiss and, consequently, turning the user into a sexual magnet. The purchaser buys an advertising dream of sexual transformation rather than a simple cake of cleansing soap.

Social fears played a role in J. Walter Thompson's ads for the first underarm deodorant, Odorno. Originally, Odorno was developed by a Cincinnati doctor to control perspiration during surgery. His daughter hit on the idea of selling it to women. The Odorno ad appeared in 1919, 2 years after Resor and Lansdowne's marriage and 1 year before Watson's arrival at the ad firm. The Odorno ad showed a man and woman embracing with the caption, "There isn't a girl who can't have the irresistible, appealing loveliness of perfect daintiness."[113] Filled with text the ad introduced readers to a new product. The ad alluded to sexuality and fear of social embarrassment. The ad opened, "A woman's arm! Poets have sung of it, great artists have painted its beauty. It should be the daintiest, sweetest thing in the world." The ad quickly went from the picture of the couple's embrace and the poetry of women's arms to the warning, "There's an old offender in this quest for perfect daintiness—an offender of which we ourselves may be ever so unconscious, but which is just as truly present. . . . For it is a psychological fact that persons troubled with perspiration odor seldom can detect it themselves." Unlike the Woodbury ad, personal transformation is replaced with protection against a natural bodily function that might reduce one's sexual appeal. Fear and sexuality were combined.

These types of ads were given scientific legitimation after Watson joined the firm and conducted a study that found that smokers with particular brand preferences could not actually distinguish between brands in a blindfolded test. The result, according to Watson, proved that consumer choice was not based on reason but on emotions. In an ad for Pepco toothpaste, Watson showed a seductive woman smoking a cigarette. The cigarette was associated with independence and assertiveness for women. The ad suggested that is was all right to smoke as long as one used Pepco toothpaste. In the words of Watson's biographer,

> the advertising copy subtly raised the fear that one's attractiveness might be diminished by the effects of smoking on the breath and teeth. Toothpaste was promoted, not as contributing to health and hygiene, but as a means of heightening the sexual attraction of the user. Consumers were not merely buying toothpaste—they were buying "sex appeal." In this sense, commodities themselves became eroticized.[114]

The methods used by the J. Walter Thompson agency were used by other firms. An ad campaign by the Williams & Cunningham agency for the first mouth wash, Listerine, showed a tearful woman clutching a handkerchief while kneeling before what was apparently a marriage hope chest. Combining social fear, sexuality, and personal transformation, the large type of the ad introduced the catchphrase, "Often a bridesmaid but never a bride." The smaller type read, "Edna's case was really pathetic one. Like every woman, her primary ambition was to marry. . . . That's the insidious thing about halitosis (unpleasant breath). You, yourself, rarely know when you have it. And even your closest friends won't tell you."[115] The use of Listerine promised personal transformation into a sexual object attractive to men.

Ads flooded magazines, newspapers, and outdoor displays with brand names associated with relief from social anxieties and personal emotions.

Soaps promised protection against body odors and blackheads. An ad for Lifebuoy soap was entitled, "Why I cried after the party." In cartoon fashion was presented "The B. O. Experience 321." In the first frame of the cartoon, a woman lamented, "I knew I was the best dancer in the hall, but after the first few dances, the men drifted away. Like every party it ended in tears for me." Later, her best friend told her that the problem was body odor or B.O. She then bathed with Lifebuoy soap and her life was magically transformed: "Lifebuoy has been an 'open sesame' into life for me. My dance program is always full. Do you wonder I am deeply grateful."[116]

Probably the most explicit play on personal fears were Scot Tissue ads, which promised to protect against Acids, Mercury, and Arsenic supposedly found in other brands. An accompanying picture showed an attentive nurse looking at a bed-ridden child with the warning, "Be careful Mother!"[117] Mothers were asked to worry about rectal disease caused by the rubbing of harsh tissues. In this manner, the advertising industry played on personal and social fears, sexuality, and promises of personal transformation to sell consumerism to the American public and eventually the global community.

In the early 20th century, advertising images of women as consumers were in sharp contrast with those envisioned by home economists. In public schools, colleges, and in industry, home economists were imagining consumption as a vehicle for liberating women from the home. Advertising images portrayed women as wracked by emotional fears that could only be quieted by the consumption of the right product. However, in both instances, women were imagined as the consumer and the man as the producer.

WOMEN'S FASHIONS AS ARTIFICIAL OBSOLESCENCE

Fashion, central to the ready-to-wear industry, became a driving force in consumerism. Prior to the rapid growth of the ready-to-wear clothing industry in the early 20th century, the middle class and poor could only afford a limited number of garments. Only the rich could spend hours at dressmakers and clothiers being fitted. The middle class and poor spent time refurbishing worn clothing and buying from second-hand shops. The purchase of sewing machines in the latter half of the 19th century made it possible for middle-class families to expand their wardrobes. However, few poor people could afford to purchase a sewing machine.[118]

Changes in fashion spurred desires to buy new products. Fashion became a form of built-in obsolescence that eventually spread to other products, such as automobiles and home products. For immigrants, ready-to-wear fashions represented the promise of American life. In *A Perfect Fit: Clothes, Character, and the Promise of America*, Jenna Joselit wrote, "For . . .

countless immigrant women . . . ready-to-wear was not only a source of personal pleasure; ready-to-wear symbolized America—its abundance and flexibility its choices and resources. Ready-to-wear, proclaimed *Vogue*, aptly capturing its essence, was 'as American as turning on—and having—hot-water'."[119]

The ready to wear industry pioneered a system of consumption based on planned obsolescence. By changing the design of a product and advertising these changes, industries put the consumer in a constant state of dissatisfaction. Satisfaction over the purchase of new shoes or dresses was short-lived if the clothing and shoe industry suddenly advertised a new fashion trend. A perfectly good pair of shoes might suddenly be put aside for new styles. The early ideologue of consumerism, Simon Patten, argued that consumer dissatisfaction was key to economic growth. He contended, "It is not the increase of goods for consumption that raises the standard of life . . . [but] the rapidity with which [the consumer] tires of any one pleasure. To have a high standard of life means to enjoy a pleasure intensely and to tire of it quickly."[120]

Schools and home economists played an important role in promoting obsolescence through changing fashions. In her history of the clothing industry, Joselit commented, "Home economists were equally didactic in their use of the fashion show, hoping to transform high school students into surefooted consumers by teaching them 'buymanship'."[121] During the 1920s, home economists promoted the idea of high school fashion shows that used live models and music. The goal, from the standpoint of home economists, was for the high school to prepare girls for the modern role of consumer. Also home economics teachers claimed fashion shows helped students improve their postures.

Fashion changes sparked a public debate. Joselit argued that the growing ready-to-wear industry in the early 20th century caused, "A broad swath of Americans, from self-styled aesthetes to certified domestic scientists . . . to [worry] about the social and moral consequences of a nation now at liberty to change its clothes—and its image—at will."[122] Before World War I, critics in popular magazines called the use of fashion to control the public mind a new form of tyranny that caused addictive consumer tendencies comparable to opium or alcohol.

Working in high schools and youth clubs, home economists in the 1920s tried to turn fashion-conscious shoppers into wise consumers. High school and 4-H club members engaged in clothing contests where they modeled clothing before panels of teachers. Prizes were given for the most economical and sensible clothing. Working with the U.S. Department of Agriculture, home economists published and distributed a series of score cards to teach students how to evaluate their clothing purchases. On the score card, 30 points were given for "general appearance," 20 points each for "suitability" and "economic factors," and 10 points each for "health aspects" and "social influence."[123]

In addition, public schools promoted fashion as Americanization for immigrants and as a means of social uplift for minority populations. An educator at Cleveland's Technical High School taught that "good taste in dress" transformed immigrants, minorities, and the poor into "efficient thinkers and workers, homemakers and good citizens."[124] New York's Hebrew Technical School promoted proper dress as part of their broader educational program. The New Jersey Manual Training and Industrial School, which served African-American youth, learned that "people dress in order to make a picture and that to make a beautiful picture the correct colors must be combined in the right proportion."[125] While criticizing the dress of African-American students at Fisk University, civil rights leader W. E. B Du Bois argued that proper dress would help the African-American community.[126]

Fashions, similar to the new American cuisine, promised democratization of consumption. With inexpensive, ready-to-wear clothing, all people could participate in changes in fashion. In the 19th century, social class distinctions were obvious between those who could or could not afford to have their clothes made by professional tailors. Later in the 20th century, the mass appeal of blue jeans blurred social class distinctions in dress. However, designer names and logos began to identify the cost of clothing. Social class distinctions in fashion shopping were clearly established in the latter part of the 20th century when the Gap Corporation created a three-tier hierarchy of clothing stores—namely, Old Navy, Gap, and Banana Republic. This model of consumer markets was borrowed from the automobile industry, which turned fashion into artificial obsolescence and made cars into symbols of their owner's social class.

EQUALITY OF OPPORTUNITY AND CONSUMPTION

Along with changing their fashions, consumers were to use education to change jobs and status. Public schools continued as an icon for equality of opportunity. Nineteenth-century Protestantism often interpreted equality of opportunity as the acquisition of wealth while continuing to uphold the values of thrift and simple living. With 20th-century consumerism, equality of opportunity was more closely tied to spending and the acquisition of products. The translation of equality of opportunity into consumerism was most visible in the buying of cars. Leaders of the auto industry consciously tied financial success to the ownership of a particular model of car. Driving on city streets and highways, cars were an outward symbol of the financial success of the owner. In addition, the industry held out the promise that everyone had an equal opportunity to move up or down the scale of success through the purchase of a particular model, such as from Chevrolet to Cadillac.

Before creating a conscious scale of financial success through car models, the industry wrestled with the idea of artificial obsolescence. Fighting consumerist trends, the opening of Henry Ford's assembly line in 1913 was dedicated to the production of a durable and inexpensive automobile. Reflecting traditional Protestant values, Ford's commitment was to a simply designed car in one color. By the 1920s, Ford's black Model T was forced to compete with the trend of using changing fashions to increase sales.

During the 1920s, General Motors introduced the idea of preplanned artificial obsolescence through annual changes in technology and model designs. The campaign for annual models was led by Charles Kettering, who believed the mission of company research was to consciously keep the auto consumer in a state of dissatisfaction. General Motor's Chevrolet, Ford's major competitor, went through styling changes to overtake Ford's Model T in sales in 1927. In the same year, Alfred Sloan, president of General Motors, adopted the principle of the yearly model change as the principle method for selling all cars. Faced with the competition from Chevrolet, Ford finally capitulated to artificial obsolescence in 1927 with the production of the Model A.[127]

General Motors pioneered the idea of using social class or status as a means to sell a car. They wanted automobile models to be outward symbols of income and not simply a machine to travel from one point to another. General Motors offered symbols of income status beginning with the humble Chevrolet and moving up the line to Pontiac, Oldsmobile, Buick, and Cadillac. This income slope created the possibility of selling cars to people who were simply in search of status. A person might be tempted to sink a disproportionate amount of their income into buying a Cadillac to achieve a public symbol of affluence.[128]

Advertising became the means for relating products with social class and changing fashions. Considered one of the most celebrated ads in advertising history, Theodore MacManus pioneered the association of status symbols with particular products and models in his 1914 ad for Cadillac. "The Penalty of Leadership," the ad proclaimed in large type, while in smaller type the copy opened, "In every field of human endeavor, he that is first must perpetually live in the white light of publicity. Whether the leadership be vested in a man or in a manufactured product, emulation and envy are ever at work."[129] A 1926 ad promised the status symbol of a Cadillac in a choice of "50 Body Styles and types" and "500 Color Combinations."[130]

While the automobile industry became noted for creating artificial obsolescence, the practice was taken up by other industries. For instance, Elgin Watch Company's ads asked, "Was your present watch in style when *Uncle Tom's Cabin* came to town?" Elgin ads cautioned that watches were

an "index to . . . business and social standing." Standard Plumbing Fixtures warned that "bathrooms have aged more in the past year than in all the twenty before." Radio ads suggested that older models "would look funny now." During the 1920s, noted home economist, Christine Frederick, found that the typical American was quickly changing homes "because they seemed obsolescent to this family so rapidly moving up on the social scale."[131]

Artificial obsolescence ensured that ownership of a product could never be completely satisfying to the consumer. Ads might promise that purchasing a particular brand would provide for personal transformation, but there would always be the disquieting knowledge that some other brand or model might indicate a superior social class or status. Keeping the consumer in a constant state of dissatisfaction added to the stressful nature of consumer society. Now the consumer was made anxious about the outward signs of their social class along with the social fears generated by advertising. The flow of brand images in the public mind created fear of body and mouth odors along with the shame of driving a lowly Ford or Chevrolet. With artificial obsolescence and advertising that related products to income, consumerism defined *equality of opportunity* as the ability to move up and down a slope of income and ability to consume products.

CONCLUSION: THE PURITAN AND THE IMMIGRANT

Anzia Yezierska's 1923 novel *Salome of the Tenements* illustrates the conflict among consumerism, traditional Protestant values, and newly arrived immigrants. By the 1920s, public schools, magazines, and newspapers were inundating the public with consumer values, fashion changes, and brand icons. The novel's main character, Sonya Vrunsky, exemplified the educated and independent women who were growing up in the mix of Protestant and immigrant cultures of the early 20th century. In many ways, she was the type of new woman that home economists were aiming for as they taught and worked in public schools, colleges, and the food industry.

In contrast to Sonya, the novel's main male character, John Manning, tried to imbue new immigrants with traditional Protestant values of simple living and hard work. Manning was a composite character drawn from the author's real-life knowledge of John Dewey, the philosopher, educator, and social reformer, and Graham Stokes, the millionaire socialist and philanthropist.[132] In fact, the novel was written a few years after the author refused to have sex with John Dewey.

John Manning, supposedly reflecting the passionless character of John Dewey, wrote to the passionate Sonya, a poor Jewish immigrant living in the teeming ghetto of the Lower East Side, "Identify yourself with your work.

Work is the only thing real. The only thing that counts. The only thing that lasts."[133]

The tensions between John and Sonya dramatize the interactions between the Protestant elite and immigrants over a world filled with an abundance of goods and new forms of leisure. Sonya embraces the new possibilities for consumption and regards consumerism as being more important than existing political ideologies. Referring to the growth of the fashion industry, Sonya made her famous statement of choice, "Talk about democracy. . . . All I want is to be able to wear silk stockings and Paris hats the same as Mrs. Astorbilt, and then it wouldn't bother me if we have Bolshevism or Capitalism, or if the democrats or the republicans win."[134]

Protestant reformers and educators feared that the morality of the nation would be undermined by the movie theaters and dance halls popping up in immigrant neighborhoods. Throughout *Salome of the Tenements*, the author highlighted the divide between the stiff morality of the Anglo-Saxon Protestant and the passionate morality of the new immigrants. The author was probably made acutely aware of this divide while attending Columbia's Teachers College and, at the same time, working as a laundress. At Teachers College, she met John Dewey, who in 1917 offered to help her publish some early writings. Her contact with Dewey, other educators at Teachers College, and social reformers working in tenement areas left her with bitter feelings about Protestant Anglo-Saxons. To her they were ice people incapable of experiencing pleasure. In the novel, a Jewish newspaper writer tells Sonya, "The Anglo-Saxon coldness, it's centuries of solid ice that all the suns of the sky can't melt. Nobody can tell what that frozen iciness is, except those that got to live with it."[135] John and Sonya symbolize the struggle between the two cultures. The author describes,

> Sonya and Manning . . . were the oriental and the Anglo-Saxon trying to find a common language. The over-emotional Ghetto struggling for its breath in the thin air of Puritan restraint. An East Side savage forced suddenly into the strait-jacket of American civilization. Sonya was like the dynamite bomb and Manning the walls of tradition constantly menaced by threatening explosions.[136]

The clash between cultures appeared in attitudes about material goods. It was the Sunday School ethic of unostentatious living and buying only necessities versus fashion and buying for pleasure. Dressed in the latest fashion, Sonya meets John in a ghetto tea room where he is bewildered by the loud noise and activity. The author describes his reaction, "Her [Sonya's] abandon, her nakedness staggered him, and John Manning, the product of generations of Puritans, retreated into his shell."[137] After Sonya declares that she was "the ache of unvoiced dreams, the clamor of suppressed de-

Protestant
ethics a
pulls a
Consumer

sires," John responds, "I am a Puritan whose fathers were afraid to trust experience. We are bound by our possessions of property, knowledge and tradition."[138] At another point in the novel, John pronounces his love for the poor's simplicity. Sonya responds, "You like the working-girl in her working dress. . . . You like her with the natural sweat and toil on her face—no make-up—not artifice to veil the grim lines of poverty?"[139] The reference to make-up reflected the growing association of cosmetic use with the liberated woman. Reminiscent of the glorification of poverty and hard work in 19th-century children's literature, John answers, "Exactly. . . . Poverty and toil are beautiful crowns of the spirit and need no setting off."[140] Later, in an act of Puritan philanthropy, John proclaimed, "The service I feel myself called upon to render the East Side is to teach the gospel of the Simple Life."[141]

In *Salome of the Tenements,* John wanted working women to avoid the fashions of ready-to-wear clothes by returning to the practice of making their own clothes. He asked Sonya to teach the "working-girl . . . to avoid, vulgar styles and showing her how beautiful it is to be simple."[142] When Sonya replied, "But they buy those gaudy styles because they're cheap and ready-made," John exclaimed, "We want to get them away from that. We want to teach them how to make their own clothes."[143]

As embodied in John, Protestant morality required a world freed from the temptation of worldly goods. The social expert, the new guardian of morality, was to control any consumption that might lead to degradation. John proudly explained to Sonya how he was using social experts to help immigrants. "The words 'social experts,' 'scientific,' 'plane of reason,' " the novel's narrator commented, "were like icy winds over her [Sonya's] enthusiasm."[144] Shortly after John's comments on social experts, Sonya concealed herself behind a pillar in a lecture room where a social expert complained about finding a woman cooking chicken after being given rations of cornmeal, rice, and macaroni. Sonya dashed from the room thinking, "So it's a crime to eat chicken if you get charity. . . . Worthy poor—those who are content with cornmeal!"[145]

For Sonya, representing the new immigrants, the promise of America was access to consumer goods. Arriving from mainly peasant villages in Southern and Eastern Europe, immigrants were surrounded by advertisements promising personal transformation and relief from social anxieties. Consumer goods and brand icons promised stability in the rapidly changing world of the immigrant. Ads targeting African-American consumers promised race pride and uplift. For many African Americans, clothes and cosmetics became part of a broader dream of achieving equal rights and equality of opportunity. Reflecting the tensions in public racial images, ads targeted for the Euro-American market continued to show African Americans in service to Whites and marginalized Native Americans as the exotic other.

Underlying these tensions was the debate over a rational versus irrational public. Regarding this debate, Stuart Ewen argued,

> At one end there was the Progressive democratic faith, which assumed that people were essentially rational beings, that could be most effectively persuaded by a . . . factual, logically framed argument. At the other end was the perspective . . . that human nature was essentially irrational and . . . that "opinion" was most efficiently shaped by scientifically informed subliminal appeals to unconscious urges and instinctual drives.[146]

By emphasizing fashion and status models, industry and advertisers treated the public as if it were irrational. The goal was to keep the consumer in a constant state of dissatisfaction. Hoping for social transformation through consumption, the buyer was often disappointed. When confronted with more prestigious models of the same product that they owned, consumers were made to feel dissatisfied. Consumerism depended on the constant desire to buy more rather than achieving satisfaction. In this climate, the public school promise of equality of opportunity offered the unattainable goal of achieving consumer satisfaction by earning more money and buying more products. The American dream became a nightmare about working hard to attain the unattainable goal of consumer satisfaction.

Chapter 3

Cowboys and Jocks:
Visions of Manliness

In the first half of the 20th century, the dominant public image of White men was sports-minded, patriotic, and patron of women as domestic consumers. Men sought their identities in leisure time activities, particularly sports. Commodified forms of leisure were male consumer activities, which included buying tickets to sporting events and equipment for golf, fishing, hunting, and other outdoor activities. Of course men participated in major decisions regarding domestic consumption. Also ads presented car purchases as joint decisions. However, men interested in fashions, particularly clothing fashions, were considered effeminate. In contrast to the 19th century, 20th-century educators and image makers drew a sharper line between homo- and heterosexuality.

Sports and other leisure time activities were to provide the new male with a means of sexual control, particularly control of adolescent sexuality. Despite the emphasis on controlling sexuality, advertising used male and female imagery to imbue consumer items with the promise of sexual fulfillment. In this particular context, consumerism became another form of sexual activity. Ironically, the Puritan effort to control sexuality resulted in making consumer items objects of sexual desire. In schools, popular magazines, and ads, the new White man was strictly heterosexual, athletically oriented, muscular, and someone separated from the supposedly more emotional world of women.

Patriotism was important to both consumerism and male identity. By the 1930s, the ideology of consumerism was related to something called the *American way of life*, which promised a high standard of living as measured by the consumption of the increased output of industrialism. Threatened by communism as an alternative to American consumerism, schools, the press, and media bombarded the public with patriotic messages. The patriotism of the 1920s was different from earlier forms. The new patriotism was a form of economic nationalism that considered the threat to America to come from alternative economic systems. In direct contact with the American Legion, the public schools linked this form of patriotism to the image of the new White male.

THE CRISIS IN MALE IDENTITY

In part, the image of the new White man that appeared at the turn of the 19th and early 20th centuries was a reaction to the image of the new woman. Some White men were outraged that women scientists, physicians, and voters were displacing manhood with womanhood. Gail Bederman claimed, "Yet the new woman did 'displace manhood with womanhood' if only because her successes undermined the assumption that education, professional status, and political power required a male body. The woman's movement thus increased the pressure on middle-class men to reformulate manhood."[1] Typical of the satirical press about the new woman, an 1897 illustration showed a woman warning her husband as he took over laundry and child-care duties, "Don't Get the Clothes Too Blue!"[2] Even as early as 1869, there were expressions of male fears that women wanted to reverse roles. A Currier and Ives lithograph showed a woman entering a carriage driven by another woman while men are depicted doing child care and the laundry.[3]

Also as Bederman indicated, White males felt a loss of independence as they increasingly worked in corporations and factories. Before the Civil War, 88% of Americans were self-employed.[4] Between 1870 and 1910, the number of self-employed White middle-class men declined from 67% to 37%.[5] As a result of work in corporate structures, doctors declared that the newly discovered disease of neurasthenia caused by excessive brain work was spreading rapidly among professional and businessman.[6] Some people advocated rigorous physical activities such as body building, sports, hiking, camping, hunting, and fishing as a cure for neurasthenia. Theodore Roosevelt, a national symbol for the new manhood, declared that the continuation of American civilization depended on men practicing, as his 1899 speech was entitled, "The Strenuous Life."[7]

In public schools, organized athletics and gym were to develop the new man. In fact, the growing educational importance of athletics and gym for boys paralleled the inclusion of home economics courses in public schools. In this context, public schools were given an important role in educating the new man and woman. Besides invigorating the body as protection against the lethargy of modern living, athletics, gym, and outdoor activities were to teach self-control of sexuality. Fearing that modern living and entertainment, particularly movies, would unleash sexual drives that would undermine civilization, educators contended that organized sports and school activities could channel sexual drives into social service activities.[8]

As consumers, according to Mark Swiencicki, between 1880 and 1930 men spent twice as much as women on leisure time activities, which amounted to about 30% of a family's disposable income.[9] The consumption of leisure time activities supports Bederman's contention that, "The growth of a consumer culture encouraged many middle-class men . . . to find identity in leisure instead of in work."[10] By the 21st century, I would contend, the TV viewing and discussion of sports, such as football, basketball, and baseball, would occupy a large amount of the time for white- and blue-collar workers.

Differences in spending between men and women on personal grooming items highlight the distinctions in personal identity. The men found their identity in leisure time activities, whereas women found it in cosmetics and clothing fashions. According to Swiencicki's figures for 1890, men spent only 30% of the total dollars spent on perfumery and cosmetics.[11] However, these figures do not diminish the importance of the male market for personal grooming items such as shavers, shaving creams, hair lotions, cologne, and skin conditioners.

With regard to clothing, men's interest in fashions reflected a growing trend to define the new masculinity in heterosexual terms. In her history of clothing, Jenna Joselit argued, "From their vantage point [men in the early 20th century], not only was it dumb to pay attention to what one wore, it was foppish or effeminate. . . . American men did not concern themselves too much with clothing lest they be thought 'pansies'."[12] The feeling that a focus on fashion threatened male images reflected the role of schools and advertising in nurturing a public image of heterosexuality as the *normal* form of sexual relations. As George Chauncey argued, "the hetero–homosexual binarism, the sexual regime now hegemonic in American culture, is a stunningly recent creation."[13] Prior to the middle of the 20th century, abnormality was primarily associated with men who acted effeminate and not with sexual relations between men. Men who acted according to the socially ascribed characteristics of being male while also engaging in sexual activities were considered normal. Chauncey contended that, "Only in the 1930s, 1940s, and 1950s did the now-conventional division of men into 'homosexuals' and heterosexuals,' based on the sex of their sexual partners, replace the division of men into 'fairies' [effeminate men] and 'normal men' on the basis of their imaginary gender status as the hegemonic way of understanding sexuality."[14] In both the proper dating practices taught in schools and the depictions of couples in advertising, heterosexuality was made the norm.

"cowboy"
(gendered image)

Advertising created gender images that contrasted the emotional consumer and dependent female with the self-controlled, athletic, and outdoor male. The cowboy came to symbolize the lost masculinity of the modern White male. Theodore Roosevelt, born and bred in New York City, tried to affirm his masculinity by buying a Western ranch and donning the garb of the cattleman and hunter. The statue outside the Roosevelt Memorial rotunda at the American Museum of Natural History in New York City bears testimony to this self-created image. Roosevelt sits snugly in a saddle in full cowboy attire with Indians standing alongside the horse.[15] This image was re-created in the 1950s in America's most famous icon of masculinity, the Marlboro Man, who was depicted consuming Marlboro cigarettes while riding horses, corralling cattle, and hanging out by the campfire.[16] Earlier this symbol of masculinity appeared in a 1913 Cream of Wheat ad with a depiction of a cowboy with a holstered revolver on horseback placing a letter in a wooden mailbox mounted on a tall post. The mailbox was marked "Cream of Wheat," and the ad's caption read, "Where the mail goes Cream of Wheat goes."[17]

Also there was a racial component to the depiction of the new man as protector of civilization. The statue outside the American Museum of Natural History depicts the masculine image of Roosevelt on horseback towering above a Native American on foot. The Indian clings to Roosevelt's saddle bag with his nose just below Roosevelt's holstered revolver. Roosevelt's White manliness is presented in sharp contrast to the subdued and conquered Native American. It is this White manliness that was supposed to lead the savage into civilization. In the late 19th and early 20th centuries, as Gail Bederman stated, "In a variety of venues and contexts, white Americans contrasted civilized white men with savage dark-skinned men, depicting the former as paragons of *manly* virtue."[18]

There was also a social class component to male identity. In the early 20th century, advertising primarily presented images of businessmen dressed in suits and ties even while lounging at home. It was these denizens of the modern corporation that needed to protect their manly identity. Corporate life, it was believed, was weakening male bodies. However, not all men in the early 20th century were businessmen who wore suits at home. Many could not afford to own a suit. By the end of the economic boom period of the 1920s, there still existed "35 to 40 percent of the non-farm population" living in poverty.[19] According to Susan Porter, only about a third of working class families owned automobiles while barely half the households had flush toilets.[20]

Among low-income males, male identity was defined in a variety of ways. For some men, union activity, including strikes and political actions, exemplified an independent and manly life. Some men established their identity by rejecting marriage and family obligations. They were *real men* who were not going to be tied down by a wife and children. Others rebelled against the industrial discipline of the factory and refused to be tied down by a job. Similar to their businessmen counterparts, these men believed that factory life was stealing their manhood. Yet rather than working and seeking their male identity in leisure time activities, these working class men simply rejected a life of steady work becoming drifters and hoboes. Many working class men maintained their sense of independence and manliness by retaining part of their wages for personal spending on smoking, drinking, and gambling.[21]

Although I do not have any statistics available, I would hypothesize that many factory workers continued to maintain their manliness, like their businessmen counterparts, by spending weekends hunting and fishing. Later, with the advent of TV, men would spend many weekend hours watching sports. Manliness could be achieved through sports as a participant or spectator. The consumption of sports became the greatest venue for maintaining a sense of manliness.

SPERMATIC POLITICAL ECONOMY AND PATRIOTISM

Advocacy of male sexual control accompanied the new patriotic efforts to defeat alternative economic systems. Puritan fear of uncontrolled male sexuality infused activities supporting the new male image, including college and high school sports, sex education courses, school clubs, and high school dating and dancing. *Self-control* was often the word used to indicate the channeling of sexual desire into other activities. Self-control was also associated with what was the male adolescent vice of masturbation. Fear of masturbation and sexual excess in marriage was based on what M. E. Melody and Linda Peterson called "spermatic political economy."[22] There was a popular belief in the late 19th century that loss of semen, through masturbation or other sexual activity, weakened the male physically and mentally. It was even suggested that loss of sperm led to feeble-mindedness and criminality. John Harvey Kellogg, producer of Kellogg cereals and operator of the Battle Creek Sanitarium, popularized the idea of seminal control in *Plain Facts about Sexual Life* (1877) with authoritative statements such as, "The seminal fluid is the most highly vitalized of all the fluids of the body, and its rapid production is at the expense of a most exhaustive effort on the part of the vital forces, is well attested by all physiologists."[23] Marital excesses and masturbation, Kellogg told his popular readership, resulted in a man finding "manhood lost, his body a wreck, and death staring him in the face."[24] Summarizing Henry Hanchett's *Sexual Health: A Plain and Practical Guide for the People on All Matters Concerning the Organs of Reproduction in Both Sexes and All Ages* (1887) in the language of political economy, Melody and

Peterson wrote, "Sex exhausts men, it saps their vitality. Semen is an 'expensive' fluid for the body to produce and so spending decisions must be made carefully."[25]

Spermatic political economy was basic to preservation of the male amid the temptations of modern urban life. (Men had to find outlets for their sexual desires that did not result in the loss of sperm.) Adding a note of romanticism to the protection of sperm loss, it was argued that sexual desire could be redirected to fighting for social and political ideals. Communing with nature through hiking, hunting, and fishing along with participation in sports would save the body and mind of the male from the deleterious loss of sperm and, at the same time, educate the male to service the country. In this sense, patriotic war became sexualized.

A good example of this new male image is the Theodore Roosevelt rotunda at the American Museum of Natural History. Roosevelt was considered one of the strongest advocates of the late 19th and 20th centuries for educating youth in manhood to overcome the debilitating effects of modern life.[26] Michael Kimmel wrote, "America's self-proclaimed and self-constructed 'real man,' Roosevelt was, as he proclaimed a completely Self-Made Man."[27] Both Roosevelt and his father worked actively to promote and expand the work of the Museum as part of their belief in the importance of contact with nature in maintaining masculine values. In the *Winning of the West*, written in four volumes in the 1880s and 1890s, Roosevelt presents the Indian wars as a test for White American males that established their superiority over Indians. It was the actual fighting that demonstrated, according to Roosevelt, the virile and heroic qualities of White males. In this sense, a willingness to fight and die in battle was the ultimate test of manhood.[28]

These masculine and patriotic values were embodied in the cowboy image on the statue of Roosevelt and the Indian outside the Roosevelt Rotunda and in Roosevelt's words etched on the interior walls. Roosevelt's linkage of nature to masculinity and war are found in the wall etching entitled "Nature," "Youth," "Manhood," and the "State." In Roosevelt's world, these four topics were interdependent. The strenuous life experienced in "Nature" was essential for the proper education of "Youth" for "Manhood." "Manhood" was essential for maintaining the civilized "State."

As president, Roosevelt put into practice—through the establishment of national parks and forests—his belief that preservation of nature was essential to maintaining White American manhood and, consequently, American ideals. In his personal life, although somewhat frail and asthmatic, Roosevelt tramped around the United States and the world exploring and hunting. The continued existence of places for men to experience the strenuous life through camping, hiking, hunting, and fishing, he believed, would ensure the continued manliness of the urban male. His statement on

"Nature" intertwines the hardy life with the conservation of resources and destiny of the nation. The romanticization of nature is eventually linked in the inscriptions of the patriotic ideal of fighting for the state. The inscription on nature reads,

Nature

There is a delight in the hardy life of the open
There are no words that can tell the hidden spirit of the wilderness that can reveal its mystery its melancholy and its charm
The nation behaves well if it treats the natural resources as assets which it must turn over to the next generation increased;
and not impaired in value Conservation means development as much as it does protection.[29]

Roosevelt's inscription on "Youth" was obviously intended for male youth. From his perspective, it was obviously manly men who were the most important beneficiaries of nature and central to the preservation of the nation. Also the statement reflected his own emphasis on sports and games while he was a student at Harvard. He believed boxing at Harvard contributed to the development of his own manliness. Games, bravery, manliness, gentleness, and character were all linked to the success of the nation.

Youth

I want to see you game boys
I want to see you brave and manly and I also want to see you gentle and tender
Be practical as well as generous in your ideals
Keep your eyes on the stars and keep your feet on the ground
Courage, hard work, self-mastery, and intelligent effort are all essential to successful life
Character in the long run is the decisive factor in the life of an individual and of nations alike.[30]

Roosevelt believed daring, courage, endurance, and ideals were essential features of manliness. Courage was a willingness to die for one's ideals. This willingness to pursue death for an ideal was a result of the training received in youth.

Manhood

A man's usefulness depends upon his living up to his ideals insofar as he can
It is hard to fail but it is worse never to have tried to succeed
All daring and courage all iron endurance of misfortune make for a finer nobler type of manhood

Only those are fit to live who do not fear to die and none are fit to die who have shrunk from the joy of life and the duty of life.

The inscription on "The State" completes the link among preservation of nature, education of youth, manliness, sports, war, and nationalism. In fact, Roosevelt classified war as the "noblest sport the world affords." As I discuss, the introduction of athletics in American high schools was considered preparation for citizenship and nationalism. From Roosevelt's perspective, and that of many of his generation, manliness meant the courage to die for ideals and the state.

The State

Ours is a government of liberty by through and under the law
A great democracy must be progressive or it will soon cease to be great or a democracy
Aggressive fighting for the right is the noblest sport the world affords
In popular government results worth while can only be achieved by men who combine worthy ideals with practical good sense
If I must choose between righteousness and peace
I choose righteousness.[31]

The Roosevelt rotunda embodies the educational ideals of masculinity at the beginning of the consumer age. These ideals were embodied in educational changes, which stressed athletics and extracurricular activities in high schools as preparation for manhood and patriotism. They also paralleled the ideas of psychologist and educators.

THE SPERMATIC POLITICAL ECONOMY OF HIGH SCHOOL SPORTS

Sports to control sexual desire

Male consumption of tickets to sporting events, sporting equipment, and the following of sporting events through the media were affirmed by theories of masculinity and spermatic political economy. Becoming a mass institution by the 1930s, the high school became a training ground for male preoccupation with sports. Crucial to the development of modern high school life was the work of psychologist G. Stanley Hall. Like others, Hall was influenced by ideas on spermatic political economy. In his classic work *Adolescence* (1904), Hall made a direct link between the control of male sexuality and the maintenance of modern civilization. For Hall, girls needed to preserve their sexual energies for reproduction.[32] In contrast, men needed to channel their sexuality into service to others and the nation. Manliness and civilization required self-control of sexual drives. Hall proposed that sports, organizations (such as the YMCA, Boy Scouts), and schools were crucial in channeling male sexuality into social service. Hall wrote, "The whole future of life depends on how the new powers [of adolescence] now given suddenly and in profusion are husbanded." Hall believed the control of sexuality was necessary for society to evolve to its modern stage. He wrote, "The whole future of life depends on how the new powers [of adolescence] now given suddenly and in profusion are husbanded." According to Hall's theory of recapitulation, each stage of individual development paralleled a stage of social evolution. Childhood—the years between 4 and 8—corresponded to a cultural epoch when hunting and fishing were the main activities of humanity. From 11 to 12, according to Hall, the child recapitulated the life of savagery. During puberty, the new flood of passions developed the social person: "The social instincts undergo sudden unfoldment and the new life of love awakens."[33]

Bederman argued, "like many of his contemporaries, [Hall] feared over-civilization was endangering American manhood. As a nationally recognized expert on pedagogy, he believed it was his responsibility to make sure American boys received a virile education that avoided overcivilized effeminacy."[34] Hall believed that a virile education, which meant the channeling of adolescent sexual drives into manly social activities, would be the panacea for most social problems: "womb, cradle, nursery, home, family, relatives, school, church and state are only a series of larger cradles or placenta, as the soul . . . builds itself larger missions, the only test and virtue of which is their service in bringing the youth to ever fuller maturity."[35]

The popular press and Hall's psychology created an image of adolescence as a romantic stage of life during which the developing sexual-social drives could lead the adolescent to either a life of decadence or a life of social service. The romantic and poetic impulses of youth, it was believed, could be captured and directed toward socially useful projects such as helping the poor, the community, or the nation. Boy Scouts, the YMCA, and other youth organizations were justified by their ability to channel the sexual-social drives of youth.

Organized sports was considered a key element in dissipating and controlling youthful sexuality. Historian Michael Kimmel captioned this change, "Restoring Masculinity by Remaking the Body." Kimmel summarized the sports movement, "Turn-of-the-century [19th to 20th] America went 'sports crazy,' as thousands of men sought to combat the enervating effects of their urban white-collar working lives with manly physiques, health regimens, and participation in sports."[36] A 1900 book ad in the leading body building magazine, *Physical Culture*, demonstrated the connection being made between sexual control and athletic activity. Entitled *Manhood Wrecked and Rescued*, the book ad promised to save men from sexual weakness and resulting self-destruction by making them "strong manly men, instead of physical and social wrecks."[37] The ad's outlined chapter summaries captured the belief that sexual activity destroyed manliness and that athletics could protect the body from sexual dissipation: "Chapter IV—A Youthful Wreck: Masturbation . . . Prevalence of this solitary vice . . . Loss of semen is loss of blood-Results of its expenditure—Seminal Emissions—Effects on the nervous system . . . Where masturbation and marital excess do their deadly work." The final three chapters of the book were devoted to "The Rescue," with an explanatory emphasis on the relationship between nervous function and muscular power. The book was sold along with a year's subscription to *Physical Culture* and a copy of Bernarr Macfadden's booklet on *Physical Training.*[38] The naked and sculpted muscular body of Bernarr Macfadden was displayed on the cover of his book, *The Virile Powers of Superb Manhood.*[39]

A 1922 poster entitled "The Sex Impulse and Achievement" of the American Social Hygiene Association captured the same belief in the relationship between athletic activity and sexual control. The poster showed a group of young men running hurdles. The caption under the picture read:

> The sex instinct in a boy or man makes
> him want to act, dare, possess, strive.
> When controlled and directed, it gives
> ENERGY, ENDURANCE,
> FITNESS.[40]

Educators expanded the public school's social activities to protect adolescent sexuality from the temptations of modernity. The 1911 report of the National Education Association's (NEA)—at the time the most influential education organization—Committee on a System of Teaching Morals stated that adolescence is "the time of life when passion is born which must be restrained and guided aright or it consumes soul and body. It is the time when social interests are dominant and when social ideals are formed."[41] The report proposed teaching morals in high school through cooperative social activities, student government, and a curriculum dealing with the relationship between the individual and society. In *The High-School Age* (1914), Irving King, professor of Education at the University of Iowa, argued that a high school education must provide the adolescent with opportunity for social service because, at the age of 16, "youth emerges from the somewhat animal-like crassness of the pubertal years and begins to think of his social relationships, his duties and the rights and wrongs of acts."[42] Reflecting a belief that education could lead youth to accept social ideals, he continued, "Every youth is . . . an incipient reformer, a missionary, impatient with what seem to him the pettiness and the obtuseness of the adult world about him." The same sentiment was echoed by Michael V. O'Shea, professor of Education at the University of Wisconsin, in *Trend of the Teens*, published in 1920. According to O'Shea, the "reformer . . . realizes that if he would get his cause adopted he must appeal to youth. . . . Youth longs for a new order of things."[43]

To a major extent, concerns about male sexuality influenced the development of the modern American high school with its trappings of organized athletics, pep rallies, cheerleaders, and extracurricular activities. The modern high school that emerged in the 1920s was quite different from the classically oriented school of the 19th century. Under the influence of new sexual concepts of youth, the National Education Association organized a commission in 1913 whose report eventually established the basic framework for the modern high school. This group, the Commission on the Reorganization of Secondary Education, issued its final report in 1918 as the now famous *Cardinal Principles of Secondary Education.*

According to the Cardinal Principles, high school athletics and extracurricular activities would channel adolescent sexuality into socially useful activities. Social cooperation, the report stated, was necessary for a modern democracy, and it could be developed through "participation of pupils in common activities . . . such as athletic games, social activities, and the government of the school."[44] Athletics was considered a key method in channeling adolescent sexuality into cooperative social activity. It taught youth how to cooperate and work with a team. This argument was one reason for the rapid growth of football in the public schools. As a team game, football fostered the coordination and cooperation needed in a corporate organization. A Seattle high school principal told the National Education Association in 1915, "In the boy's mind, the football team is not only an aggregation of individuals organized to play, but a social instrument with common needs, working along common lines, and embodying a common purpose."[45]

Comparisons to war and corporate life made sports into a metaphor for modern life. Likening competitive sports to war persisted from the 1890s into the 21st century. At the turn of the 19th to 20th centuries, the father of modern football, Walter Camp, claimed there was a "remarkable and interesting likeness between the theories which under lie great battles and the miniature contests of the gridiron."[46] The competition of the playing fields was equated to the competition of capitalism. However, that competition, as in sports, needed to be contained within the organization needs of corporate life. Writing in *Outlook*, Cunningham LaPlace argued that team competition taught students the "subordination of the unit to the total, the habit of working with his fellows, of touching elbows."[47] Theodore Roosevelt made a direct comparison between life and team sports: "In life, as in foot-ball game, the principle to follow is: Hit the line hard; don't foul and don't shirk but hit the line hard . . . [sports are] a means of preparation for the responsibilities of life . . . [and teach] qualities useful in any profession."[48] As a church-going man observed in the 1920s, "Life is a football game, with the men fighting it out on the gridiron, while the minister is up in the grandstand, explaining the game to the ladies."[49]

SEX EDUCATION

Ironically, despite the efforts of educators and moral reformers, adolescent sexuality seemed to be heightened with the development of the high school as a mass institution. By bringing together all adolescents, the high school made possible a teenage culture that focused on the rituals of dating, sex and, eventually, a teenage consumer market. Athletics was only one part of the high school program designed to control adolescent sexuality. Another was sex education.

The addition of sex education to the school curriculum was a logical step in attempts to control adolescent sexuality. One goal of the American Social Hygiene Association, organized in 1905, was to get sex education into the schools. Influenced by the social hygiene movement, the NEA endorsed sex education courses for the schools.[50] In 1926, the NEA's Committee on Character Education recommended sex education as a means to combat the decline of the family and regulating sexual impulses for the good of society. Its report gave the purpose of human life as: "The creation of one's own home and family, involving first the choice and winning of, or being won by, one's mate." Sex education was to prepare youth to fulfill this purpose. "The recent activities," the report states, "in sexual and social hygiene are in the nature of forerunners to this work."[51]

The type of sex education advocated by the NEA was modeled on the work of a member of the NEA's Character Education Committee, Thomas Galloway. Galloway was Associate Director of the American Social Hygiene Association Department of Educational Measures and the author of its official training manual, *Sex and Social Health: A Manual for the Study of Social Hygiene*. He was also author of a number of other books, including *The Sex Factor in Human Life* and *Biology of Sex*.

Galloway's preface to the official sex education training manual, *Sex and Social Health*, suggested using it to guide community discussions, as a textbook for parent–teacher groups and teacher training programs, and as a reference book.[52] The stated premise of the manual was that "reproductive processes and the associated sexual impulses are not individual but social privileges and phenomena."[53] Paralleling the psychological theories of G. Stanley Hall, the manual argued that sexual energies should not be repressed, but should be channeled into socially constructive activities. In making this argument, the manual emphasized the necessity of controlling male sexuality because men were considered the pursuers in sexual relations. In fact, the manual stated that, "Defense and chivalry in males are probably correlated with this tendency of pursuit, biologically."[54]

Also similar to Hall, the manual considered the control of male sexuality as the key to maintaining civilization and modern democracy. Using the concept of redirected sexual energy, the manual described the sexual underpinnings of democracy. It asserted that sexual drives contributed to the development of social and unselfish motives, which made possible a cooperative society. Using a social definition of democracy, the manual contended that a cooperative spirit, growing out of sexual energy directed toward the good of society, was the basis for a modern democracy: "Clearly this sense of the worth of social sacrifice and democracy, which is so largely the gift of the sex and reproductive processes, can in turn be applied most effectively to the guidance of sex impulses themselves."[55]

The manual contended that sexual energy permeated all social activities, and the goal of sex education was to direct this energy into socially constructive activities. The manual rejected the idea of repressing because it could result in the breakdown of character and the molding of submissive and obedient children.

The manual made a sharp distinction between male and female sexuality. Male sexuality was portrayed as aggressive and requiring more control. Male assertiveness was related to localized sexual energy in the "generative organs," whereas female sexuality was less localized and less intense. The combination of biological factors and social repression resulted, according to the manual, in women being more "capable of control [of sexual drives], of suppression, and of refinement into more intellectual and aesthetic forms than . . . most men." The role of women was to restrain the sexual drives of men. The manual argued that proper feminine qualities included "purity as a social obligation, a restraining rather than an inciting attitude toward the male, and a sense of obligation for conserving and 'mothering' life."[56]

The purpose of both sex and marriage was reproduction. In the words of the manual, sex control is necessary for "proper home functioning, which includes the comfort and happiness of all, maximum development of the mates, proper child production, and effective personal and social education of children." Sexual intercourse outside of marriage should be avoided because of its potential threat to the stability of the family. The manual stated that physical "intercourse . . . without the social sanction of formal marriage . . . , wholly ignores the interest of society in all questions of sex and reproduction."[57]

For these reasons, the manual stated, sexual abstinence, except among married couples, was necessary for the good of society. The manual informed the reader, "If abstinence is desirable or necessary, it is primarily because of the effects of sex behavior on the home, on the emotional qualities in the individual upon which the success of the home is based, and on the larger society which depends on the home and on personal character."[58] The manual made a similar argument when it warned that sexual intercourse outside the institution of marriage not only weakened the family structure, but caused diseased and defective individuals, prostitution, and the shame of an illegitimate pregnancy. Premised on the idea that sexual intercourse was a social privilege, the goal of sex education, as stated in this American Social Hygiene Association manual, was to educate people so they would have sexual intercourse only within the confines of marriage. Interestingly, the manual urged teaching about venereal diseases because "they make an appeal to fear."[59] Regarding adolescent sexual energy, the manual called for draining the energy away from sexual thoughts and activities to constructive interests: "If young people are given many wholesome, attractive enterprises which strongly appeal to them personally during the whole of childhood and adolescence, there is much less likelihood that they will be drawn into sexual or other errors and excesses."[60]

HIGH SCHOOL DANCES AND DATING:
CREATING A NEW CONSUMER MARKET

By the 1930s, capstone of high school activities was the senior prom. The senior prom symbolized the shift of youth activities from relatively unsupervised dance halls to the controlled environment of the school. The prom experience was also a consumer experience with the unending requirements of grooming and dressing. The prom culminated the high school's dating and dancing rituals. Educators considered high school dating rituals as a prelude to marriage and the foundation for a consumer family.

High schools sponsored dances because moral reformers and educators worried that the wrong dancing in the wrong place threatened youthful morality. This worry persisted from the 1890s through the flapper age of the 1920s, the swing period of the 1930s and 1940s, and, of course, the blossoming of rock and roll in the 1950s. The "dance craze," as Kathy Peiss called it in *Cheap Amusements,* resulted in the opening by 1910 of over 500 public dance halls in New York City and 100 dancing academies instructing over 100,000 students. A 1912 survey found that the vast majority of those attending urban dance halls were between the ages of 13 and 20.[61] A major part of this group would eventually find their dancing activities relocated from the dance hall to the school gym.

One can imagine the horror of Protestant reformers and educators when faced with dancing with full body contact and various forms of shimmying. In the 19th century, the waltz was considered scandalous despite the requirement of 4 inches of separation between partners and that eyes be directed over the partner's shoulders. In contrast, youth in dance halls engaged in what was called *tough dancing*, which included the slow rag, lovers' two-step, and turkey trot.[62] Kathy Peiss described, "Tough dancing not only permitted physical contact, it celebrated it. Indeed, the essence of the tough dance was its suggestion of sexual intercourse. As one dance investigator noted obliquely, 'What particularly distinguishes this dance is the motion of the pelvic portions of the body, bearing in mind its origins [i.e., in houses of prostitution]'."[63]

Reformers and educators not only worried about dance styles, but also the environment of the dance halls. The Committee of Fourteen, a Protestant reform agency concerned with urban vice, sent its investigators into the commercial dance halls of the 1910s. One shocked investigator reported, "I saw one of the women smoking cigarettes, most of the younger couples were hugging and kissing . . . they were all singing and carrying on, they kept running around the room and acted like a mob of lunatics let loose."[64]

Amusement parks posed another challenge for reformers and educators. In the 1890s, dance pavilions on piers and beaches were the most popular places on Coney Island. One investigator described, "thousands of girls who are seized with such madness for dancing that they spend every night in the dance halls and picnic parks."[65] Another observer commented at the different types of dance halls, "in the most fashionable there is a good deal of promiscuous intercourse, flirting and picking up of acquaintances, but the dancing itself is usually proper and conventional; in the Bohemian, behavior is free and pronouncedly bad forms of dancing are seen."[66]

As a result of the dance hall atmosphere, the Women's Branch of the Brooklyn Mission in 1901 campaigned against immorality and prostitution at Coney Island. In 1912, the West End Improvement League of Coney Island joined the crusade. Reverend Mortenson of the Society of Inner Mission and Rescue complained about bawdy dance halls, movie pictures, and rowdyism on the beach. Over time commodified sexuality replaced dance halls. Penny machines were introduced to measure kisses. The Tunnel of Love and the Canals of Venice provided opportunities for couples to embrace. The Steeplechase Park built in 1897 provided rides, such as the Barrel of Love, the Dew Drop parachute ride, and compressed air jets to lift women's skirts.[67]

As commercial enterprises created new leisure time activities, other youth recreation was offered in chaperoned community centers and clubs. Efforts were made to limit the sale of alcohol. The New York public Recreation Commission suggested having older women chaperone younger ones at dance halls and movies. Under pressure from community organizations, some movie houses set aside special seats for single women. To lure youth away from dance halls, settlement houses provided social activities, including regulated and chaperoned dances.[68]

In 1902, John Dewey proclaimed before the NEA that the public schools should become the new social centers. Dewey wanted to provide an alternative social world to the dance halls and saloons. However, Dewey's concept of the social center went one step beyond protecting the working class from immorality. He saw it as a method to keep people working harder in a world of mass production. In contrast to the consumer-oriented approach of Patten, Dewey emphasized the social meaning of work. He told the NEA meeting that the school as a social center, "must interpret to [the worker] the intellectual and social meaning of the work in which he is engaged; that is must reveal its relations to the life and work of the world."[69]

Prior to Dewey's speech, schools and parks were opening social centers. In 1897, New York City organized its after school activities into social centers. The Chicago park system created social centers in their field houses and provided for adult clubs and choral groups. Public schools in Milwaukee opened their doors to evening adult programs. In 1913, the Russell Sage foundation reported that almost half of the school superintendents they contacted reported the creation of school social centers. Schools were built to accommodate evening activities, including chaperoned dances. In 1912, the president of the Western Municipal League of Boston wrote regarding social centers, "it is our endeavor to make our city a true home for the people, it is not enough that we should merely make it a house. . . . We must ensure that there shall be within it recreation, enjoyment, and happiness for all."[70]

High school activities created a shared experience for youth. In *From Front Porch to Back Seat: Courtship in Twentieth-Century America*, Beth Bailey argued that the high school standardized youth culture in the United States. A common youth culture was spread by radio and magazines. Beginning in 1935, this national White youth culture was confirmed by surveys conducted by the American Institute of Public Opinion. Bailey concluded, "From about the late 1930s on, many young people knew to the percentage point what their peers throughout the country thought and did. They knew what was normal."[71]

High school activities provided an alternative to the commodified pleasures of the dance halls, amusement parks, and movies. In the process, high school activities became a new form of consumerism involving the purchase of athletic equipment, club materials, and special clothing such as lettermen's jackets. The school prom represented the coming together of consumerism and the attempts to control the sexuality of youth.

Leading up to the prom were ritualized dating behaviors that emerged from the high school culture of the 1920s and 1930s. High school textbooks and marriage manuals helped create a formalized dating ritual that involved both control of youthful sexuality and selection of a mate for marriage. Dating involved an economic and sexual exchange. In "Rate Your Date: Young Women and the Commodification of Depression Era Courtship," Mary McComb wrote, "Generally, men were expected to pay for their date's entertainment, transportation, and meals. Women were expected to repay men with varying levels of sexual favors, usually a chaste kiss good night."[72]

While young men paid for the date, young girls bought dresses, shoes, and makeup. In purchasing these products, young women commodified the process of selecting a husband. McComb contended, "Women not only rewarded men with sexual favors, but young females in the 1930s and early 1940s fashioned themselves into commodified beings who existed in a heterosexual marketplace of exchange."[73] The commodification of marriage selection through ritualized high school dating was spelled out in Frances Strain's 1939 marriage text, *Love at the Threshold: A Book on Dating, Romance, and Marriage.* Strain advised, "Besides being fun, single dating defines a person and brings out his or her capacity. . . . It's like selling— you must be alert to the other person's responses. An appropriate turn of the phrase, and everything is won. Too much high pressure, perhaps, and everything is lost."[74]

High school marriage texts and manuals built sexual boundaries around dating. According to McComb, every book during this period dealt with the issue of petting, which meant anything from hand holding to sexual acts short of actual penetration. All the books warned against promiscuous petting. High school girls were cautioned that heavy petting would lead to a decline of their dating value in the marketplace. Women were given the task of ensuring that petting did not go too far. They were warned that boys tended to sit around and talk about their sexual exploits. The worst thing that could happen to a girl was to become an object of locker room discussions. Girls were told to achieve a balance between being known as an "icicle" or a "hot number."[75]

The high point of the high school dating ritual was the prom. In *Prom Night: Youth, Schools, and Popular Culture,* Amy Best argued that as a growing number of youth attended high school, "School clubs, school dances, and student government increasingly became a significant part of the kids' lives."[76] Proms became widespread in the 1930s when the high school became a mass institution. They were considered a poor or middle-class version of the debutante ball, which instructed youth in proper dating and mating rituals. Amy Best contended, "Proms were historically tied to a schooling project used to govern the uncontrollable youth. By enlisting you to participate in middle-class rituals like the prom, schools were able to ad-

(margin, handwritten, sideways): Constructions of gender & consumerism

vance a program that reigned in student's emerging and increasingly public sexualities."[77]

Proms opened new vistas for consumerism, particularly female consumerism. Shopping for the right dress became an important part of the prom ritual along with the purchase of makeup, shoes, lingerie, handbags, and jewelry. Among teenage girls, there were countless discussions about what to buy and how to fix one's makeup and hair.[78] Eventually prom-oriented magazines appeared, such as *Your Prom* and *Teen Prom*, to guide both prom manners and consumerism. These magazines surveyed readers with consumer-oriented questions such as, "How many stores will you visit when shopping for a prom dress?" and "Would you be interested in looking at gowns like these for other special occasions such as homecoming?"[79]

Protestant reformers and educators changed the direction of the commodification of youth's leisure time from commercial dance halls to attendance at high school dances and proms. These efforts did not end the commercialization of youth's leisure time activity or their sexual activity. The end result, as exemplified by the prom, was to create a controlled consumer market. The emergence of the high school as a mass institution created a common experience for youth across the nation. This common experience inevitably created a common culture related to the high school experience.

By bringing teenagers together, the high school formed a teenage consumer group that was noted by the publication of the first issue of *Seventeen* magazine in 1944. The magazine's editors, reflecting the development of the high school, assumed the existence of a teenage market. Their goal was to shape teenage female spending patterns. Estelle Ellis, the promotional director of *Seventeen*, stated, "Of course the emphasis was on consumption—the buying power of this age group."[80] Articles in *Seventeen* preached the importance of education in politics and world affairs along with proper consumption.

In summary, the high school's institutionalization of youth, extracurricular activities, athletics, home economics, sex education and marriage courses, dances, and the prom helped establish gender roles. The high school male's image was that of the muscular athlete who, while keeping up with his studies, found his identity in leisure time activities. Too much focus on scholarship or the arts without active participation in the world of jocks opened the door to charges of being a pansy or queer. Male youth bought sexual favors on dates by assuming the role of paying for transportation, food, and dinners. Girls prepared themselves for future consumption by focusing on clothes and makeup. Similar to the male image, girls were to do well in school while projecting an image of primarily worrying about boys and consumption.

PATRIOTISM AND ECONOMIC NATIONALISM

The new male image included a patriotic scorn for economic alternatives to consumerism, particularly communism. The new man was imagined as sports minded, rugged, sexually controlled, and loyal to consumer capitalism and his nation. Patriotic exercises, history and social studies courses, and character education were to dedicate men, particularly future businessmen, to corporate spirit and "100% Americanism." Referring to the image of the businessman of the 1920s, the report of the 1926 Committee on Character Education of the NEA declared, "This is why 'live wires' and 'go-getters' are such heroes to the bulk of the people; in and of itself all this is quite legitimate, and indeed moral."[81] The object of character education was to form live-wires and go-getters for the expanding corporate world of business. Besides defining gender roles, the high school world of football, basketball, cheerleaders, student government, assemblies, clubs, and rallies promoted school spirit, which was considered the underpinning of the corporate male personality.

School and corporate spirit were accompanied by a spirit of Americanism. Leading the Americanism campaign in public schools was the American Legion. Topping the list of resolutions at the American Legion's first convention in 1919 was a resolution against "Bolshevism, I.W.W., radicalism . . . [and] all anti-Americanism tendencies, activities, and propaganda." Targeting its Americanism campaign at the public schools, the American Legion eventually joined arms with the NEA in a campaign for citizenship education.[82]

While the public schools were educating their version of the 100% American businessman, the newly founded public relations industry was issuing probusiness editorials and articles for inclusion in newspapers and magazines. According to the leading distributor of these probusiness materials, the purpose was to reduce "the volume of legislation that interferes with business and industry . . . to discourage radicalism by labor organizations" and to "campaign against any socialistic propaganda of whatever nature."[83]

Reflecting the same goal as the probusiness public relations campaign, the U.S. Commissioner of Education, John Tigert, declared in 1921 his "determination to crush out of the schools communism, bolshevism, socialism, and all persons who did not recognize the sanctity of private property and 'the right of genius to its just rewards'."[84] Teachers and administrators were called on to purge schools of all subversive ideas. Writing in the 1930s, historian Howard Beales expressed his belief that the reason a War Facts Test was given to New York high school teachers in 1919, which asked about Russian communism and the sources for such information, was to identify teachers with radical views.[85] In another study by Beales published in 1941, he ranked the relative influence of various organizations interested in purging schools of subversive ideas. "On the whole," he wrote, "the American Legion seems to be the most important. Next come benefactors of the school, the D.A.R., the Chamber of Commerce, and 'other patriotic organizations,' including in the South the United Daughters of the Confederacy."[86]

In 1921, the NEA formed a permanent Committee on Character Education to work in cooperation with the American School Citizenship League and the NEA Committee on the Teaching of Democracy.[87] In 1926, the Committee on Character Education issued its report, which was reprinted and distributed as a bulletin of the U.S. Bureau of Education.[88] The report stressed the importance of cooperation and group activity by claiming, "The most profoundly moral lives are those in which the I is most completely merged into the We." The integration of the I into the We, the report argued, would result "in achievement, success, life-career. This is an impressive phase of moral development and furnishes a powerful motive for conduct."[89] The businessman's achievements, according to the report, would motivate the school boy. In discussing the motivational power of dreams of a successful career, the report stated, "It [success] has powerful appeal to 'man on the street,' who loves to hear about 'doing big things,' and probably dreams more or less about doing big things himself." The report claimed that the public worships successful people who are live-wires and go-getters.[90]

The involvement of the American Legion in high school education and its connection with the NEA strengthened efforts to educate a patriotic go-getter and spark-plug businessman. In March 1919, the American Legion started in Paris at a meeting called by Theodore Roosevelt, Jr. to organize a World War I veterans' organization. The organizing members worried that U.S. military personnel were being exposed to radical economic ideas that would aid the spread of Bolshevist ideas. William Gellerman concluded in his study of the American Legion's involvement in education, "Ex-soldiers were restless. Bolshevism had triumphed in Russia. American leaders both at home and abroad were worried. They were afraid that ex-servicemen might organize along Bolshevistic lines, and exercise such power as to threaten the status quo in America. The American Legion was organized to prevent any such catastrophe."[91]

The organizational structure of the American Legion maximized opportunities for influencing both local and national educational policy. Whereas membership was attached to local American Legion posts, policymaking was centralized. Legion leaders wanted to present a united front. The membership of the American Legion during the 1920s grew from 845,146 in 1920 to 1,153,909 in 1931. By 1923, the Legion had established 11,129 local posts.[92] Within this organizational structure, the Legion's National Americanism Commission dictated its Americanism campaign to local posts.

In the official version of the organization's history as told by Russell Cook, National Director of the Legion's Americanism Commission to delegates at the 1934 NEA convention,

> The members of the American Legion were rudely awakened to the necessity of more general education while serving the flag of our country on the battlefields of the World War. At no other period in our national history has the importance of education been more pronounced than during the war when members of the Legion experienced a handicap which a lack of schooling placed upon comrades.[93]

The inability to read orders, he claimed, caused deaths among the troops. Voicing concern about the problem of illiteracy among the foreign-born, he recounted how the Americanism Commission had originally sought the NEA's help "in establishing an annual program in which the American people might dedicate themselves each year to the ideal of self-government based upon an enlightened citizenry. Out of that thought was born American Education Week." Reminding the NEA of the Legion's dedication to the education of the foreign-born, he told the delegates, we "realized that aliens in this country must have help in fitting themselves to accept the responsibilities of American citizenship and in understanding and solving the problems of everyday life in America."[94]

The American Legion influenced students through political censorship of teachers and textbooks and by supporting patriotic exercises. These activities were controlled by the Legion's Americanism Commission. The Commission was formed at the Legion's first convention in 1919. The founding resolution stated, "the establishment of a National Americanism Commission of the American Legion to realize in the United States the basic ideal of this Legion of 100% Americanism through the planning, establishment and conduct of a continuous, constructive educational system. . . ."[95]

The resolution listed the following goals in the promotion of 100% Americanism:

1. combat all anti-American tendencies, activities and propaganda;
2. work for the education of immigrants, prospective American citizens and alien residents in the principles of Americanism;
3. inculcate the ideals of Americanism in the citizen population, particularly the basic American principle that the interests of all the people are above those of any special interest or any so-called class or section of the people;

4. spread throughout the people of the nation information as to the real nature and principles of American government;
5. foster the teaching of Americanism in all schools.[96]

As part of its Americanism campaign, local Legion members were urged to weed out subversives from local school systems. The 1921 Legion convention passed a resolution calling for state laws to cancel certificates of teachers "found guilty of disloyalty to the government." In addition, Legion members were asked to volunteer the names of subversive teachers to local school boards. In 1919, the National Americanism Commission warned that, "We have those who believe that the red, white and blue presided over by the eagle shall be replaced by the red flag with the black vulture of disloyalty and international unrest perched upon its staff. Through the schools and through the churches the radicals are now seeking to put across their policies."[97]

In 1921, the National Americanism Commission joined with the NEA to sponsor American Education Week. Henry J. Ryan, Chair of the Joint Advisory Committee of the NEA and the American Legion, and National Director of the Americanism Commission for 1921–1922, explained to the delegates of the 1921 NEA convention the reasons for the Legion's interest in supporting an American Education Week. "America is God's last chance to save the world," he told the delegates. "We can save it only by giving to every boy and girl in America an equal opportunity for education . . . opportunity to learn of that government . . . so that . . . they will be able to say, 'We learned to love our country at school'."[98]

In 1925, the American Bar Association and the Daughters of the American Revolution (DAR) also joined in sponsoring American Education Week. In that year, one day of Education Week was called Equal Opportunity Day, devoted to making "Democracy safe for the world through universal education."[99] The DAR participated in American Education Week because "reverence for the nation's founders and interest in schools fit in with our conservation of the values of the past, and the constructive growth of the future."[100]

During American Education Week, educators and representatives from local Legion posts, DAR chapters, and the American Bar Association cooperated in sponsoring a series of activities supporting the public school and projects for education in Americanism. In 1925, American Education Week emphasized instruction on the U.S. Constitution and the building of patriotism. In 1926, each day in American Education Week was designated by descriptive titles such as, "For God and Country Day," "Constitutional Rights Day," "Patriotism Day," "Equal Opportunity Day," "Know Your School Day," and "Community Day."[101]

The Legion tried to shape students' political ideologies by sponsoring essays around patriotic and antiradical themes. In 1923, the assigned topic in the contest was, "Why America should prohibit immigration for five years";

in 1924, it was, "Why Communism is a menace to Americanism." The American Commission argued that their school awards were an "effective antidote for the teachings of those groups opposed to the patriotic principles embraced by the American Legion." In addition to these activities, local Legion posts promoted flag education and the saying of the Pledge of Allegiance in local public schools.[102]

In the 1920s and 1930s, the American Legion, the D.A.R., the Women's Christian Temperance Union, and religious organizations monitored the content of public school textbooks. In the 1930s, Howard Beales recorded the feelings of an author of American history texts regarding the impact of these organizations: "In trying to guard against criticism and opposition, authors are driven to sins of omission and commission." After describing how he added material of little importance to his history texts and deleted other material because of pressure from outside advocacy groups, such as the American Legion, the textbook author told Beales, "And, if any author tells you he is not influenced by such pressure, that he tells 'the truth, the whole truth and nothing but the truth' as far as he knows it, don't you believe him. He is a conscious or unconscious liar."[103] Also textbooks conformed to state laws requiring an education for patriotic citizenship. For instance, the Lusk Laws passed by the New York State legislature in 1918 prohibited any statements in textbooks fostering disloyalty to the United States. The law established a state commission to examine books in "civics, economics, English, history, language and literature for the purpose of determining whether such textbooks contain any matter or statements of any kind which are seditious in character, [or] disloyal to the United States." A 1923 Wisconsin law prohibited any textbook "which falsifies the facts regarding the war of independence, or the war of 1812, or which defames our nation's founders or misrepresents the ideals and causes for which they struggled and sacrificed, or which contains propaganda favorable to any foreign government." An Oregon law banned any textbook that "speaks slightingly of the founders of the republic, or the men who preserved the union, or which belittles or under values their work."[104] In *Civic Attitudes in American Schools* (1930), Bessie Louise Pierce concluded that, "Most makers of courses of study are united in their belief that the main aim of instruction in American history is the development of a vivid conception of American nationality and a high sense of patriotism and civic religion."[105]

THE CLEAN-SHAVEN BUSINESSMAN:
ADVERTISING IMAGES OF THE NEW MAN

The high school's ideal of the sports-minded, patriotic businessman was duplicated in advertising images. In general, ads most often portrayed generic businessmen who were either admiring the consumption of women, stoically using or modeling a product, or acting as an expert. Regarding early 20th-century ads, Roland Marchand summarized, "Men appeared almost as frequently as women, but often in nondescript, standardized parts as husbands or as businessmen at work . . . men rarely assumed decorative poses or exaggerated bodily proportions. Their hands exemplified the contrast between the functional grasp of the male and the ethereal gesture of the female."[106] Advertising agents avoided any suggestion of effeminacy in the male image. Ads implied that the competitive world of business made men *true men*, and agencies "worried that the attempt to pretty him up for the collar ads and the nightclub scenes would sissify and weaken man's image, tailoring it too much to feminine tastes."[107]

Some traditional Protestant advertising men linked images of the businessman with theology. Advertising executive Bruce Barton popularized the idea that businessmen represented a form of muscular Christianity. In *The Man Nobody Knows*, Barton's best selling 1925 book—it outsold F. Scott Fitzgerald's *The Great Gatsby*—Jesus Christ was portrayed as the exemplary business and advertising man.[108] Barton's muscular, Christian business and advertising man could be seen in various forms in magazine and newspaper advertisements in the early 20th century.

Bruce Barton wrote his tract on business, advertising, and muscular Christianity while heading the firm Batten, Barton, Durstine & Osborn (BBDO). Born in 1886, Barton's father was a Protestant minister who rode a church circuit through rural Tennessee. After working on magazines, he was attracted to advertising during World War I while writing fundraising copy for the Salvation Army, YMCA, YWCA, and other nonprofit organizations. In 1919, he joined Alex Osborne and Roy Durstine in opening an advertising agency that, in the early 1920s, landed important accounts such as General Electric, General Motors, Dunlop tire, and Lever Brothers. Throughout the 20th century, the agency remained in the top 10 of advertising companies as measured by earnings.[109]

Barton's muscular Christ exemplified the division taking place between the effeminate world of the fairy and pansy and the new man. Barton's Christ was tough and lived in the tradition of Theodore Roosevelt's "the strenuous life." In a chapter entitled "The Outdoor Man," Barton described Christ driving the money changers out of the temple: "As his right arm rose and fell, striking its blows with that little whip, the sleeve dropped back to reveal muscles hard as iron. No one who watched him in action had any doubt that he was fully capable of taking care of himself."[110] Barton claimed that Christ's muscularity was a result of 30 years of carpentry. Unfortunately, from Barton's perspective, the Bible never provided any details about Christ's physical condition. Barton complained that, as a result, many of the paintings of Christ depicted a "frail man, under-muscled, with a soft face—a woman's face covered by a beard."[111] Barton's portrayal of traditional representations of Christ sounded very much like the 1920s' descriptions of the fairy or pansy. To prove Christ's manly and rugged being, Barton cited four characteristics. The first was that health "flowed out of him to create health in others." The other three characteristics clearly outlined the image of the new man:

1. The appeal of his personality to women—weakness does not appeal to them.
2. His lifetime of outdoor living
3. The steel-like hardness of his nerves[112]

This manly Christ became, as one of Barton's chapters is entitled, "The Founder of Modern Business." What did Christ discover that made Christianity a great business? "You will hear that discovery," Barton wrote, "proclaimed in every sales convention as something distinctly modern and up to date. It is emblazoned in the advertising pages of every magazine."[113] Referring to an advertisement for the *greatest* car company in the world, which I assume was General Motors because it was his company's account, he claimed the key to success was good service, a willingness to understand the life of the lowly worker, and extra effort. Christ's life represented these qualities, and modern businessmen, as muscular Christians, needed to learn the same lessons. Barton listed Jesus Christ's winning business methods:

1. Whoever will be great must render great service.
2. Whoever will bind himself at the top must be willing to lose himself at the bottom.
3. The big rewards come to those who travel the second, undemanded mile.[114]

Of course from Barton's perspective, Christ was able to sell his religion because of good advertising methods. These advertising methods involved service to others. Barton imagined the following advertising headlines:

PALSIED MAN HEALED
JESUS OF NAZARETH CLAIMS RIGHT TO FORGIVE SINS
PROMINENT SCRIBES OBJECT
***
DEFENDS PUBLICANS AND SINNERS
JESUS OF NAZARETH WELCOMES THEM AT LUNCH
***
JESUS OF NAZARETH WILL DENOUNCE
THE SCRIBES AND PHARISEES IN THE
CENTRAL SYNAGOGUE

TO-NIGHT AT EIGHT O'CLOCK
SPECIAL MUSIC[115]

The image of the new man and muscular Christian appeared in advertising copy as what Marchand called the *generic businessman*. Along with BBDO, almost all ads presented men dressed in suits even while relaxing at home. The bodies under these suits appeared muscular. All of the male faces were clean shaven with chiseled features. None of the male faces was similar to those Barton disdained in paintings of Christ, such as "like a woman's face covered by a beard." In ads for women's products, men were often shadow figures admiring some aspect of the featured woman.

Being clean shaven became a mark of the new man. Although mustaches lingered on, beards disappeared from images of the new man. Clean shaven became the norm for White males. In fact, the clean-shaven male became a symbol for patriotic Americans as I discovered in the 1960s when, in my youthful rebellion, I grew a beard. Despite countless centuries of men wearing beards, including the portrayal of religious figures with beards, the beard became the sign of radicalism in the America of the 1960s. Without even opening my mouth to spout a political doctrine, people would immediately associate my beard with anti-Viet Nam war protests. A clean-shaven American male was associated with patriotism, acceptance of the American way of life, and morality. Just as the suit became the uniform for the corporate male, a clean-shaven male became the corporate standard for grooming.

In a 1913 ad for the Arrow Collar Man, three *manly* men wearing ties are shown, with one seated holding a cane, another holding a tennis racquet, and the third holding a leash connected to the studded collar of a bull dog. Looking distinguished, the man with the cane sported a small mustache, whereas the others were clean-shaven outdoors men.[116] In Helen Resor's famous ad for Woodbury's Facial Soap, a clean-shaven and suited man is shown kissing the hand of the featured woman with the caption, "A skin you love to touch." The man was shown behind the woman, and his upper body is only partially visible.[117]

The introduction of the Gillette Safety Razor in 1905 quickly linked the marketing of a brand-named product with the image of the new man, particularly the clean-shaven new man. The new disposable safety razor threatened the traditional masculine social life of the barbershop where many middle-class men went to be shaved. However, within the context of the new corporate life, the safety razor promised greater independence for men to manage their own grooming. Similar to home economists who wanted to save the family from unsanitary cooking conditions, King Gillette, the inventor of the safety razor, promised to save men from the unsanitary conditions of the barber shop. In a 1907 ad, King Gillette claimed, "When you use my razor you are exempt from the dangers that men often encounter who allow their faces to come in contact with brush, soap and barbershop accessories used on other people."[118]

Gillette ads actually taught men how to be clean shaven under any conditions. A series of ads in 1910 demonstrated how to shave to sailors, outdoorsmen, railroad travelers, and others who could not go to a barbershop. One 1910 ad used fear of sexual rejection to send home the message that men could always be clean shaven under any conditions: "A bridegroom on the Canadian Pacific acquired a three-days' growth of beard. Despair was written on his face. A kindly gentleman loaned him a Gillette— and received the united thanks of two fond hearts."[119] The accompanying illustration denoted the racism implied in this male image. On the left of the illustration, the distressed young man was shown talking to the older man. On the right, the young man was shown shaving. Bridging these illustrated sections was an African-American porter shown holding the hat and cane of the older man. The early Gillette ads also emphasized that men who could remain clean shaven represented progress. The previously discussed ad urged readers, "Be progressive. Keep Gillette on your home washstand— take it with you when you travel. . . . Life is brighter when a clean face is an every morning habit."[120]

It seemed inevitable that this new tool for the new man would eventually be linked to sports, particularly from the standpoint of advocates of the new manliness like Theodore Roosevelt, the real man's sport of boxing. With the advent of radio, American minds would be haunted, including this author's mind, with the following jingle:

Gillette Razor Blades

Announcer: *Look sharp!*
Sound: Prizefight bell
Announcer: *Feel sharp!*
Sound: Prizefight bell
Announcer: *Be sharp!*
Sound: Prizefight bell
Announcer: *Use Gillette Blue Blades . . . with the sharpest edges ever honed.*[121]

The new man and new woman confronted each other in a 1927 ad for S.O.S. cleaner. This ad encompassed many of the aspects of the new gender images, including the supportive role of the home economics expert, the generic businessman, and the consuming wife. A fully suited man with a tie was shown sitting on a couch with his legs crossed looking doubtfully at his standing wife. He is clean shaven and appears muscular under his clothing. The wife, with short hair and wearing a flapper dress, juts her chin out defiantly at the husband as she exclaimed, "You think I'm a flapper but I can keep house." Below this scene was a small, round photo of the domestic science expert Mary Dale Anthony, who was described in the ad as "Adviser on kitchen and household cleaning problems to thousands of women." Anthony informed the reader, "Leave it to the modern girl to speak her mind . . . alert and eager to learn . . . looking for new time-savers. Girls today want more leisure, and they get it by using short-cuts."[122] In this ad, the strong and silent man remained the authority in the house, whereas consumer wife claimed greater freedom through consumption.

Two of BBDO's ads for General Motors featured similar clean-shaven men in suits. One 1925 ad was for the General Motors Acceptance Corporation, which pioneered the installment buying of General Motor's cars. In the ad, a woman was seated at a salesman's desk with the salesman—clean shaven in suit and tie—explaining the installment plan. Her husband, also clean shaven in suit and tie, is standing and listening. His standing position demonstrates his authority over his seated wife. However, as symbolic of the new woman, the wife was participating in the purchase of the car.[123] In another 1925 ad for General Motor's Chevrolet, there was a similar scene, except in this case the husband was seated. The wife's hands were poised expressively in the air while the husband had one hand clinched and the other firmly placed on the desk.[124] In both cases, the salesman was providing the service that Bruce Barton believed was the key to Jesus Christ's success as a businessman.

THE COWBOY IMAGE

Schools and advertising upheld the image of the ideal or normal as being a clean-shaven White businessman dressed in a suit who was sports-minded, patriotic, energetic, and rugged in appearance with his personal identity formed through leisure time activities. However, another image was that of the cowboy. For Theodore Roosevelt, the cowboy symbolized the American manliness that was lost with the passing of the frontier and the rise of urban and corporate America. After World War II, this cowboy image was reflected from the screen by John Wayne whose characters embodied patriotic masculinity.[125] It also found its place in the icon of the Marlboro Man.

Removed from the dusty plains of cattle ranching, the modern day version of the cowboy was the jock. Clean shaven and manly, the modern jock was primarily a spectator who most often listened or watched sporting events on radio or TV. With a mind filled with sports statistics, the corporate man could safely commune with fellow males without engaging in the potentially explosive topic of politics. Indeed, the modern corporate man in suit and tie could compare the competitive world of business with the competition of the sports field. Also sports were somehow patriotic, with each game starting with the playing of the national anthem. Besides spectatorship, the new male could find leisure time relaxation in a round of golf, fishing, or hunting. Fulfilling the dreams of Theodore Roosevelt, a man could take his family camping in a national forest or park and relive the frontier experience of cooking over an open fire.

This was the gendered world that many American men of the 20th century encountered in public schools, advertising, and media. Of course there were exceptions. Rebels showed their disdain for this image by wearing long hair, beards, beads, and tie-dyed shirts and pants, and by displaying pierced noses, ears, and tongues. Sometimes these alternative images of masculinity represented a scorn of the patriotic values associated with the sports-loving and clean-shaven *real male.* Alternative clothing and facial hair possibly indicated a variety of dissenting positions, including left-wing politics, anticonsumerism, anti-Americanism, and antisports.

CONCLUSION: RUDOLPH VALENTINO AND THE EROTICIZATION OF AMERICAN SOCIETY

Ironically, the efforts of Puritan leaders and advertising agencies infused sexuality into American institutions and consumer items. The high school was transformed from a purely academic institution to one responsible for controlling the sexual life of teenagers. As a result of athletics, cheerleading, dances, dating, clubs, and marriage and sex education courses, the high school, in fact, became a center of adolescent sexuality. The folklore of the teenage girl giving up her virginity on prom night illustrated the eroticization of the institution. The climax of academic studies was accompanied by the consummation of a relationship between high school lovers.

Sexual themes of denial and fulfillment used to sell products also eroticized those products. The Gillette safety razor became an object for heightening sexual pleasure when it received the "united thanks of two fond hearts" by allowing the honeymooner to shave off a 3-day beard. Underarm deodorant, mouth wash, tooth paste, Wonder Bread, cleaning products, cosmetics, and a host of other products were advertised as either protecting a romantic relationship or ensuring the attentions of a new lover.

As a result, the promise of consumption was often sexual fulfillment. The promise of a high school education was an income that opened the door to consumerism. A goal of schooling was providing equality of opportunity to earn money and consume. Therefore, indirectly, education promised a fulfillment of sexual desires by providing an income that could purchase products advertised to enhance sexuality or gain a sexual partner. Consequently, both the social and academic life of the modern high school promised sexual fulfillment.

Of course the eroticization of American society was complicated by the racial and heterosexual nature of the new man. As a host of historians have argued, the most important being Gail Bederman, Michael Kimmel, and William Pinar, the new male image included a vision of the White male bringing civilization to the rest of the world.[126] This image suggested that African-American men were not real men and therefore should submit to the civilizing effect of White men. In part, the lynching and castration of African-American men in the late 19th and early 20th centuries for supposed sexual impositions on White women were based on the assumptions by White men that African-American men could not practice spermatic political economy. Unlike the new White man, African-American men, in the minds of most Whites, could not control their sexual passions. Consequently, it was the duty of White men, according to this reasoning, to restrain African-American men's lustful nature by public displays of violence. The same attitudes existed toward Indian men as exemplified by the statue of the proud practitioner of spermatic political economy, Theodore Roosevelt, seated on his horse above the conquered Indian as a symbol of the civilizing effects of White men on Indian men.

The violent actions against African-American men occurred while advertising images placed them in subservient positions to Whites. In the Gillette ad, the African-American train porter holds the White man's coat as the older White man ensures the continued sexual activities of the honeymooners by teaching the young man to use a safety razor. This implies that the proper role of the African-American man was to help the White man fulfill his civilized and officially sanctioned sexual acts.

The movie star, Rudolph Valentino, I believe best represented the complex sexual and racial image of the new man and the eroticization of American society. As a public figure, Valentino was a 1920s sex symbol for many White female moviegoers while being despised by most White males. Over 100,000 mostly female mourners visited his open coffin after his premature death in 1926 at the age of 31. The cult of Valentino continued years after his death and included a mysterious Woman in Black bearing roses who annually visited his crypt.

Although Valentino's movie career began in 1918 with small parts, his fame and female following began with the release of *The Sheik* in 1921. His biographer Alexander Walker contended that the female attracted to Valentino's performance was "the liberated 'New Woman' of the 1920s who wore her skirts shorter and her hair bobbed, who smoked, danced, drank from her beau's hip flask and took up every fad or craze of a novelty era." Also, according to Walker, Valentino's portrayal of the Sheik appealed to traditional women who wanted the thrill of uninvited seduction.[127]

In contrast to the image of the new man, Valentino's *character* was the barbarian who, although manly and rugged, was possessed by uncontrolled sexuality. The movie fantasy portrayed a man who seduced women after kidnapping them. It was a rape fantasy without a rape. In the movie, the Sheik kidnapped Lady Diana Mayo and brought her to his tent. "Why have you brought me here?" she asked. "Are you not woman enough to know?" he responded.[128] A militant feminist, Lady Diana was humiliated by the Sheik until she agreed to trade her riding pants for a skirt and lost her militant attitudes. In the seduction scene, Lady Diana proclaimed, "I am not afraid with your arms around me, Ahmed, my desert love, MY SHEIK."[129] With these lines, the independent woman succumbed to the preying nature of the barbarian.

The film encompasses many important issues regarding race and the image of the new man. First, the Sheik turned out not to be a barbarian, but the abandoned child of a Scottish nobleman, the Earl of Glencarryl. This resolved the potential racial problem in the 1920s of a non-White man seducing a White woman. It also resolved the social class issue with both partners coming from upper class backgrounds.

However, the fantasy image of the seductive and sexual Sheik did not match the ideal public image of the sexually restraint White man transmitting civilization around the world. This clash in images might have been a reason that many male moviegoers despised the seductive screen image of Valentino. A male writer in the 1922 issue of *Photoplay* wrote, "I hate Valentino! All men hate Valentino. . . . I hate him because he's the great lover of the screen; I hate him because he's an embezzler of hearts. . . . I hate him because he's too good looking."[130] Male moviegoers considered on-screen seductive approaches to women as effeminate despite that the Sheik and most other roles played by Valentino presented a muscular and adventuresome male. There is certainly nothing necessarily effeminate about kidnapping women for the purpose of seduction.

The conflict between the screen image of Valentino and the public image of the new man was explained by his biographer Alexander Walker: "The truth was that Valentino had made lovemaking into too onerous and time-consuming a task for American males to emulate. He had shown the Latin trait of infinite consideration in his courtship which requires an equivalent amount of time, patience, and vanity. It wasn't the American ideal, at least it wasn't the American *male* ideal."[131]

Valentino's public displays of athleticism were attempts to overcome charges of effeminacy made by the press. Similar to Theodore Roosevelt, Valentino chose boxing as proof of his masculinity. Frequently, after public comment that he appeared effeminate in his screen role as a lover, he would give public demonstrations of boxing. In one photo made for public consumption, the famous boxer Jack Dempsey was shown referring to a fight between Valentino and an unnamed opponent.[132] In addition, he distributed photographs of his muscular body and his exercise routine.

However, no matter how many boxing demonstrations, his screen presence was still considered effeminate by many men. Advertising images that came close to Valentino's screen image were just shadowy figures in ads for women's cosmetics and personal care items. In contrast, most other advertising images of clean-shaven generic businessmen did not show the passionate gestures and sexuality that Valentino displayed on the screen.

Ironically, from the perspective of the future, it was Valentino's seductive and emotional qualities that made American White men uneasy. Valentino's screen image did not practice spermatic political economy. His screen characters shared themselves with many women, and they focused attention on sexual relationships rather than channeling sexuality into sports, adventure, and civilization building. On the screen, Valentino was not the sexless cowboy riding across the plains to fight Indians. Ironically, many men thought of Valentino as being a *fairy* or *pansy*.

Valentino's personal issue with masculinity was as complicated as his screen image. There was a difference, of course, between the fantasy life of the screen and the real life of the actors. As movies impacted the world of personal fantasies, moviegoers became more and more interested in the lives of their off-screen heros and heroines. In many ways, moviegoers wanted the fantasy of the screen to be replicated in movie actors' lives. Consequently, the movies developed two fantasy worlds. One was on screen and the other was in the supposed glamorous lives of movie stars.

Off-screen, Rudolph Valentino seemed confused about his own masculinity. As George Chauncey argued in his history *Gay New York*, the public image of manliness in the early 20th century made sharp distinctions between heterosexuality and homosexuality, with heterosexuality presented as the norm. You were either gay or straight. There was no room in this male image for bisexuality. Valentino's life suggested that he was not sexually attracted to women or, as his biographer suggested, Valentino might have been impotent.[133] In real life, Valentino did not have raging love affairs with a multitude of women. He was divorced from his first wife after she locked him out of their bedroom on their wedding night. No reason for this action was ever provided, but the marriage was not consummated. His second marriage was to a lesbian who supposedly exercised domineering powers over his personal and professional life. Most of his personal companions were young men.

Whether gay, bisexual, or impotent, Valentino wrestled with the image of the new male. Just before his death, an editorial in the Chicago *Tribune* accused him of debauching "American manhood by the 'unmasculine' image he had popularized."[134] He was so angered by the editorial that he immediately organized for newspaper reporters a boxing match with a sparring partner. Alexander Walker suggested that the incident might have contributed to his early death by aggravating a gastric ulcer that, along with a ruptured appendix, caused his death.[135]

Valentino's lavish public funeral was the first time a movie star's death was given as much attention as that of a president or other major public figure. The debate about Valentino's masculinity on and off the screen highlighted inherent problems of the new male image. Heterosexuality, manliness, sports-mindedness, sexual control, and patriotism embodied in a clean-shaven businessman in a suit was the dominant image of manhood in the 1920s.

Valentino and other movie stars also stimulated consumption fantasies. Movie stars were portrayed as living lavish lives filled with expensive clothes, homes, cars, travel, parties, and sporting activities. Movie fans and aspirant actors could imagine living a celebrity's glamorous life of personal intrigue and drama and, most important, access to limitless consumer goods. In the 1920s, males were considered effeminate if they were interested in shopping and Valentino. This changed by the 1940s and 1950s, as I discuss in chapter 6, when *Esquire* and *Playboy* magazines made the Valentino image of the male lover and shopping acceptable to heterosexual men.

Commodification of Leisure and Cultural Control: Schools, Movies, and Radio

There were sharp differences between the owners of commercial media and advocates of leisure time activities that would provide moral uplift, enhancement of workers' endurance, and motivation to work harder to consume more recreational products. The problem for the latter group was that commercial movies and radio were driven by the profit motive to maximize their audiences. Media owners discovered that dramatic portrayal of sex and violence ensured the sale of their products. Educators and moral leaders were horrified when they discovered that these new cultural tools were creating a sexual revolution and possibly inciting violent acts. The compromise in this struggle was an emphasis on *family values* in commodified forms of leisure that eventually found expression in the building of Disneyland in the 1950s.

The moral and economic arguments for commodified leisure were discussed by economist Simon Patten in a series of 1907 lectures before the Charity Organization Society of the City of New York. Patten warned, in the same tone as 19th-century Sunday School books, that "Drinking and the new sedative pleasures of smoking and saloon card-games are the vices of a faulty economic system, and an unintelligent attempt to enrich an impoverished, alien situation."[1] The "impoverished" and "alien situation," according to Patten, was urban life, which separated the worker from the invigorating and rejuvenating influence of rural life. Most urban activities, Patten argued, "are irrational and extravagant, for they sate appetite and deaden acute pain without *renewing force or directing vigor toward the day's work* (italics added)."[2] The central question, according to Patten, was: "How shall activity be made pleasurable again, and how shall society utilize the working-man's latent vitality in order to increase his industrial efficiency and give to him the rewards of energies, now ineffective, within his body and mind?"[3]

Patten suggested activities that were both reinvigorating and created a motivation to work. He called on educators and social reformers to influence leisure time activities. Of great importance, he argued, was the ability of commodified leisure to cause people to work harder. In Patten's words, entertainment "is to fix the spurs that prick to work. A circus, a national holiday, a camp meeting, arouse country people sharply and suddenly to a need of ready money. Coney Island attracts the city man as soon as he has achieved a bare subsistence."[4]

Advocating the investment by educators and philanthropists in "people's theaters," he argued that the spur to work harder should be combined with moral lessons. In this context, Patten made one of the strongest statements for the role of commodified leisure in a consumer society. "Their zest [the workers'] for amusement urges them to submit to the discipline of work, and the habits formed for the sake of gratifying their tastes make the regular life necessary in industry easier and more pleasant."[5] However, Patten's prescription for leisure time activities had to be reconciled with traditional Protestant morality. This issue was aggravated by the desire by producers of commodified leisure to enlarge their audiences by offering, from the standpoint of traditional Protestantism, immoral entertainment.

While agreeing with Patten, many educators worried that movies, and later radio, threatened the school's control of national culture and morality. In the early 19th century, common school leaders argued that the schools could unite the population by teaching a common set of moral and political principles and through the mutual contact of students. This role was continued when schools adopted Americanization programs for late 19th-century immigrants. Americanization efforts included home economists who tried to standardize American cooking and change immigrant diets. The same commitment to ensuring a common national culture occurred with the swirling new social world of the high school student.

Profit-seeking movie companies challenged the sexual codes that high schools were teaching in sex and marriage courses and in school activities. Seeking to expand their audiences, early movie makers discovered that sex sold tickets. As University of Chicago sociologist Harold Blumer reported in the 1920s, after reading student journals about going to the movies, "They [the journals] force upon one the realization that motion pictures provide, as many have termed it, 'liberal education in the art of loving'."[6]

Radio provided a similar challenge. There was general agreement that the power of broadcasting to enter homes fundamentally effected American culture. Consequently, school people wanted government and educator controlled broadcasting. In the end, commercial interests won, ensuring an increasing role for advertising in promoting consumerism. Radio and TV helped sell consumerism to the American public. ✗

Movies and radio were part of the revolution in leisure time activities. In the late 19th and early 20th centuries, the majority of leisure activities shifted from family, church, and community gatherings to activities requiring the purchase of recreational products and admission tickets to events and establishments, such as movies, professional athletic games, commercial dance halls, and amusement parks. This shift was a result of urbanization, declining hours of work, and new technologies, including movies, radio, and TV. Industrialization and urbanization created a clear separation between work and leisure activities. Workers left the factory seeking evening and holiday entertainment. In the early 20th century, young and single workers went to movies, dance halls, and saloons. These workers confronted a conflict between a media industry promising escape from the tedium of work and educators and moral reformers demanding that media should provide moral instruction.

MOVIES: PROFIT VERSUS MORAL INSTRUCTION

Similar to newspapers, movies increased the public sharing of a common experience. People meeting from different parts of the country, and eventually the world, could relate through a common movie experience. Movie posters joined other city reading and sparked complaints about sensationalism similar to the earlier ads of P.T. Barnum. John Collier, a cofounder of the National Board of Review or, as it was sometimes called, the National Board of Censorship, complained, "Why I saw the Passion Play in moving pictures recently advertised by a poster showing the elopement of a modern couple in evening dress over a garden wall."[7]

Opening first in immigrant and working class neighborhoods, social reformers believed movies and movie theaters were undermining public morality. It was estimated that, prior to 1910, three fourths of the moviegoers crowding nickelodeons and small store-front theaters were working class. In New York City, nickelodeons increased from 50 in 1900 to 400 by 1908, and daily attendance reached 200,000.[8] Typical of moralistic reactions to nickelodeons was the 1911 Chicago Vice Commission's warning: "Investigations by individuals interested in the welfare of children have pointed out many instances where children have been influenced by the conditions surrounding some of these shows. Vicious men and boys mix with the crowd . . . and take liberties with very young girls." Examples were a nickelodeon owner who assaulted 14 young girls, and a 76-year-old man who enticed young girls to attend movies. The Chicago Vice Commission reported the

statement of an unnamed movie critic: "I think the nickel theater is a re-
cruiting station for vice. In the first place from the type of pictures often
shown there; in the second place from the association."[9]

Some feared that movies would cause working class and immigrant audiences to engage in acts of civil disobedience. Films that prompted concern
included *The Candidate* (1907), in which workers threw dirt at an affluent
politician after a speech and he was later beaten by his discontented wife. In
Down with Women (1907), an upper class male declared women incompetent and condemned women's suffrage. Later in the movie, he encountered women in a variety of occupations, from musician to lawyer to taxi
and truck driver. Eventually, he was saved by one woman and defended in
court by another. Greedy landlords were condemned in *The Eviction*
(1907), and workers in labor-management struggles were treated sympathetically in films like *The Iconoclast* (1910).[10] Bankers and factory owners
were frequently criticized in early silent films.[11]

By the 1930s, pro-working class and anti-upper class themes disappeared
from most U.S. films. According to film historian Terry Christensen, "One
movie maker, however, remained sympathetic with workers, immigrants,
and the downtrodden in general as they struggled to withstand the pressures of an urban, industrial society. He was, of course, Charlie Chaplin."[12]

Fears of moral decay, social unrest, and the strengthening of class consciousness prompted demands for censorship. There were two approaches
to the issue of censorship. Some people wanted to remove scenes from movies, whereas others wanted to turn movies into another form of moral education. In addition, there was a debate about whether the government
should take an active role in censorship or whether censorship should exercised by the movie industry.

Advocates of government censorship wanted removal of scenes and words
that might teach audiences how to commit crimes, cause them to participate
in some form of social disturbance, contribute to immorality, or promote
sexual promiscuity. However, those advocating self-censorship wanted films
to teach moral lessons. They wanted movie scripts changed at the time of
production so that explicit moral lessons could be taught to audiences.

The first censorship laws requiring police review and licensing of movies
were passed by the City of Chicago in 1907. In 1909, the law was challenged
when Chicago police refused to license *The James Boys* and *Night Riders*. The
Illinois Supreme Court accepted the police's argument that censorship of
films was necessary to maintain social order. In the words of the Court, the
two films "represent nothing but malicious mischief, arson, and murder.
They are both immoral, and their exhibition would necessarily be attended
with evil effects upon youthful spectators."[13]

Most government-operated censorship boards reviewed films and then
decided whether to license them for distribution. Obviously the film indus-

try resented the process of government censorship because it delayed distribution and created the possibility that each municipality or state would require different standards. Delays and constant editing increased costs. In the 1920s, Will Hays, as president of the Motion Picture Producers and Directors Association (MPPDA), argued against government censorship on the grounds that there was lack of agreement on standards. This was exemplified by state laws prohibiting the showing of a woman smoking a cigarette. According to Hays, these laws "might eliminate any scene of a social gathering happening in another state." In another instance, a lawyer on one censorship board would not allow any scenes that depicted lawyers as unethical or crooked. In another example, Hays wrote, "Scenes of strike riots were ordered eliminated from news reels in one state at the same time newspapers were using photographs of the exact incidents recorded in the films."[14]

In 1915, the U.S. Supreme Court reaffirmed the necessity of government censorship for maintaining social order. The case involved the Mutual Film Corporation's complaint that Ohio required all films to be submitted to a state censorship board, which resulted in delayed distribution. The lawyers for the company argued that censorship before distribution was a violation of the Free Speech Clause of the First Amendment. In a decision that was not overturned until the 1950s, the U.S. Supreme Court ruled that, "We immediately feel that the argument is wrong or strained which extends the guarantee of free speech to the multitudinous shows which are advertised on the billboards of our cities and towns, and which regards them as emblems of public safety." In the words of the Court, movies represented a potential threat to public safety: "Their [the movies'] power of amusement, and it may be, education, the audiences they assemble, not of women alone, but together, not only adults only but of children, make them the more insidious in corruption by pretense of worth. . . ."[15]

Comparing state censorship to public schools, Ellis Oberholtzer, Secretary of the Pennsylvania State Board of Motion Picture Censors, argued in 1921,

> The efforts which are made to convert the unlikeliest of young human beings at school into useful citizens are many. From the care of their teeth and the public feeding of them . . . to the purely education processes. . . . I for one fail to see, therefore, how by any fair system of reasoning we can be held to be without some duty to inquire into the course of the film man with his 15,000 or more picture houses . . . at the door of each inhabitant.[16]

Similar to the public schools' role in protecting morality, he believed the government should censor movies by removing any scenes that might result in lawlessness and the moral decay of the citizenry. As an advocate of gov-

[handwritten note: ✓ schools should teach morality, not film, radio, TV]

ernment censorship, Oberholtzer rejected the use of movies to consciously teach morality. He quoted from a British Board of Film Censors report:

> It is said for such films that they serve to warn the public against the dangers of the abuse of drugs, but the Board decided that there being no reason to suppose that this habit was prevalent in this country . . . , the evils of arousing curiosity in the minds of those to who it was a novel idea far outweighed the possible good that might accrue by warning the small minority who indulged in the practice.

Declared Oberholtzer, "I am, therefore, not to be beguiled by the protestations of such a picture man. I have met him and he resembles a teacher less than any one I have ever seen."[17]

[handwritten mark: ✳] Schools, Oberholtzer declared, should remain the central government agency for teaching morality. Rejecting movies as a source of moral lessons, he stated, "It is clear that a theater is not a proper place for the inculcation of such lessons, or the theater man a proper person to bear such delicate messages to the young. We have the church, the school, the home and our social organizations. . . ."[18]

In contrast to government censorship, advocates of self-regulation wanted films to teach audiences moral and social lessons. They criticized government censorship because it only removed negative scenes without controlling the general theme of a film. Through self-regulation, movies could become another form of public education. The strongest champion of this approach was John Collier of the National Board of Review. The National Board of Review was organized after New York City police, under orders from the mayor and chief of police, closed 550 movie houses on Christmas in 1908 for violating Sunday closing laws as part of a larger crusade against vice. In reaction to police actions, theater owners organized the National Board of Review hoping that self-censorship would stop future vice raids. Officially organized in March 1909, the Board received financial support from the film industry, which hoped that Board approval would ensure a movie's nationwide acceptance and, consequently, avoid problems with government censors. Board members wanted movie reform, like schools and settlement houses, to improve urban life. The majority of members of the executive committee of the National Board of Review were wealthy Protestant males, including Andrew Carnegie, Samuel Gompers, presidents of major universities, and "representatives from the Federal Council of Churches, the YMCA, the New York School Board, the Society for the Prevention of Crime headed by the most powerful vice crusader in the city, the Rev. Charles Parkhurst, and the moralistic Postal Inspector, Anthony Comstock."[19]

The Board's guiding principles were presented by Collier in a magazine series in *The Survey*. As Collier explained, the Board's censorship code stressed the importance of always teaching morality by showing good winning out over evil. "The results of the crime [as depicted in a movie]," the Board's code stated, "should be in the long run disastrous to the criminal so that the impression is that crime will inevitably find one out. The result [punishment] should always take a reasonable proportion of the film." The code stressed the importance of teaching that the government was the protector of public morality. "As a general rule," the code stated, "it is preferable to have retribution come through the hands of authorized officers of the law, rather than through revenge or other unlawful or extra-legal means." In keeping with the Protestant leadership's concern about sexual morality, code standards would "not allow the extended display of personal allurements, the exposure of alleged physical charms and passionate, protracted embraces," and it also disapproved "the showing of men turning lightly from woman to woman or women turning lightly from man to man in intimate sexual relationships."[20]

From John Collier's perspective, government censorship would impede the potential of movies as a form of public education. "The challenge of the old and the institution of the new," Collier wrote, "are a responsibility of the drama, no less than is the inculcation of accepted virtues. . . ."[21] The heavy hand of government censorship, Collier insisted, undermined art's social role by applying absolute standards. "Until censorship can discriminate, can limit the audience, can prescribe the destination of the censored product," he wrote, "it is nothing but a bludgeon-like imposition, by some element [government censors] momentarily in power of its prejudices on the mass of the people." As an example, Collier used a movie scene showing a boy torturing a cat. Although the board prohibited depiction of brutality, these scenes were approved because they were "essential in a plot dealing with the relation of defective mentality to juvenile crime. The boy who is here shown torturing a cat is later restored by medical treatment to normality."[22]

As government officials and reformers grappled with the potential impact of movies on the public mind, school people worried about competing with movies for student attention and adapting films for use in the classroom. The early reaction of both reformers and educators set the stage for the movie industry's adoption of self-censorship codes in the 1930s. Self-censorship codes became standard for most forms of commodified leisure.

EDUCATORS AND MOVIES: COMPETITION OR CONSUMER ITEM

Movies were both a threat to educators and a new consumer item to be used in classroom instruction. Some educators worried that movies would replace schools in controlling culture and morals. "In less than twenty years, the motion picture business has secured a hold on the minds of people," declared Peter Olesen, school superintendent from Cloquet, Minnesota, before the 1914 NEA meeting. Olesen claimed the influence of movies was "almost equal to that of the school and the daily press." Olesen warned that movies might actually possess a stronger hold on the mind of the child than did the schools. "I believe," he observed, "that one reason why it is hard to interest some children in school today is that their minds have been filled and their imagination thrilled with too vivid motion pictures, and, when these children come to school, they are disappointed because the teacher cannot make the subject as interesting as a motion-picture show."[23]

At the same NEA meeting, movies industry officials announced their entry into school markets. Alfred Saunders, manager of Colonial Picture Corporation's Education Department, gave a promotional speech entitled, "Motion Pictures as an Aid to Education." One of the first movie industry representatives to speak to the NEA, Saunders wanted to sell films to public schools. After reviewing available movie projectors and films suitable for schools, he claimed that, "every school that is equipped with a projecting machine may cover the cost of it by allowing the parents to attend exhibitions in the evening."[24]

In response, some educators contended that movies would enhance classroom instruction. David Snedden, Commissioner of Education for Massachusetts and a pioneer in industrial education, argued that movies could present real-life images for classroom instruction. Snedden realized that the "cheapening and vulgarizing of the motion picture, schools and other educational agencies have been loath to attach to it the importance which it deserves."[25] Yet, he stressed, pressure from the education world on the movie industry could result in films that were of instructional value. Snedden's position was echoed by Nathaniel Graham, school superintendent from South Omaha, Nebraska, who contented, "We all believe that encouragement by this body of educators will result in motion pictures being made available for every department of school work. Who can tell in how short a time motion pictures will be as great an accessory to education as is the printed text?"[26]

The debate over competition for the minds of students and the use of movies as educational aids continued into the 1920s and 1930s. Similar to government officials and Protestant social reformers, however, educators remained uneasy about this new form of commodified leisure.

MARKETS, FINANCING, AND THE CONTENT OF MOVIES

The social tensions caused by the advent of movies were similar to the cultural clashes between Protestants and Jewish immigrants portrayed by Yezierska in *Salome of the Tenements*. Looked down on by established American wealth, the film industry became an outlet for the entrepreneurial skills of recently arrived immigrants and their children. Working their way out of the tenements of New York, Boston, and other American cities, Neal Gabler, in *An Empire of Their Own: How the Jews Invented Hollywood,* chronicled the lives of Jewish immigrants and their children who founded the major movie studios and produced films that shaped the consciousness of Americans.[27] Protestant reformers and educators perceived the movie industry as corrupt because of immigrant domination. Typical of the feelings of the Protestant leadership was Henry Ford's complaint in a 1921 issue of the *Dearborn Independent* that, "As soon as the Jews gained control of the 'movies,' we had a movie problem, the consequences of which are not yet visible. It is the genius of that race to create problems of a moral character in whatever business they achieve a majority."[28]

Concerned about their ability to market movies to middle-class Protestant families and raise money to finance their expanding industry, immigrant movie makers decided to create an industry organization headed by a prominent Protestant political leader. This desire was increased with the public scandals of movie stars. In 1920, the nude body of screen star Olive Thomas was found on the floor of a Paris hotel, her death due to an apparent drug overdose. Shortly afterward, comedian Fatty Arbuckle was accused of the rape and murder of starlet Virginia Rappe at a party in San Francisco. In the same year, after director William Desmond was murdered, it was discovered he had been leading a double life under two names and had two wives and two sets of children.[29]

In response to the general attitude of the Protestant establishment toward the movie industry and the scandals, movie makers took their cue from another form of commodified leisure—the baseball industry—by organizing the MPPDA in 1922. After being plagued with numerous bribery scandals in the 1910s, the baseball owners hired Judge Kenesaw Mountain Landis to act as a czar over the industry. Landis was given the task of *cleaning up* baseball and improving its moral image. Using this model, Louis Selznick assumed leadership in organizing the MPPDA. Selznick was a Ukrainian Jew who, in 1912, after immigrating to Pittsburgh and entering the jewelry business, became a partner in the recently organized Universal Pictures.[30]

Searching for someone to head the MPPDA who would please Protestant leaders, studio owners selected William Harrison Hays, an elder of the Presbyterian church from Indiana and former National Chairman of the Republican Party. Protestant, midwestern-born, and politically well connected, Hays was an ideal public relations leader for the industry. The MPPDA was an organization created to help immigrant entrepreneurs function in a Protestant environment that was hostile to both immigrants and Jews.

The growing concentration of the movie industry made it possible for the Hays Office, as it was called, to exercise a *dictatorship of virtue* over the content of American films. In the 1920s, the Big Eight film companies that formed the MPPDA made 90% of American films, whereas in 1912, 60 firms had been in operation in the United States. The Big Eight included Paramount, 20th Century Fox, Loews (M-G-M), Universal, Warner Brothers, Columbia, United Artists, and Radio-Keith-Orpheum (RKO).[31]

In the 1920s, movies became the largest portion of the recreation budget for average American families. Large cities averaged one movie seat for every five to seven people in their population. Furthermore, the composition of movie audiences changed during the 1920s. In 1912, 25% of the movie audiences were clerical workers and 5% were from the business classes, whereas in the 1920s included increasing numbers from the middle class.[32]

As movies became the major form of commodified leisure, reformers and educators demanded greater control over the information and ideas contained in movies. The Hays office responded by organizing a public relations office, a public information department, and a title registration bureau. Hays used the public relations department to establish ties with groups critical of films. At the first meeting of the MPPDA in June 1922, Hays appointed Protestant reformer Lee Hanmer of the Russell Sage Foundation to chair the Committee on Public Relations, which included representatives from the Camp Fire Girls, the Boy Scouts, the General Federation of Women's Clubs, the International Federation of Catholic Alumnae, the Young Men's Christian Association, and the National Education Association.[33]

The Hays Office was concerned about calls for government censorship. Protestant evangelical groups often laced their attacks on movies with statements about the low morality of immigrants. Sounding anti-Semitic, Protestant evangelist Billy Sunday campaigned in 1921 for laws that would close movie theaters on Sunday. He preached that, "No foreign bunch can come over here and tell us how we ought to observe the Lord's Day. The United States at heart is a God-fearing and a God-loving nation and most of our laxity on this point I lay at the door of those elements which are a part of our population, but are not assimilated."[34] In 1920, the Reverend Wilbur Crafts crusaded for Sunday closing legislation at the federal level with the claim that movies, despite their production in the United States, were causing a Europeanization of America.[35]

There were also claims that movies caused public violence and race riots. The years immediately following World War I were punctuated with a number of public bombings. In addition, major race riots occurred in northern cities. Fearful of race riots and social disorder, government codes restricted racial themes and the portrayal of criminal acts. In his study of censorship laws, Richard Randall found that most laws prohibited movie scenes containing obscenity, indecency, and immorality. In addition, many laws banned scenes that would promote racial, religious, or class prejudice. Reflecting the concern that movies taught people how to commit criminal acts, many censorship codes called for removal of scenes that involved "incitement to crime," "portrayal of criminal behavior," and "disturbance of the peace."[36] *The Nation* magazine reported that, in 1921, the Kansas State Board of Review banned from movies all scenes of race riots in Tulsa, Oklahoma, although newspapers carried front-page pictures. The Kansas board also prohibited any mention of the Ku Klux Klan. These actions were taken against newsreels. The words "Probe of murders laid to Klan" were censored from newsreels in Ohio, according to *The Nation*.[37] Consequently, censorship laws inhibited the production of movies dealing with social issues.

Between the enactment of the first municipal censorship law in Chicago in 1907 and the 1930s, a wave of municipal and state censorship laws spread across the country. Between 1922 and 1927, 48 bills on movie censorship were introduced into state legislatures, and prior to the 1950s there existed at various times 90 municipal censorship boards. The most important municipal boards were located in Chicago, Detroit, Memphis, Atlanta, and Boston.[38]

World War I disrupted the European movie industry leaving U.S. companies in a dominant role in global markets. By 1919, over 90% of the films shown in Europe and virtually all films shown in Latin America were made in the United States. Foreign distribution caused American movie makers to avoid portraying any foreign nation in a negative manner for fear that the film would be banned from that country. The desire to protect foreign markets played a major role in the self-censorship standards adopted by the movie industry in the late 1920s and 1930s. Standards banned negative portrayal of foreign governments or the people of foreign nations.[39]

EDUCATORS, YOUTH, AND THE MOVIES *Film censorship*

Educators claimed that movies were harming American youth. In response, Will Hays appeared before the NEA in July 1922 within 6 months of assuming leadership of the MPPDA. Hays pledged acceptance of the challenge of the American mother to provide worthy entertainment for American youth.[40] Hays' appearance did little to ease educators' apprehensions. A 1923 editorial in *The Elementary School Journal* complained that after Hays' speech little effort was made to involve educators directly in the movie industry. The writer complained the movie industry only wanted educators to preview and publish a list of approved movies and help develop a market for classroom films. Noting that "the motion picture has come to be one of the most important sources of influence over the public mind," the writer argued that it "behooves everyone who is interested in the creation of sound attitudes among people at large and especially among pupils to study the problems which motion pictures have created."[41]

The NEA created a special committee to work with the MPPDA. This committee received direct financial support from the MPPDA. The committee was chaired by a leading educational psychologist, Charles Judd of the University of Chicago. Its membership included public school representatives from around the country. The MPPDA financed a meeting in New York between members of the committee and representatives of the movie producers. In addition, the MPPDA provided $5,000 for the committee to investigate the use of films for classroom instruction.[42]

The NEA committee's report regarded schools as a new market for films. As a result, the NEA created a Department of Visual Instruction to study the classroom use of movies. The MPPDA, hoping to extend the commercial life of films, asked educators to review old movies for classroom instruction. The movie industry hoped this would extend the commercial live of films. The MPPDA sponsored committees of teachers to select portions of old films that could be used in classrooms.[43]

Building on this cooperation, Colonel Jason S. Joy, MPPDA's Director of Public Relations, told the delegates to the 1927 NEA annual meeting, "The motion picture today is catering to the American family." As part of this effort, he stated, "the industry has been concerned for some time now in finding out exactly what the effect of pictures is—on behavior, as an educator, and as a force for good." Joy cited a Columbia University study of audiences in 12 different New York City theaters. The study found that on average only 8% of movie audiences were under the age of 17 and school-age children attended movie houses on the average 1.15 times per week. Based on these figures, Joy concluded movies had little effect on children. More important, Joy claimed movies had educational and moral value. Ten of the most popular movies selected by children in the study included *Beau Geste*, *Ben Hur*, and *The Scarlet Letter*.[44]

Dismissing claims that movies had a negative effect on children, Joy outlined what the movie industry was doing to make movies more attractive to educators and families, such as making films of literary classics. Joy told the NEA, "This growing intimacy between the motion picture and the book has met with general although not universal approval. There have been those who feared that many people would 'take their reading out in looking'."[45] However, he argued in reference to a report by the New Jersey Library Association, movies stimulated greater interest in reading the classics and historical novels. In addition, classics made into movies became more accessible to the general population. "Books on the shelves of libraries," he told the NEA, "make it possible for men to attain a certain amount of knowledge and information by hard work and application. But the moving picture, presented as an amusement, will in a few years make it impossible for any average man or woman to remain ignorant."[46]

films to educate!

children + movies

Despite the MPPDA's claim that movies had educational value, educators continued to complain about the detrimental effects of movies on children. For many educators, the harmful effects of movies were proved by the results of a series of research findings commonly referred to as the *Payne Studies.* The public uproar caused by the publishing of this research contributed to the movie industry's decision to enforce a self-censorship code.[47]

The Payne studies were organized in 1928 under the leadership of W. W. Charters, Director of the Bureau of Educational Research at Ohio State University. Twelve studies were completed and published under the sponsorship of The Payne Fund. In addition, Charters wrote a summary volume in 1933. The research was carried out by a formidable array of social scientists and educators and published in a series of volumes by the Macmillan Company.[48]

Reprinted seven times between 1933 and 1935, James Forman's (1933) *Our Movie-Made Children* popularized the Payne studies' findings and created general public concern about the effects of movies on children and youth.[49] The public was shocked by the finding that movies had a detrimental effect on the health of children by disturbing sleep patterns. Working with the Bureau of Juvenile Research in Columbus, Ohio, researchers in a state institution wired children's beds to measure restlessness during sleep. The children were divided into different groups. One group drank coffee at 8:30 p.m. Another group underwent sleep deprivation by being kept up *movies* until midnight and then awakened early in the morning. (This part of the *disturb* experiment ended after complaints by matrons of the institution.) A third *sleep* set was taken to the movies prior to going to bed. Researchers found that movie attendance caused as much disturbance during sleep as drinking two cups of coffee at 8:30 p.m. "We can conclude" the report stated, "from our results that seeing some films does induce a disturbance of relaxed, recuperative sleep in children to a degree which, if indulged in with sufficient frequency, can be detrimental to normal health and growth."[50] The results of this study led Charters to warn, "Thus it appears that movies selected unwisely and indulged in intemperately will have a detrimental effect upon the health of children."[51]

Another finding was that children retained information from movies over long periods of time. A group of second and third graders remembered, at the end of 6 weeks, 90% of what they remembered from a movie on the day they saw it. Researchers also concluded that movies had a significant effect on the conduct and attitudes of children. One study compared the behavior of children who attended movies four to five times a week with those from similar economic and social backgrounds who went to movies twice a month. Those who frequently attended movies, compared with those who attended infrequently, had lower deportment grades in school, did more poorly on school subjects, and were rated lower in reputation by their teachers. A study of children living in congested areas of New York City found similar results. The researchers concluded from the statistics gathered in the study "that for this population there is a positive relationship between truancy and delinquency and frequent movie attendance."[52]

The studies confirmed the increasing role of movies in leisure time activities. As part of the Payne Studies, 55,000 children in 44 communities in Ohio were surveyed regarding movie attendance. It was found that children between the ages of 5 and 8 attended movies an average of 0.42 times a week, and for 8- to 19-year-old children the average was 0.99. The study determined that the average boy between the ages of 8 and 19 attended 57 pictures a year, whereas the average girl attended 46 movies. The specter of weekly movie attendance by youth heightened fears about the effects of movies.

The studies confirmed the belief that movies increased promiscuity and crime rates. In *Our Movie-Made Children*, Forman concluded, "A number of adolescent and youthful criminals give circumstantial accounts of their path to, and arrival at, criminality, and, rightly or wrongly, but very positively, they blame the movies for their downfall." Forman reported that girl inmates in an institution for sex delinquents attributed "to the movies a leading place in stimulating cravings for an easy life, for luxury, for cabarets, road-houses and wild parties, for having men make love to them and, ultimately, for their particular delinquency."[53]

MOVIES AND THE SEXUAL REVOLUTION

Was the 1920s' sexual revolution caused by movies, eroticized ads, new sex manuals, high schools, or changing concepts of women? There was a definite shift in the sexual behavior among youth. Despite structuring high schools around principles of spermatic political economy, youth engaged in more sexual activities. In *Intimate Affairs: A History of Sexuality*, John D'Emilio and Estelle Freedman concluded, "Sexual innovation played a key role in this new [1920s] world of youth. Particularly in coeducational institutions, heterosocial mixing became the norm. Young men and women mixed casually in classes, extracurricular activities, and social spaces, with a great deal of freedom from adult supervision."[54] Statistics showed an increase in sexual activity. In a 1939 survey of college-educated women, only 26% of the respondents born between 1890 and 1900 reported engaging in premarital sex, compared with 69% of those born after 1913.[55] The Kinsey studies of the early 1950s showed a steady increase in the number of women achieving orgasm in marriage beginning with the cohort born in the first part of the 20th century. Kinsey found that more than a third of the women born before 1900 remained clothed during sex, in contrast to 8% of those born during the 1920s.[56]

While high school sex education courses were preaching abstinence from sex until marriage, warning of venereal diseases, and avoiding any discussion of sexual techniques to enhance sexual pleasure, popular sexual manuals were appearing that undermined the concept of spermatic political economy and promoted the idea of female orgasm. In addition, Margaret Sanger was advocating birth control to free women from feminine slavery. In *The Pivot of Civilization* (1922), Sanger argued that birth control would raise economic standards for the poor by reducing the number of children in a family and allowing women more free time for self-development. She contented that birth control would allow women to achieve sexual pleasure, and, consequently, the sexual joy of partners would help achieve an "earthly paradise."[57] In *Happiness in Marriage* (1926), Sanger extolled the importance of sexual rapture and rejected the idea that sexual intercourse depleted bodily strength. Instead, she argued that sexual intercourse revitalized the body.[58] The best-selling marriage manual of the 1920s, Joseph Collins' *A Doctor Looks at Love and Live*, rejected earlier concerns about masturbation and declared it a healthy activity. He hoped for a future with less restrictive morality. Other books of the period carried the same message along with suggested techniques for improving love making, including oral sex.[59]

Many educators were convinced that movies were causing the sexual revolution. One Payne study focused on the relationship between changes in sexual behavior and movies. The study asked 1,800 high school and college students, office employees, and factory workers to keep journals on the effect of movies on their lives. A male college sophomore recounted, "She would make me go with her to see [a movie] . . . and then when we returned home she made me make love with her as she had seen the other two on the screen." Another college male wrote, "The technique of making love to a girl received considerable of my attention, and it was directly through the movies that I learned to kiss a girl on her ears, neck, and cheeks, as well as on the mouth." A statement in the journal of a female high school sophomore was typical of those found in other journal by girls her age: "I have learned quite a bit about love-making from the movies."[60] The author of the study, Herbert Blumer, concluded that movies were taking over the fantasy world of youth. He claimed that 66% of 458 journals written by high school students provided evidence that movies were linked to sexual daydreaming.

Another Payne study concluded that aggressive female sexual behavior portrayed in movies did not conform to the public values of the 1920s. To compare public values with those in movies, Charles Peters, professor of Education at Pennsylvania State College, divided the population into 14 categories ranging from middle-aged college professors to western Pennsylvania miners and their wives and children. Each group rated movie scenes according to whether they thought the content was above or below standards of public morality and political attitudes. They were asked to judge movie scenes according to (a) democratic attitudes and practices, (b) treatment of children by parents, (c) kissing and caressing, and (d) aggressiveness of a girl in lovemaking.[61]

Only the fourth movie portrayal, "aggressiveness of a girl in lovemaking," was rated as below general moral standards. "Treatment of children by parents" and "democratic attitudes and practices" in movies were rated by all categories as above the average standards of society. "Kissing and caressing" movie scenes were found to parallel general moral standards.

All studies seemed to confirm fears that movies were undermining public morality. The Catholic Church's Legion of Decency joined the fray by ordering parishioners to avoid immoral movies. Organized in 1933, its founding recommendation included the strong words, "The pest hole that infects the entire country with its obscene and lascivious moving pictures must be cleansed and disinfected: The multitudinous agencies that are employed in disseminating pornographic literature must be suppressed."[62] The Legion of Decency, with the support of the Catholic hierarchy, asked Catholics to sign a pledge that they would "remain away from all motion pictures except those which do not offend decency and Christian morals."[63] The pledge opened with a call for unity in protesting the threat to youth, country, home life, and religion, and it included a promise to boycott objectionable magazines and books. The signer of the pledge promised to condemn movies that were promoting a "sex mania in our land" and to "do all that I can to arouse public opinion against the portrayal of vice as a normal condition of affairs, and against depicting criminals of any class as heroes and heroines, presenting their filthy philosophy of life as something acceptable to men and women."[64]

MAKING MOVIES SAFE

Despite the moral criticism, large attendance attested to the popular appeal of movies. The movie studios were supplying a product that the public was buying. Yet faced with prospect of government censorship, the movie industry wanted to sell movies and placate those calling for censorship. Will Hays tried to achieve this balance after a storm of religious protest over the 1923 best-selling novel adapted to the screen as *West of the Water Tower*, which dealt with illegitimacy and a dissolute clergyman. Hays convinced members of the MPPDA to allow his office to review all books and plays that might interest movie producers.[65]

Fearing additional government censorship, the MPPDA established a mechanism for self-censorship. In 1927, the Hays Office adopted a list of

Don'ts and Be Carefuls. In 1930, this list was replaced by a more extensive "Code to Govern the Making of Talking, Synchronized and Silent Pictures." The 1930 code was enforced by a 1934 agreement among members of the MPPDA that all movies prior to their release had to be approved by a new office of Production Code Administration.

A writer of the movie code, Martin Quigley, argued in *Decency in Motion Pictures* that films were a form of public education that should establish ideals in the minds of audiences. He rejected that art should be allowed to freely develop.[66] The code's text stated that films appealed to the masses and, therefore, were different from other forms of art. Similar to public schools, everyone was exposed to the movies. The code distinguished between art forms appealing to particular social classes and those with mass appeal. Movies, the code stated, attracted "every class—immature, developed, undeveloped, law abiding, criminal." The ease of distribution allowed movies to reach "places unpenetrated by other forms of art." Consequently, the code's writers argued, "it is difficult to produce films intended for only certain classes of people . . . the exhibitor's theaters are built for the masses, for the cultivated and the rude, the mature and the immature, the self-respecting and the criminal. Films, unlike books and music, can with difficulty be confined to certain selected groups. . . . Psychologically, the larger the audience, the lower the moral mass resistance to suggestion."[67]

The code's authors recognized movies as a new form of public education that might replace the school's control over national culture and morality. The code echoed Patten's earlier arguments that commodified leisure should promote the well-being of workers. The code's text differentiated between the morally uplifting qualities of baseball and golf and the degrading qualities of cockfights and bullfighting. The code stated, "correct entertainment raises the whole standard of the nation, Wrong entertainment lowers the whole living conditions and moral ideas of a race."[68]

The code's self-censorship standards can be divided into: (a) religious, (b) moral, (c) offensive to certain individuals, (d) criminal, and (e) political. The guidelines for religious content in movies dealt with situations that might offend organized religious groups. Moral guidelines were concerned with the portrayal of good and evil and specific sexual situations. The standards for content "offensive to certain individuals" referred to scenes that might spark racial tensions or might be objectionable to some people or organized groups. Guidelines for criminal scenes emphasized the importance of showing crime as objectionable and ensured that scenes did not teach the audience how to commit crimes. The political restrictions of the code dealt with attitudes toward the law, the justice system, the U.S. political system, and foreign countries.

The following divides the 1927 code into the prior categories.[69]

Film Censorship

Don'ts and Be Carefuls (1927)
Shall Not Appear in Movies

A. Religious
   1. Pointed profanity ... this includes the words *God, Lord, Jesus, Christ*
   2. Ridicule of the clergy
B. Moral
   1. Children's sex organs
   2. Any licentious or suggestive nudity
   3. Any inference of sex perversion
   4. White Slavery
   5. Sex hygiene and venereal diseases
   6. The sale of women or a woman selling her virtue
   7. First-night scenes
   8. Man and woman in bed together
   9. Deliberate seduction of girls
   10. The institution of marriage
   11. Excessive or lustful kissing
C. Offensive to Certain Individuals
   1. Miscegenation (sex relations between the White and African-American races)
   2. Scenes of actual childbirth
   3. Brutality and possible gruesomeness
   4. Actual hangings or electrocutions as legal punishment for crime
   5. Apparent cruelty to children and animals
   6. Branding of people and animals
   7. Surgical operations
D. Criminal
   1. Illegal traffic in drugs
   2. Sympathy for criminals
   3. Use of firearms
   4. Theft, robbery, safe cracking, and dynamiting of trains, mines, buildings, and so on (having in mind the effect that a too-detailed description of these may have on the moron)
   5. Technique of committing murder by whatever method
   6. Methods of smuggling
   7. Rape or attempted rape
E. Political
   1. Willful offense to any nation, race, or creed
   2. Use of the flag

3. International relations (avoiding picturizing in an unfavorable light another country's religion, history, institutions, prominent people, and citizenry)
4. Attitude toward public characters and institutions
5. Sedition
6. Titles or scenes having to do with the law enforcement or law-enforcing officers

The 1930 code expanded on the 1927 code by emphasizing the importance of showing the triumph of good over evil. Its first general principle stated, "No picture shall be produced which will lower the moral standards of those who see it. Hence the sympathy of the audience shall never be thrown to the side of crime. wrong-doing, evil or sin." Good people were always to be rewarded. In this movie-made world, cowboys in white hats always beat the bandits in black hats. The code stated that movies must avoid scenes where "evil is made to appear attractive or alluring and good is made to appear unattractive."[70] Distinguishing between sympathy for a crime or sin as opposed to sympathy for the plight of a sinner, the code warned against the sympathy of the audience being directed toward behavior that would generally be considered a crime or sin.

Supporting the religious vision of good struggling against evil, the second general principle of the 1930 code stated, "Correct standards of life, subject only to the requirements of drama and entertainment, shall be presented." In the code, "If motion pictures consistently hold up for admiration high types of characters and present stories that will affect lives for the better, they can become the most powerful natural force for the improvement of mankind."

The third general principle promoted positive images of laws and governments. It stated, "Law, natural or human, shall not be ridiculed, nor shall sympathy be created for its violation." *Natural laws* were defined as the principles of justice dictated by a person's conscience. The code specified that audience support should always be created for government laws and warned against movies that were sympathetic to the commission of crime and did not favor the law. In addition, according to the code, "The courts of the land should not be presented as unjust." Although individual court officials might be portrayed in movies as unjust, the code warns that "the court system of the country must not suffer as a result of this presentation."

Hollywood's movie code made movies into another form of public education. It provided a means for turning the most consumed leisure time product into moral and political lessons. Standing before the 1939 meeting of the NEA, Will Hays accurately claimed, "That educators and motion picture producers have certain specialized and mutual interests in the motion picture as a purveyor of ideas and motivator of activities even the layman has come to realize." Hays contended that the movie code had established an enduring truce between educators and the movie industry. The movie code, he stated, required that in films, "crime, wrongdoing, evil, or sin shall not be made attractive; that correct standards of life shall be presented; that law, natural or human, shall not be ridiculed, or sympathy created for its violation." It was the standards of this code, Hays maintained, that made it possible to bring together the world of the movies and the schools as purveyors of ideas.[71]

The movie code represented one resolution of the tension between the public's desire for commodified forms of leisure and the desire by educators and Puritan reformers to make leisure time activities supportive of an efficient industrial and moral society. The advent of radio sparked another conflict over cultural and moral control.

THE TRIUMPH OF ADVERTISING:
COMMERCIAL RADIO

The triumph of commercial radio, and eventually commercial TV, over government or educator-operated media, created a close link between advertising and entertainment. In general, movies were free of ads except for ads about coming movies and in later years the practice of product placement in films. With commercial radio and TV, listeners and viewers wanting to be entertained had to accept constant interruptions from commercials. To compete for listener and viewer attention, ads had to be as entertaining as the media programming. Eventually ads and entertainment would merge in the form of programs devoted to selling products. As described in chapter 7, Walt Disney pioneered this method on TV by devoting full-length programs to the Disneyland theme park and to the making of Disney movies. Commercial media assisted in the integration of consumerism into all aspects of American life.

Educators realized the importance of commercial media to shaping American culture. How could the school compete with a media that could enter every home with continuous entertainment? In addition, educators worried about the domination of business values as advertising became more potent with catchy jingles to haunt the public mind, such as "I'm Chiquita Banana and I've come to say . . ." and "Halo, everybody, Halo/Halo is the shampoo that glorifies your hair."[72] Initially, the struggle was over educator versus commercial control of the air waves. After educators lost that battle, the struggle was over the content of advertising-driven radio programs.

Reflecting the debate over the commercialization of radio, the August 1933 headline on the theatrical trade journal *Variety* announced: "BRITISH

VS. AMERICAN Radio Slant, Debate Theme in 40,000 Schools."[73] The pro-industry *Variety* considered the debate theme part of an antiradio propaganda campaign being waged by educators, religious groups, and nonprofit organizations against commercial broadcasting. *Variety* used *antiradio* when referring to opponents of commercial radio who wanted the federal government to license more educational and nonprofit radio stations. Antiradio groups worried that profits were determining radio programming and that, consequently, commercial radio was destroying American national culture.

The central issue in the high school debates was whether radio should be privately owned and financially supported by advertising or, like the British system, operated by the government and supported by taxation. Commercial radio networks worried that with an estimated attendance of 100 persons at each debate, as many as 4 million people might hear the question being discussed. "Many, perhaps most," *Variety* lamented, "of these people have been unaware of the existence of the question."[74]

While educators worried that the crass commercialization of privately operated radio would subvert American culture, the radio industry claimed that commercial programming fostered a democratic culture by allowing listeners to vote for the type of culture they wanted by turning the radio knob to their favorite programs. Operated as a business, industry leaders argued, commercial radio responded to the choices made by listeners. What educators wanted, they argued, was to impose a culture on the population. In opposition, private broadcasters claimed, commercial radio reflected listeners' choices and, consequently, was fostering the development of a truly democratic culture.

The debate between educators and commercial radio interests reached a peak in the early 1930s. By then commercial radio networks dominated the airwaves. However, they operated under a constant fear that government action might take away their newly established dominion. They were particularly concerned about educators who, in addition to voicing concerns about the decline of national culture, were fighting mad over their recent loss of radio licenses resulting from government favoritism toward commercial radio. The Radio Act of 1927 created the Federal Radio Commission (FRC), which in 1928 adopted a new allocation plan favoring stations with more financial resources, the most expensive equipment, and the most varied programming. This decision favored commercial broadcasters. By 1937, the number of radio licenses held by educational institutions declined from 202 to 38.[75]

Commercial networks worried about a vocal coalition of educators, religious organizations, and other interested groups that were demanding 25% of all broadcasting licenses be given to nonprofit institutions. Leading this movement was the National Committee on Education by Radio. Formed in 1930, the Committee was funded by the Payne Foundation and had representatives from 11 major national educational organizations, including the National Education Association, the National Catholic Education Association, the American Council on Education, the National Association of State Universities, and the National Council of State Superintendents of Education.[76]

Advertising was a central concern of the National Committee on Education by Radio. When the Committee met in May 1934, Jerome Davis, a faculty member at the Yale Divinity School, complained about the cultural values disseminated by radio advertising: "Children are told that when they drink Cocomalt they are cooperating with Buck Rogers and heroine Wilma. . . . I am not questioning the quality of Cocomalt, but the outrageous ethics and educational effects of this advertising on the child mind." Davis contended that programs planned "for the younger generation on an educational instead of a profit basis, the dramatic adventures of historical figures in American life—those who have really contributed something to the welfare of the nation and the world—could be told."[77]

Joy Elmer Morgan, chair of the Committee, echoed Davis' sentiments: "You will discover that the advertising agency is taking the place of the mother, the father, the teacher, the pastor, the priest, in determining the attitudes of children."[78] Based on a pursuit of profits, she argued, radio entertainment was destroying positive cultural values: "America today is operating on a momentum which was acquired in the days before radio. It is operating on a momentum which the people acquired before the motion picture began teaching crime and gambling and the cheap and flippant attitude toward the verities of life." Morgan worried about the effect on the United States of a generation raised on commercial media. "No one knows what will happen," she warned, "when this country comes into the hands of those who have been exposed to the propaganda of the money changers and to the debasing material which they have broadcast into the lives of the people."[79]

In response, commercial broadcasters launched a campaign to prove the educational worth of commercial radio. At the 1934 NEA's annual meeting, Merlin H. Aylesworth, president of the National Broadcasting Corporation (NBC), spoke on "Radio As a Means of Public Enlightenment." Aylesworth contended that radio had joined the church, home, and school as a source of public enlightenment. Using questionable numbers, Aylesworth claimed that 50% of network radio was educational.[80] At the 1934 FCC hearings, William Paley, president of Columbia Broadcasting System (CBS), defended commercial radio in a talk entitled, "Radio As a Cultural Force." Driven by market forces, Paley argued, commercial radio responded to listeners' desires. Commercial radio had to win and hold audiences. Also radio had to appeal to a mass audience. In contrast, newspapers could be written for special audiences, whereas radio required universal appeal. Consequently, Paley maintained, radio programs appealed to the emotions and self-interest of listeners as well as their intellect.

Regarding the control of mass culture, Paley declared that a democratic culture required control by the audience. Commercial radio was democratic because it was based on listener selection. "We cannot assuredly," Paley argued, "calmly broadcast programs we think people ought to listen to . . . and then go on happily unconcerned as to whether they listen or not."[81] Paley criticized educational radio for being based on aristocratic assumptions. Quoting from an article he wrote for the *Annals of the American Academy of Political and Social Sciences,* Paley contended that an aristocratic concept of education emphasized learning for learning's sake. In his words, "Experience has taught us that one of the quickest ways to bore the American audience is to deal with art for art's sake, or to deify culture and education because they are worthy gods."[82] Commercial radio, he claimed, was part of a democratic culture and that scholars who thought the goal of education should be learning for learning's sake would be shocked that "we even went so far as to classify a broadcast of the World's Fair opening as an educational program."[83]

Paley considered direct experience of events a form of democratic learning. Paley claimed that CBS devoted 2,207 hours to educational programming during the first 9 months of 1934. Using the same reasoning, NBC argued that "Amos 'n' Andy" was educational and had the actors perform a comedy routine before the FCC as an example.[84] Paley named CBS's "American School of the Air" and "Church of the Air" as educational radio programs. Paley went on to argue that, for "radio's democratic audience," history should be presented as a living experience and science should not be discussed as abstract theory, but "as an answer to the daily needs of man in his struggle with his environment."[85]

In summary, Paley defended commercial radio by invoking the idea of the marketplace and free choice, and claiming that radio would ensure the worthy use of leisure time. "It is worth repeating here," Paley concluded his presentation to the FCC,

> we conceive of education by radio not in the narrow classical sense, but in the broadest humanitarian meaning. Nor, in our democratic society, is culture merely a matter of learning the difference between Bach and Beethoven . . . but it is equally a knowledge of how to rear a family in health and happiness— or to spend leisure wisely and well.[86]

Paley and educators agreed that radio was an educational force in developing a national culture. Where they differed was over the control and form of this new means of mass education. Both groups wanted control over radio programming. Educators on the National Committee on Education by Radio believed that intellectual leaders should determine what was good or best for the education of the general public. However, leaders in the radio industry justified their control by claiming that, if education over radio were to be effective, it had to be packaged as entertainment that appealed to the masses. One issue not stressed by the radio industry was that programming also had to appeal to the sponsor. Would the advertising sponsors determine the content of radio?

CONSUMERISM, CRIME, AND VIOLENCE ON CHILDREN'S RADIO

Ads on children's radio programs provided fertile ground for training future consumers. Having lost the battle over advertising-driven media, educators and some public members turned their attention to the content of children's radio. Violent radio programming was increasingly being used to capture the listener's interest. Advertising revenues depended on the size of the radio audience. Local radio stations reacted to the complaints of educators and parents. For instance, in December 1934, Thomas Rishworth, director of radio station KSTP in St. Paul, Minnesota, asked the local Parent–Teachers Association (PTA) to stop their glib criticism of children's radio programs and offer constructive advice. He was tired of hearing complaints that radio broadcasts disturbed children with tales of blood and gore, causing them to toss and turn in their sleep, and making them miss meals when their favorite programs were on the air.[87] Within a week, representatives of the PTA, Boy Scouts, and other community organizations met with Rishworth. At the meeting, John Donahue, a probation officer in St. Paul, warned that radio programs like "Jack Armstrong" caused law-breaking tendencies among the communities' children by the portrayal of likeable villains.[88] The meeting ended with a call for boycotts of advertisers and strict censorship of radio listening by parents. *Variety* reporters were surprised by the vehemence of the reaction. *Variety's* original story gave the impression that Rishworth would easily handle the critics of children's radio. After critics announced a boycott of advertisers, a *Variety* article entitled "Air Reformers After Coin" claimed that critics in St. Paul wanted to make money by peddling their own scripts to commercial sponsors.[89]

Rishworth's meeting exemplified the protests against children's radio that began shortly after the NBC broadcast on April 6, 1931, of the first children's radio serial "Little Orphan Annie." Serialized adult mystery drama began in 1929 with "True Detective Mysteries." The most popular of the mysteries, "The Shadow," appeared in the same year as "Little Orphan Annie." Children could listen to both the evening mystery programs and late afternoon children's programming: CBS broadcast "Buck Rogers in the Twenty-fifth Century" in 1932; in 1933, the "Lone Ranger" and "Jack Armstrong, the All-American Boy" made their debuts. By 1938, the most popular children's serials included the previously mentioned programs plus "Dick Tracy," "Don Winslow of the Navy," "Terry and the Pirates," and "Tom Mix."[90]

Historian Raymond Stedman argued, "The agitated fantasy of 'Buck Rogers' must have been at the heart of many of those articles expressing worry about radio's effect on young minds."[91] In the daily fantasy series, Buck Rogers battled fleets of spaceships, missiles, death rays, and other futuristic weapons to save the universe from destruction. In contrast, "Tom Mix" provoked little apprehension in parents. "Tom Mix" was a classic cowboy drama of the 1930s with the good cowboy Tom Mix always defeating the evil cowboy. The epigram of "Tom Mix" was, "Lawbreakers always lose. Straight shooters always win. It pays to shoot straight!" The sponsor, Ralston Cereals, tried to win parental support by placing promotional advertising in *Parents Magazine*.[92] Even programs emphasizing the conquest of evil were considered disturbing to children. In the first episode of the "Lone Ranger," the hero was restored to health by his faithful Indian companion after being shot in an ambush that left his five companions dead. "The Shadow" opened with the chilling question: "Who knows what evil lurks in the hearts of men? The Shadow knows."[93]

Parents Magazine led public complaints about radio violence. A 1933 editorial was accompanied by a cartoon of a frightened young girl listening to a radio broadcasting, "Scram! Don't Shoot! Kidnapped! They're Going To Kill Me! Help! Murder! Bang! Bang! Kill Him! Police!" The editorial urged parents to write sponsors protesting the quality of the children's program.[94]

Parental complaints about children's radio were voiced at meetings of PTAs and women's clubs. In February 1933, the Central Council of the PTA of Rochester, New York, issued a public warning that radio broadcast "crime ideas harmful to the moral fibre of children and the bloodcurdling situations tend to excite youngsters in a manner to interfere with their sleep."[95] The PTA sent protests to local stations with hints of a boycott of advertisers. A few months later, the California State PTA issued a list of *bad* radio programs and called for unofficial censorship of programs broadcast between 5 p.m. and 8 p.m—the prime hours for children to listen to radio. The California PTA expressed concern about "all programs emphasizing killing, robbing, impossible or dangerous situations."[96]

The National Council of Women, representing 28 national women's organizations, joined the public outcry against radio by organizing the Women's National Radio Committee headed by Mrs. Harold V. Milligan. The organization's concern was sparked by a study conducted by the Woman's Club in the wealthy Westchester County, New York, community of Scarsdale.[97] In 1933, protests erupted in Scarsdale against children's radio after a committee of Scarsdale women met at Teachers College, Columbia University and rated 40 children's programs. They found only five programs that were suitable. The rest were condemned for keeping "children in emotional suspense and [for] excit[ing] them so they can't sleep." The committee publicly objected to mystery thrillers because "children don't just hear it and forget it, but they carry the story in their mind from day to day, or week to week."[98] To provide an alternative to existing children's programs, the Scarsdale Woman's Club wrote an unsuccessful radio serial entitled "Westchester Cowboys."[99]

Mrs. Harold Milligan laced her attack against children's radio with strong feminist language. In a 1935 letter to *Variety*, she described the Committee as a coordinated effort by women to register their complaints against radio, which in her words was "man-made" and "man-regulated."[100] The following year at a national radio conference she declared, "Women vote, and they have influence on public opinion, yet big business does very little to indicate its willingness to earn the respect of millions of women who are serious about the one problem—children's programs on the radio."[101] Also at issue was advertising. Milligan charged advertisers with exploiting children as consumers. Urging parents to counter the work of advertisers, she reported, "Some parents have met the 'box-top' problem by suggesting that if the child wants the prize offered for sending in a certain number of box tops, he pay for the package out of his own allowance."[102]

The Women's National Radio Committee gave awards for good children's radio. Some went to programs that could not find commercial sponsorship, such as CBS's historical program "Wilderness Road." Some member organizations of the National Council of Women sponsored radio programs. The American Legion Auxiliary sponsored a radio dramatization of James Truslow Adams' *The Epic of America* and offered prizes for the best children's essay on "What the 'Epic of America' Has Taught Me About the Future of America."[103]

NBC responded to criticism by announcing in February 1933 that it would "blue pencil" radio scripts with criminal themes to keep children from mimicking unlawful actions.[104] *Variety* announced that August, "Commercials are yielding to the agitation of PTA associations."[105] The Jello's advertising agency shifted sponsorship from horror programs to a radio version of *The Wizard of Oz*. Members of other advertising agencies expressed surprise that protests had not started sooner because horror was overdone on radio. Radio networks mounted a public relations campaign as noted in this *Variety* headline: "Radio Wants Clubwoman Good Will: Offer Transmitters to Gals with Messages." The CBS Chicago affiliate, WBBM, offered free air time to local women's clubs, the DAR, and PTAs.[106]

In 1935, the FCC responded to complaints from PTAs and women's clubs. *Variety* described, "Deluged with bleats from educators and parents, Commish [FCC Chairman] is agreed that if broadcasters do not move on their own to cook up more satisfactory entertainment for children, the government must apply the whip." Pressure came from the White House and Congress to do something about "Goose-Pimple Kid Shows." *Variety* claimed, "Kids' programs of blood-and-thunder type appear doomed under new drive."[107]

By May 1935, the FCC radio cleanup was in full swing. Its efforts extended beyond children's radio. Admitting that it could not directly censor radio, the FCC let radio stations know that it was concerned about the following types of programming and advertising:

1. lotteries
2. fortune tellers
3. racing tips
4. blood and thunder kids' programs
5. birth control compounds
6. fat-removing compounds

MAKING COMMODIFIED LEISURE SAFE
FOR AMERICANS

In 1935, CBS announced a self-censorship code.[108] NBC reacted to CBS's announcement by claiming it had adopted a similar code in 1934.[109] However, NBC did not pull together its broadcasting standards into a single booklet for public distribution until 1939. Prior to 1939, NBC distributed broadcast standards in personal letters to advertisers.[110]

President Paley broadcast the CBS codes over the Columbia network on May 14, 1935. Paley reminded listeners that radio permeated the lives of most Americans. "You hear the voices of Columbia," Paley said, "for many hours each day. These voices are familiar in your home, perhaps in your workshop, and even in your automobile and the restaurants and theaters you visit." Paley described the close relationship between listeners and radio: "These voices are frequently more familiar comrades than some of your closest personal friends." After painting a picture of the intimate and personal relationship between the listener and the broadcaster, Paley went on to describe the general outlines of the new broadcasting code.[111]

CBS Reference Library files indicate that the self-censorship code was part of a well-orchestrated public relations campaign. The code was immediately distributed to important public leaders, and their responses were carefully collected and used in public relations announcements. The code was distributed with an announcement that CBS was employing Professor Arthur Jersild of Columbia University Teachers College as a consulting psychologist for children's programming.

Appropriately, Professor Jersild's major area of research was children's fears. In a book coauthored with another child psychologist, Frances Holmes, Jersild wrote, "The use of fear-inspiring materials in books, radio programs, and moving pictures designed for children might, no doubt, be controlled to some degree by rigid censorship." He continued, this type of censorship might protect some individuals at the expense of others. Therefore, he felt parents of susceptible children should exercise control over their movie going and radio listening.[112]

Of central importance for the future of children's radio programs was the code's emphasis on providing children with moral and social heroes. The code recognized the importance of hero worship in a child's life. "Superman," "The Lone Ranger," and "Tom Mix" exemplified the heroic model recommended in the CBS code. Like the movie code, the CBS code also emphasized the importance of not teaching children antisocial behavior by presenting crime and criminals in a positive light. In addition, the code tried to answer complaints from women's clubs about the quality of advertising on children's programs.

The code recognized that CBS "does have an editorial responsibility to the community, in the interpretation of public wish and sentiment, which cannot be waived."[113] Using this justification, the code identified themes and dramatic treatments that would be excluded from children's programs:

1. The exalting, as modern heroes, of gangsters, criminals, and racketeers will not be allowed.

2. Disrespect for either parental or other proper authority must not be glorified or encouraged.

3. Cruelty, greed, and selfishness must not be presented as worthy motivations.

4. Programs that arouse harmful nervous reactions in the child must not be presented.

5. Conceit, smugness, or an unwarranted sense of superiority over others less fortunate may not be presented.

6. Recklessness and abandon must not be falsely identified with a healthy spirit of adventure.

7. Unfair exploitation of others for personal gain must not be made praiseworthy.

8. Dishonesty and deceit are not to be made appealing or attractive to the child.[114]

Indicating the future of children's radio, the code made hero worship a central theme. For children of elementary school age, programs were to provide entertainment of a moral nature. The code noted that children's literature provided "heroes worthy of the child's ready impulse to hero worship, and of his imitative urge to pattern himself after the hero model." Literature of this sort, the code claimed, "succeeds in inspiring the child to socially useful and laudable ideals such as generosity, industry, kindness and respect for authority. . . . It serves, in effect, as a useful adjunct to that education which the growing and impressionable child is absorbing during every moment of its waking day."[115]

Released in 1939, the NBC code banned advertisements dealing with speculative finances, personal hygiene, weight-reducing agents, fortune tellers, professions, cemeteries, alcoholic beverages, and firearms.[116] Children's programs were to stress law and order, adult authority, good morals, and clean living. Like the CBS code, heroes were to play a role in shaping children's morality. The NBC code stated, "The hero or heroine and other sympathetic characters must be portrayed as intelligent and morally courageous . . . and disrespect for law must be avoided as traits in any character that may be presented in the light of a hero to the child listener."[117] In addition, programs were to emphasize mutual respect, fair play, and honorable behavior. Adventure programs were prohibited from using themes of kidnapping, torture, extreme violence, horror, superstition, and "morbid suspense."[118]

By the end of the 1930s, those attending movies and listening to the radio received the same message about the triumph of good over evil. In the case of radio, moral messages were being conveyed through the adventures of superheroes. The moral and political message of radio in the second half of the 1930s was the ultimate triumph of good, the importance of obedience to the law, and patriotism.

CONCLUSION: CONTROLLING COMMODIFIED LEISURE

In the first half of the 20th century, movies and radio, using self-censorship codes, achieved Simon Patten's objective of creating forms of commodified leisure that would spur consumption while maintaining traditional Protestant morality. It was commercial radio, and later TV, that played the major role in driving a consumer economy by tying entertainment directly to ads. Through radio and TV, Americans learned to accept a commercialized fantasy world where products were inseparable from entertainment.

Of course media would later change, and the self-censorship codes would be modified as the Protestant hegemony was challenged. More sex, violence, and social criticism would appear on movie screens and radio and TV programs. However, these changes did not stop the spread of advertising and consumer values into almost all aspects of American life. Certainly, the most important aspect of commercial media was its training of the public to accept advertising and consumer values as part of the American way of life.

Chapter 5

The American Way and the Manufacturing of Consent

[handwritten annotations: 1920s Walter Lippmann → critical for democracy / 1980s Noam Chomsky → critique of hegemony / -"consumerism" becomes "American way of life"]

Schools, advertising, commercial media, and public relations campaigns created a spontaneous association between consumption and the American way of life. By the 1950s, the fantasy world of most Americans was filled with consumer objects. A 1959 *Saturday Evening Post* magazine cover showed a young couple sitting under a tree gazing into a night sky illuminated by a full moon. Floating among a host of stars was their dream world consisting of a house, swimming pool, two cars, pets, two children, power drill, refrigerator, washer and dryer, stove, toaster, electric coffee pot, waffle maker, iron, TV, sound system, and vacuum cleaner. The cover's artist, Constantin Alajalov, had originally planned to have the couple staring at castles floating in the air. Yet, capturing the spirit of America, he replaced castles with consumer items.[1]

Beginning in the 1930s, the newly founded public relations profession was enlisted in a campaign to create an automatic association in people's minds among Americanism, free enterprise, and consumption. In the 1920s, the famous political theorist Walter Lippmann characterized this process as an attempt to "manufacture consent."[2] In the 1980s, this phrase was again made popular by Noam Chomsky's critical study of the control of public opinion, *Manufacturing Consent: The Political Economy of the Mass Media*.[3] Whereas Chomsky was critical of attempts to manufacture consent, Lippmann and public relations experts considered it essential for a democratic society.

The term *public opinion* had a specific meaning for public relations professionals. The term was popularized by Walter Lippmann's (1922) book

Public Opinion.[4] In this context, opinion referred to attitudes about the world that were *not* products of rational deliberation. Public opinion was considered an irrational force. In the writings of Lippmann and public relations experts of the 1920s and 1930s, public opinion was created by pictures, words, and symbols. Public opinions set the stage for experiencing and interpreting the world. Experience was filtered through preexisting opinion. In Lippmann's words, "For the most part we do not first see, and then define. We define first and then see. . . . We imagine things before we experience them. And these preconceptions . . . govern deeply the whole process of perception."[5] Therefore, the control of public opinion referred to the preparation of the public mind to interpret events in a distinct manner.

American business, working with public relations experts, tried to infuse into public opinion the "American way of life" and the "American dream" as preconceptions about the good life and the United States. To help mold public opinion, public relations experts used advertising, schools, and media. This chapter traces efforts to create a spontaneous association in the public mind among Americanism, free enterprise, and consumerism. I begin by discussing the rise of the public relations industry and its efforts to create a positive image of American business in the public mind and to link consumption to personal fulfillment and the good life.

SELLING THE "AMERICAN WAY" IN SCHOOLS AND ON BILLBOARDS

Launched in 1936, the American Way public relations campaign was designed to counter the growth of radical and antibusiness attitudes during the 1930s' depression years. Business' efforts to introject particular economic ideas into the school curricula paralleled the Americanism campaign of the American Legion. The National Association of Manufacturers (NAM) spearheaded business' public relations efforts. A 1936 internal NAM memo contended that public opinion was not based on rational discourse. The memo stated, "Public sentiment is everything—with it nothing can fail; without it nothing can succeed. . . . Right now Joe Doakes—the average man—is a highly confused individual."[6] The memo went on to argue that Joe Doakes should be resold the advantages of a competitive economy. The next year, the NAM began a national campaign placing billboards in every U.S. community over 2,500 declaring either "World's Highest Standard of Living—There's no way like the American Way" or "World's Highest Wages—There's no way like the American Way."[7]

An early American Way advertisement captured the meaning of the campaign:

WHAT IS YOUR AMERICA ALL ABOUT?
Our American plan of living is simple.
Its ideal—that works—is the greatest good for the greatest number.
You . . . are part owner of the United States, Inc. . . .
Our American plan of living is pleasant.
Our American plan of living is the world's envy.
No nation, or group lives as well as we do.[8]

Also in 1937, the National Industrial Council, the newly formed public relations arm of the NAM, issued a diagram for a "Suggested Community Program to Create Better Understanding of Local Industry." The diagram depicted a local public relations committee composed of manufacturers, merchants, civic clubs, churches, bar associations, and educators. Conspicuously absent from this committee were labor union representatives. According to the diagram, the local committee was to hire a publicity director to spread the probusiness message.

The diagram clearly connected the segments of the community to be used for controlling public opinion. This schema corresponded to what founder of the public relations profession Edward Bernays called "the wires which control the public mind"[9] The diagram showed wires leading from the publicity director to schools, newspapers, radio, civic speakers, clubs, open house meetings for workers in factories, and theaters. These wires to the public mind, Bernays suggested, resulted in "regimenting the public mind."[10]

Already feeling the influence of local American Legion officials, the NAM suggested that publicity directors introduce probusiness ideas into schools through the medium of printed materials for school libraries and classrooms by sparking an interest in studying local industries and using movies and slides. In 1937, Lewis H. Brown, president of the Johns–Manville Corporation, declared, "We must with moving pictures and other educational material carry into the schools of the generation of tomorrow an interesting story of the part that science and industry have played in creating a more abundant life for those who are fortunate to live in this great country of ours."[11] He warned that teachers knew more about Karl Marx than the inner workings of local factories.

By the time the NAM focused on schools, the public relations profession had adopted a number of techniques for controlling public opinion. Visualizations and symbols were considered a method for galvanizing public opinion without generating debate. The use of trusted leaders was a means of building public confidence for an idea or product. For example, Bernays' recommended that bacon be sold by having a physician testify as to its health benefits. Also Bernays argued that a public relations campaign should be directed toward a person's desires and emotions rather than reason. The symbol could be used to evoke positive emotions.

To avoid public debate, public relations relied on emotional rather that rational persuasion. For instance, the NAM placed ads in practically every

Advertising Consumerism & Am. way of life (handwritten)

community in the United States. The billboards offered only slogans. True to the principles of visualization and appealing to emotions, the billboards proclaimed "World's Highest Standard of Living" and showed a happy White family of four riding in a car. Through the car's front windshield was a smiling clean-shaven father wearing a suit and tie next to his grinning wife. In the rear seat were equally happy children. Hanging out the window was a white dog. Next to the car was the slogan, "There's no way like the American Way." Billboards proclaiming "World's Highest Wages" showed an aproned White mother standing in a doorway looking out at her clean-shaven husband dressed in a suit, tie, and hat tossing their blond-haired daughter into the sky.[12] There were no suggestions as to why the "American Way" provided the "World's Highest Standard of Living" and the "World's Highest Wages."

In the schools, the NAM conducted a public relations campaign to create in the public mind an interrelation and inseparability between free enterprise and democracy. On the surface, these two ideas were distinct. Free enterprise, of course, was an economic doctrine, whereas democracy was a political principle. Many European countries practiced varying forms of democratic socialism. In other words, a democratic government might have a socialized economy. A totalitarian government might allow for free enterprise. Believing that emotions rather than reason controlled public opinion, the 1939 NAM public relations committee declared as its task to "link free enterprise in the public consciousness with free speech, free press and free religion as integral parts of democracy."[13]

With the goals of creating positive reactions to American business and an involuntary connection in the public mind between free enterprise and democracy, corporations and the NAM flooded classrooms with printed material and movies. The NAM distributed to schools a series of booklets entitled *You and Industry*, which were designed to connect readers' positive emotions to the American industrial system. In 1937, the NAM began distributing to 70,000 schools a newsweekly, *Young America*, which contained articles such as "The Business of America's People Is Selling," "Building Better Americans," and a "Your Local Bank."[14] A 10-minute film, *America Marching On*, was distributed to schools with the message, "America marching upward and onward to higher standards of living, greater income for her people, and more leisure to enjoy the good things of life as the greatest industrial system the world has ever seen began to develop."[15]

PROPAGANDA AND FREE SPEECH IN SCHOOLS

As the NAM was targeting its public relations at schools, some educators were telling students that propaganda was not a problem in a democratic society because of the freedom to debate different subjects. Contrary to the public relations view of an irrational crowd, these educators were operating on the assumption that the U.S. public was capable and willing to engage in rational political discourse. In the early 1930s, educators showed interest in protecting free speech as they worried about the increased role of propaganda in forming public opinion. "The present age might well be called the age of propaganda," wrote the Commission on Character Education for the 1932 yearbook, *Character Education,* of the Department of Superintendence of the NEA. "With the development of the press, the cinema, and the radio, instruments have been forged through which ideas, attitudes, and philosophies may be quickly impressed upon vast populations," continued the Commission. "And in every society there are powerful minority groups struggling for the control of these instruments and bent on conserving or grasping special privileges of all kinds."[16]

Concerned about citizen education, the Educational Policies Commission conducted a survey of school instruction September 1939 and January 1940. The Educational Policies Commission was a joint venture started in 1935 by the NEA and the American Association of School Administrators to improve education for democratic citizenship. The survey, *Learning the Ways of Democracy: A Case Book in Civic Education,* provided snapshots of the actual ideas and values that a large sample of American high schools were trying to disseminate to their students at the outbreak of World War II. The survey found that high schools emphasized the study of public opinion as protection against the propaganda of totalitarian governments.

The survey found that many social studies classes were investigating issues related to public relations methods and government propaganda. For instance, a ninth-grade unit on public opinion in the Cleveland public schools focused on free speech and the censorship of newspapers, radio, and movies. Students studied "The Struggle for Personal and Political Liberty."[17] Twelfth-grade classes in Rochester, New York, discussed, "What serious questions exist in American democracy today concerning public opinion?" In reference to the repressive measures used during the Red Scare of the 1920s, students were asked, "What is a 'red scare'? Look up the Lusk Laws 1921 in New York State."[18] A study guide for the eighth grade in Schenectady, New York, stressed the importance of using actual concrete information in forming opinions. According to the guide, "in a democracy where free speech and free press are so highly prized, this is very important." The guide called for a study of newspapers, magazines, books, radio, and motion pictures as agencies "which aid in opinion expression and formation."[19]

Study guides included sections dealing with threats to freedom of speech. The high school study guide for Rochester, New York, contained a unit that opened with the question, "What serious problems exist in American democracy today concerning public opinion?" The guide listed the following topics:

current threats to civil and political liberty;
academic freedom and discussion of public problems in the classroom;
extension of procedures of scientific thought to public and personal problems.[20]

Commission members were pleased by the discussion of controversial issues
and wrote, "Freedom of discussion of controversial subjects is more than a
right. . . . If citizens do not have this right, they are unable to make intelligent decisions, and control passes into the hands of those individuals who
are adroit enough to attain positions of power and influence."[21]

While the free speech issues were debated in classrooms, the American
Legion continued to work with the NEA to weed out so-called *subversives*
from schools. At their 1935 annual convention, the American Legion
passed a resolution against "the advocacy in America of Nazism, Fascism,
Communism, or any other isms that are contrary to the fundamental principles of democracy, as established under the Constitution of the United
States." Local branches of the Legion's Americanism Commission were ordered to give close attention to possible subversive activities in their communities.[22]

The Legion continued advocating the firing of disloyal teachers and demanded that teachers take loyalty oaths. The Legion considered any opposition to loyalty oaths as the work of subversive elements in American society. In 1935, the Americanism Commission reported that eight states
passed legislation requiring loyalty oaths of teachers. Other reports indicated that by 1935, 20 states required teachers' loyalty oaths. In the same
year, Congress passed an appropriation bill containing a rider forbidding
the payment of salary to any teacher spreading communism doctrines. The
rider kicked off a storm of protest lasting until 1937, when President Roosevelt got the act repealed.[23]

PROTECTING ADVERTISING AND LINKING FREE
ENTERPRISE TO DEMOCRACY

Criticism of textbooks and educators by the American Legion, and business
and advertising organizations typified efforts to ensure that the schools
taught the American way of life. These groups were particularly concerned
with educators who were identified with the doctrines of social reconstructionism. Social reconstructionism originated with a speech given by
George Counts, a professor at Columbia University Teachers College, at the
1932 annual meeting of the Progressive Education Society. Originally
called "Dare Progressive Education Be Progressive?", the speech was distributed in pamphlet form with the controversial title of "Dare the Schools

1932 : Counts criti gives capitalism

Build a New Social Order?" Counts criticized capitalism for being "cruel and inhuman" and "wasteful and inefficient." He argued that the development of modern urban-industrial society made obsolete concepts of competition and rugged individualism. A new economic system, he argued, would free people from poverty. Counts urged teachers to assume leadership in the reconstruction of society. Counts stated, "If democracy is to survive, it must seek a new economic foundation. . . . Natural resources and all important forms of capital will have to be collectively owned."[24]

Counts supported democracy and rejected communism and totalitarianism. The problem was that he attacked free enterprise when business was implanting the seed that democracy could only survive with free enterprise. In 1934, Russell Cook, Director of the National Americanism Commission, warned delegates to the 1934 NEA convention, "In the last few years there has grown up a movement in which too many of our teachers are creating ideas in the schoolroom for what is called a new social order." Referring to social reconstructionists, Cook told the convention, "The American Legion is opposed to that movement. We say that it is not the mission of the teacher to lead the child into believing we should have a new social order. . . ."[25]

Soc. recon, texts ↓ Harold Riggs

Some textbooks were criticized for containing social reconstructionist ideas such as Harold Rugg's textbook series. Augustin Rudd, who campaigned to get Harold Rugg's textbooks off the market, blamed the supposed deterioration of public schools and their infiltration by subversives on progressive education. In 1940, Rudd was made chairperson of the newly organized Guardians of American Education. The organization's goal was to defeat "left-wing . . . educational leadership . . . [which is trying to replace] our American way of life . . . [with] a 'new social order' based on the principles of collectivism and socialism."[26] Particularly distressing to Rudd were statements in the social reconstructionist journal, *The Social Frontier,* calling for economic planning and presenting society as a collective organization. Rudd objected to a lead editorial that argued, "For the American people the age of individualism in economy is closing and the age of collectivism is opening. Here is the central and dominating reality in the present epoch. . . ." To Rudd and other members of patriotic organizations, social reconstructionism was a subversive plot to undermine American capitalism. Rudd was particularly upset by an April 1935 issue of the *Social Frontier,* which proclaimed: "The end of free enterprise as a principle of economic and social organization adequate to this country is at hand."[27]

1927-31

In sharp contrast to NAM's public relations efforts, Harold Rugg's social studies series emphasized collective action and planning. In the 1920s, the series began as pamphlets integrating the teaching of history, economics, and sociology to junior high school students. Between 1927 and 1931, Rugg pulled together the pamphlets into six 600-page books for senior and junior high school students. Published by Ginn and Company from 1933 to

Rugg's S.S. texts

1936, the series was expanded to include Grades 3 through 6. At the peak of their popularity in 1938, the series sold 289,000 copies. Rugg estimated that, during the 1930s, the books were used in over 5,000 schools by several million school children. After public attacks on the books, annual sales plummeted to 21,000 copies.[28]

A series' goal was educating children to assume intelligent control of their institutions and environment. The books did not advocate communism or socialism, but they did argue that intelligence should be applied to planning the economy and operating public institutions. U.S. history was presented as the transformation of an individualistic agrarian society to a collective industrial society. Rugg's message was that modern urban and industrial society required cooperative planning. In the modern world, corporations, factories, public institutions, and urban living all depended on cooperative behavior. In addition, the complexity of modern life required cooperative planning to achieve economic and social goals.

Rugg's ninth-grade textbook, *Citizenship and Civic Affairs*, claimed the "American Spirit" evolved from individualism to cooperation.[29] Rejecting the premise that free enterprise and Americanism were synonymous, Rugg's series brought on the wrath of patriotic organizations and individuals. A typical reaction were the words of a large middle-aged woman at a 1940s' public hearing on the textbook series: "I am here, not thinking that I was going to be at all, but I am and I want to say just a few words. Righteousness, good government, good homes and God—most of all, Christ—is on trial today." Although she admitted not reading any of the Rugg books, she proclaimed, "You can't take the youth of our land and give them this awful stuff and have them come out safe and sound for God and Righteousness." At another meeting, according to Rugg, a twenty-year-old youth leapt into the air waving his arms and shouting, "If you let these books go in and if what I've heard is true, it'll damn the souls of the men, women and children of our state."[30]

The business community's reaction to Rugg's books was orchestrated by B.C. Forbes, financial writer and founder of *Forbes Magazine*, through editorials distributed nationally in Hearst-owned newspapers. In a 1939 articles, Forbes called Rugg's books, "viciously un-American. . . . [Rugg] distorts facts to convince the oncoming generation that America's private-enterprise system is wholly inferior and nefarious." In words that must have made the textbook industry shudder, Forbes wrote, "I plan to insist that this anti-American educator's textbooks be cast out. . . . I would not want my own children contaminated by conversion to Communism."[31] In his syndicated Hearst newspaper column, Forbes asked the question every week during the war years: "Are too many educators poisoning the minds of the younger generation with prejudiced, distorted, unfair teachings regarding the American system of economy and dazzling them with overly-rosy pictures of conditions in totalitarian countries?"[32]

RUGG AND CONSUMERISM → *Be skeptical of advertising*

Lessons on evaluating advertising were a unique feature of Rugg's books. The advertising industry was concerned because the lessons prepared public opinion to be skeptical of advertising claims. The Advertising Federation of America, the public relations arm of the industry, distributed pamphlets entitled, "Facts You Should Know About Anti-Advertising Propaganda in School Textbooks." The pamphlets criticized the Rugg books for turning students against advertising.

Both the Rugg books and the reaction of the Advertising Federation of America typified the consumerist concerns of the 1930s. During the depression years, consumer organizations tried to educate the public about false advertising claims and shoddy consumer products. Highlighting the anti-advertising crusade was the 1931 publication of *Ballyhoo* magazine featuring satirical comments on ads and advertising, including the Ten Commandments of Advertising: "10. Thou shalt covet thy neighbor's car and his radio and his silverware and his refrigerator."[33] This surprisingly successful magazine was followed by books criticizing the wastefulness of American consumerism, including F. J. Schlink's *100,000,000 Guinea Pigs* (1933) and James Rorty's *Our Master's Voice* (1934).[34] In 1929, the Consumer Research organization was founded, which in the early 1930s spawned the establishment of the Consumers Union.

It was in this anti-advertising climate that the Advertising Federation of America worried about the Rugg books. In 1939, the Federation declared that critics of advertising were "those who prefer collectivism and regimentation by political force."[35] The Advertising Federation claimed that communism was the basis for anti-advertising attitudes and the development of the Consumer Union. During this period, the House Committee on Un-American Activities held hearings that linked consumer rights efforts to communism. The Consumer Union survived by focusing on product testing and publishing the *Consumer Report*.[36]

The Advertising Federation's anti-Rugg pamphlet objected to an opening section in Rugg's series on advertising because it bred distrust of widely advertised products. The section opened:

> Two men were discussing the merits of a nationally advertised brand of oil.
>
> "I know it must be good," said one. "A million dollars' worth of it is sold each year. You see advertisements of that oil everywhere."
>
> The other shook his head. "I don't care how much of it is sold," he said. "I left a drop of it on a copper plate overnight and the drop turned green. It is corrosive and I don't dare to use it on my machine."[37]

In April 1940, the president of the Advertising Federation sent a letter to major advertisers that opened: "Advertised products are untrustworthy!

That is the lesson taught to the children in 4,200 school systems by a social science textbook of Professor Harold Rugg of Teachers College, Columbia University."[38]

The American Legion joined ranks with the Advertising Federation with a 1940 pamphlet, originally published in the *American Legion Magazine*, by O.K. Armstrong entitled, "Treason in the Textbooks." In the pamphlet, a cartoon depicts Rugg as a devil putting colored glasses over children's eyes. The caption on the picture stated, "The 'Frontier Thinkers' are trying to sell our youth the idea that the American way of life has failed." The Legion article and pamphlet also listed several other books and *Scholastic Magazine* as being subversive.[39]

As head of the Guardians of American Education, Augustin Rudd believed Rugg's textbooks would undermine American institutions. Formed in 1940, the Guardians of American Education wanted to preserve American traditions. The association urged parents to: "Examine your child's textbooks, Demand to see the teacher's guides. . . . Look for subversive material in . . . books or courses." Regarding Rugg's series, Rudd wrote, "He [Rugg] was one of the principal architects of the ideological structure known as the 'new social order'." From his faculty position at Columbia University Teachers College, Rudd stated, "His propaganda and doctrines were spread throughout the United States. He also exercised a strong influence . . . through his Teachers' Guides, which interpreted his economic, political and social philosophies to thousands of classroom teachers using his social science courses."[40]

There was a dramatic reaction to these public criticisms. In September 1940, *Time Magazine* reported that members of the Binghamton, New York school board called for public burning of Rugg's textbooks. The article reported, "But last fortnight Rugg book burnings began to blaze afresh in the small-town, American Legion belt. In rapid succession, the school boards of Mountain Lakes and Wayne Township, New Jersey, banished Rugg texts that had been used by their pupils for nearly 10 years. Explained Wayne Township's Board Member Ronald Gall: "In my opinion, the books are un-American but not anti-American. . . ."[41]

Particularly dramatic were events in Bradner, Ohio, where the community divided over the issue of teaching communism in the schools. According to a Cleveland newspaper account of the events, "The rural Red hunt . . . has resulted in: explosion of a dynamite charge and the burning of a fiery cross in front of the home of . . . [the] school board president. The explosions and cross burning were accompanied by the spectacle of school board members shoving books into the school furnace."[42]

Rugg's publishers, Ginn and Company, sent him on a national tour to defend the series. At public hearing in Philadelphia, a participant pointed his finger at Rugg and shouted, "There sits the ringmaster of the fifth columnists in America financed by the Russian government. I want you people to look at him."[43] Rugg felt frustrated at public meetings by the open admission by critics that they had never read any of his books. Person after person at these hearings, Rugg wrote, would begin their statements with the phrase: "1 haven't read the books, but. . . ." The phrase would be followed with comments such as, "He's from Columbia, and that's enough"; "I have heard of the author, and no good about him"; and "my brother says the schools and colleges are filled with Communists."[44]

The demise of the Rugg books demonstrated the power of public relations campaigns to associate in the public mind anything critical of the United States' economic and political system with un-Americanism and communism. Similar to the automatic association between democracy and free enterprise achieved by the NAM's public relations efforts, part of the public now instinctively associated progressive education with un-Americanism, communism, and socialism. This pattern of public opinion continued after World War II as anticommunism became a standard for evaluating school textbooks and curricula.

EDUCATING THE CONSUMER-CITIZEN

War time dampens dissent and criticism. World War II provided an opportunity for public relations efforts in schools to sell business' message under the flag of patriotism. The key element of this message, similar to the billboards planted around the country by NAM, was that the American economic system provided the highest *economic* standard of living. This standard of living was measured by the ability to consume. The Secretary of NEA's Educational Policies Commission, William Carr, declared in a March 1941 article in the *Nation's Business* that public schools would cooperate with business in teaching "Americanism," "economic literacy," and "personal economics" while preparing "youth for personal work." Economic literacy meant teaching about the economic system of the United States, whereas personal economics meant the education of the consumer. Linking consumption, Americanism, and business, Carr wrote, schools have "provided a highly literate and educated population . . . constituting the world's greatest consuming markets."[45]

Consumer education was promoted in schools by local Chambers of Commerce. Their efforts matched the NAM's plan for using schools to foster positive public opinion about American business. According to Carr, 360 local Chambers of Commerce were helping local schools promote an understanding of the American economic system. Combined with citizenship education, these programs were intended to create an instinctive association of business with patriotic Americanism. Also Chambers of Commerce helped local schools mount consumer education programs or, as it was called, *efficiency in personal economics.* These consumer courses emphasized the management of personal buying power. Schools were training people to be good buyers.

In 1942, the NAM took its public relations campaign directly to the National Education Association. Declaring a "new era of understanding" between business and the schools, Walter Fuller, Chairman of the NAM's Board of Directors and President of Curtis Publishing, proclaimed at the 1942 NEA meeting, "Just as the first responsibility of industry today is to produce the weapons of war . . . so the responsibility of education is to make available an increasing manpower, especially to meet the needs for skilled men and women."[46] This new understanding resulted from a series of joint conferences between the NAM and the NEA.

Also the federal government launched a massive program to push the public schools in the direction of serving industry. In 1941, the Office of Education organized a defense vocational training program enrolling 1 million women and men. By 1942, the numbers had increased to 3 million. The U.S. Commissioner of Education hoped the close relationship established between education and employment would be carried over into peacetime. In a speech to the 1943 NEA convention, he told delegates, "Probably the most basic lesson we are learning in the schools in wartime is that boys and girls gain educationally from contact with the real world of work."[47] The four major contributions of the schools, according to Commissioner Studebaker, were citizenship training, vocational education, training for community service, and building national unity.

THE WAR OF ECONOMIC SYSTEMS

After World War II, the American Way became a major theme in the cold war between the United States and the Soviet Union. The cold war was portrayed as a clash between free enterprise and communist economic systems under the banner of American and Soviet nationalism. The winner in this battle would be the system that produced the most consumer goods. In schools, censorship of textbooks and the weeding out of so-called *subversive* teachers centered on economic issues. For those on the political right, subversives were supporters of government intervention in the economy, whereas true Americans supported free enterprise. Also the teenage consumer market rapidly expanded after World War II. Teens were learning at an early age how to be good consumers. Many affluent teens were growing up in new suburban developments where the shopping mall was becoming the center of consumer desires.

The famous 1959 "kitchen debate" between Vice President Richard Nixon and Soviet Premier Nikita Khrushchev at the American Exhibition in

Moscow provided a public lesson in economic differences. Looking at an American kitchen in a model of a six-bedroom ranch house, Nixon explained to Khrushchev the advantages of the U.S. economic system and the meaning of American freedom: "To us, diversity, the right to choose . . . is the most important thing. We don't have one decision made at the top by one government official. . . . We have many different manufacturers and many different kinds of washing machines so that the housewives have a choice. . . ."[48] As Historian Elaine Tyler May argued, both leaders lumped the consumer race with the arms race and space race. It was a test of the superiority of their economies. Khrushchev claimed that his nation would reach the American standard of living in 6 years.[49]

Imbued with the idea that the American Way meant increased consumption through free enterprise, the cold war was to be won through the purchasing of goods for the home. The early 20th-century image of the consumer wife and earner husband now played itself out in the tensions of the cold war. As May wrote, "Although they may have been unwitting soldiers, women who marched off to the nation's shopping centers to equip their new homes joined the ranks of American cold warriors."[50]

In schools, censorship efforts reinforced the equation of Americanism with free enterprise economics. After helping to drive the Rugg books off the market, the Guardians of American Education distributed American Legion articles on communist subversion directly to public schools. They also continued their campaign to associate progressive education with communism and un-Americanism by distributing an article by Kitty Jones entitled, "How 'Progressive' Is Your School?" The article restated claims that progressive and critical education undermined Americanism and free enterprise.[51]

Ironically, it was a 1952 workshop at Columbia's Teachers College that convinced Kitty Jones that progressive education and the professors at Teachers College were destroying the American way of life. After examining her local school district in Tenafly, New Jersey, she charged that progressive education caused illiteracy and juvenile delinquency. She claimed that nine textbooks used by the Tenably system "favor[ed] the Welfare State and Socialism . . . follow [ed] the Communist line, and . . . [were] written by Communist sympathizers and . . . members." Although the school system eventually rejected her charges, the episode propelled Jones into the national spotlight and created an audience for her 1956 book, *Progressive Education Is REDucation*, coauthored with Robert Olivier. The book contained descriptive chapter titles such as "Making Little Socialists."[52]

America's Future, Inc., located in New Rochelle, New York, was a distributor of Jones' book and articles. During the 1950s, America's Future combed textbooks for evidence of subversion. According to historian Mary Anne Raywid, America's Future was one of four organizations created to maintain the tax-exempt status of the Committee for Constitutional Government. The others were America's Future, the Free Enterprise Foundation, Fighters for Freedom, and the original Committee for Constitutional Government. According to Raywid, the goals of all four organizations were characterized in the following platform of Fighters for Freedom:

> Pitilessly expose Communism . . . and stop the march to fascism or socialism.
> Restore the American incentives to work, own, and save.
> Protect every individual's right to work where he will. . . .
> Safeguard our system of free, untrammeled, competitive markets.
> Stop using taxpayers' money to compete against private enterprise.[53]

Visiting America's Future's offices in 1961 and 1962, two newspaper reporters, Jack Nelson and Gene Roberts, were told by the president, Rudolf Scott, that the organization was trying to force publishers to make changes by documenting supposed errors. The main concern was textbook coverage of economic liberalism. "The whole thing of liberalism in the textbooks," Scott told the reporters, "has been an evolution, taking place over the past decade or two. But we are going to change that."[54]

Using committees of educators and business people, America's Future reviewed textbooks with an eye for liberalism and left-wing philosophies. Typical of these reviews was one by Hans Sennholz, Chairman of the Department of Economics at Grove City College in Grove City, Pennsylvania. Sennholz complained that an economics text, *American Capitalism,* made "no mention . . . of the minimum wage legislation that keeps millions of Americans unemployed, or ever-rising unemployment compensation that destroys the incentive to work."[55] In his reviews, Russell Kirk, a professor of political science at Long Island University, objected to textbooks mentioning what he called the *god-term* democracy. He warned that a "besetting vice of democracies is their tendency to submerge the individual in the mass; aristocratic republics are far more concerned for individuals."[56]

The quarterly newsletter, *Educational Reviewer,* inundated publishers with accusations, such as the charge that Frank Magruder's high school text, *American Government,* attacked the free enterprise system and presented a view of democracy that led "straight from Rousseau, through Marx, to totalitarianism." National radio commentator Fulton Lewis, Jr., used portions of the review on a coast-to-coast broadcast with the comment, "That's the book that has been in use in high schools all over the nation, possibly by your youngster." Attacks on the textbook occurred throughout the country; the book was eventually banned in Richland, Washington; Houston, Texas; Little Rock, Arkansas; Lafayette, Indiana; and the entire state of Georgia.[57]

The American Textbook Publishers Institute tried to defend their products in a 1950s' pamphlet, *Textbooks Are Indispensable.* However, this pamphlet suggested that publishers "avoid statements that might prove offensive to economic, religious, racial or social groups, or any civic, fraternal, patriotic or philanthropic societies in the whole United States."[58] A unique part of this warning was its reference to an economic group, which of course could be organized labor or business. The general climate for textbooks was summarized in 1960 by the Deputy superintendent of the District of Columbia school system, Lawson Cantrell: "We try to make sure that the books we select are not objectionable to anyone."[59]

CIVIC CONSUMERISM: THE NEW TEENAGE CULTURE

"Civic consumerism" was Kelly Schrum's description of the editorial message for teenagers in *Seventeen* magazine in the late 1940s and early 1950s.[60] Scrum defined *civic consumerism* as "combining one's democratic role as active citizen with one's duty as a responsible and active consumer."[61] During the late 1940s and 1950s, she argued, "Voting and democracy, as well as pride in America and the right to buy goods, were common themes through this period, a reflection of both lingering war rhetoric and the beginning of the Cold War."[62] Corresponding to earlier concerns with controlling adolescent sexuality through high school activities, advertisers hoped to channel teenage sexuality into consumerism. Ads for girls displayed clothing and other products that would enhance their dating potential. Boys directed their consumer sexuality at cars with the hope that the *hot car* or *hot rod*, a term with interesting sexual overtones, would result in the hot date.

The post-World War II era witnessed the appearance of the affluent high school student. The 1930s' teenage culture, spawned by the mass institutionalization of youth in high school, lacked spending power. Between 1900 and 1940, the percentage in high school of those between 14 and 17 years of age increased from 11% to 80%.[63] After World War II, spending patterns changed as symbolized by the publication *Seventeen* magazine with its slogan, "Teena means business." Similar to their mothers, teenage girls were a primary target for marketers. The word *teenager*, according to Kelly Schrum, was invented by marketers. At first marketers experimented with *teenster* and *Petiteen*; then *teenager* was popularized during the 1940s to mean a group defined by high school attendance. In a crass commercial effort, *Seventeen* magazine advertised the potential teenage market with slogans such as, "When is a girl worth $11,690,499."[64] Sounding like an illusion to prostitution, the slogan referred to the amount of money spent on teenage ads.

Was a national teenage culture a result of advertising? Certainly advertising provided national models for White teenagers to emulate. African-American, Native American, and Mexican-American youth were not subjects of these early ad campaigns. One can imagine teenagers fantasying about themselves looking like the youth in national ads. The ads provided models of dress and lifestyles. Also they carried messages about teenage sexuality.

Consider a 1950's Seven-Up ad that played on the concept of *going steady.* In the 1950s, dating rituals of teenagers included going steady, which was similar to a preengagement rite. The boy gave the girl an ankle bracelet, varsity jacket, or other consumer adornment to indicate that they would date only each other or, in the language of the times, they were going *steady.* Violation of the going steady agreement could result in a pseudodivorce. The going steady process mirrored the marriage and divorce practices of adults.

In the Seven-Up ad, a neatly dressed White teenage couple holding Seven-Up bottles are standing next to a jukebox. Above them the ad proclaimed, "It's great to 'go steady' with this COOL, CLEAN, TASTE!" Playing again on the theme of the couple's relationship, the text of the ad declared, "Here's the drink that's fun to be with-it has such a *sparkling personality.* . . . For a really 'cool' date . . . make yours 7-Up."[65] Other ads played directly to female sexuality. A 1945 *Seventeen* perfume ad embodied sexuality in the brand name, illustration, and text. The ad for Vigny's "Beau Catcher" perfume shows a young girl in a wind-blown and revealing skirt holding a string that is wrapped around a "Beau Catcher Date Book." Two other strings are tied to the product icon and a bottle of perfume. The ad's text states, "Vigny's Beau Catcher Perfume fills your date book. It's the saucy scent that won't take 'no' for an answer."[66]

A national White teenage culture was created through the common high school experience and national advertising. *Seventeen* magazine sold advertising on the basis that teenagers shared a common public mind. Magazine copy claimed, "Teena is a copycat—what a break for you. . . . She and her teen-mates speak the same language . . . wear the same clothes . . . use the same brand of lipstick."[67] The magazine included in their proclamation of a national teenage market a message that youth were responsible citizens. In other words, teenagers were responsible consumer-citizens.

Adolescent sexuality was central to teen ads and public concerns. Ironically, the high school heightened teenage sexuality by putting them within close proximity of each other. Advertising added to this concentrated sexuality by playing on themes of dating and relationships. *Seventeen* tried to balance this blatant sexuality with advice that discouraged heavy necking and petting. It also stressed the importance of political involvement, patriotism, and maintaining knowledge of current events. Scrum concluded that the general message was for teenage girls to practice civic consumerism.

Of course advertising placed sexuality at the center of teenage life by following its long tradition of playing to feelings of personal inadequacy. Similar to the fears implanted in adult women in the 1920s, teenagers were confronted with the possibility of being dateless because of body odors, bad breath, and unfashionable hair styles and clothing. The purchase of deodorants, mouth washes, cosmetics, hair products, and fashionable clothing promised the necessary sexual appeal.

The teenager was a cold warrior in training. Dating was to lead to marriage, the purchase of a home, and all of its necessary appliances. One could imagine the teenage girl and boy standing next to Nixon as he explained the advantages of American home appliances to Khrushchev. Swept up in the spirit of patriotism, this chaste and consumer-oriented teenage couple would marry and demonstrate the advantages of the American economic system.

THE AMERICAN WAY: TV AND COMIC BOOK CODES

In the 1950s, teenagers and children were the first generation raised on TV ads. While TV ads stimulated consumption, programs supported the American Way. In 1951, the TV industry's organization, the National Association of Broadcasters (NAB), adopted a self-censorship code. The code was in response to pressures similar to those that affected radio in the 1930s. Both the PTA and *Parents Magazine* wanted to "get rid of tele-violence." At the time of code's adoption, programming included a long list of gore and mystery shows such as, "Lights Out," "Suspense," "Danger," "The Clock," "The Web," "Tales of the Black Cat," and "Man Against Crime." The 1951 code was adopted because, in the words of the NAB, "[of the] threat of government censorship."[68]

Similar to earlier movie and radio codes, the 1951 TV code emphasized the importance of creating a public image of a moral world where crime was always punished and the law and police were given respect. Under the code, marriage was to be respected and illicit sex was not to be presented as commendable. Drunkenness and narcotic use were only to be depicted as vicious habits. Horror for its own sake and lewdness were forbidden. No words were to be used that might offend any race, color, creed, or nationality except to combat racial prejudice. The Code emphasized the need for "respect for the special needs of children, for community responsibility, for the advancement of education and culture, for the acceptability of the program materials chosen, for decency and decorum in production, and for propriety in advertising."[69]

In addition, advertisers imposed codes that supported the American Way and free enterprise. For instance, Procter & Gamble, the major sponsor of soap operas, required that their programs supported patriotism and never tarnished the image of government agents and members of the U.S. armed forces. If a character in a program attacked "some basic conception of the

American way of life," then a rebuttal "must be completely and convincingly made someplace in the same broadcast." In addition, the image of business was to be protected. A Procter & Gamble memo stated,

> There will be no material on any of our programs which could in any way further the concept of business as cold, ruthless, and lacking all sentiment or spiritual motivation. If a businessman is cast in the role of villain, it must be made clear that he is not typical but is as much despised by his fellow business men as he is by other members of society."[70]

Also advertisers worried about sponsoring any program that might be considered communist or an attack on the American way of life. Of particular concern were criticisms from the American Legion, which in 1948, through its Americanism Commission, started a newsletter, *Summary of Trends and Developments Exposing the Communist Conspiracy.* The newsletter told readers to "organize a letter-writing group of six to ten relatives and friends to make the sentiments of Americans heard on the important issues of the day. Phone, telegraph, or write to radio and television sponsors employing entertainers with known [Communist] front records." The newsletter stated in bold type: "DON'T LET THE SPONSORS PASS THE BUCK BACK TO YOU BY DEMANDING 'PROOF' OF COMMUNIST FRONTING BY SOME CHARACTER ABOUT WHOM YOU HAVE COMPLAINED. YOU DON'T HAVE TO PROVE ANYTHING. . . . YOU SIMPLY DO NOT LIKE SO-AND-SO ON THEIR PROGRAMS."[71]

Local Legion posts joined a supermarket campaign to convince sponsors not to employ entertainers listed in the book, *Red Channels: The Report of Communist Influence in Radio and Television.* The book's introduction warned that "Cominform and the Communist Party USA now rely more on radio and TV than on the press and motion pictures as 'belts' to transmit pro-Sovietism to the American public." Issued in 1950, the book was produced by the American Business Consultants, publishers of *Counterattack, the Newsletter of Facts to Combat Communism. Counterattack* started in 1947 by three former agents of the Federal Bureau of Investigation. Besides warning of a communist conspiracy, the newsletter listed names found in articles in the communist newspaper, *The Daily Worker.*[72]

In 1951, a supermarket campaign began when a reader of *Red Channels* and *Counterattack*, Eleanor Buchanan of Syracuse, New York, enlisted her father, Laurence Johnson, who owned four supermarkets, to work with the local American Legion Post. In one letter to the Legionnaires, Buchanan wrote, "Dad and I were pleased that you agree manufacturers can be persuaded to remove Communist sympathizers from their advertising programs on radio and television. As you gentlemen pointed out in our meeting last Friday, the task is too great for me alone. I am grateful for your aid."[73]

Besides owning four supermarkets, Laurance Johnson was an official in the National Association of Supermarkets. This created the impression that he could influence stores around the country and, because of the cooperation of the local Legion post, he had power in the national organization of the American Legion as well. Consequently, the sponsor, Amm-i-dent Toothpaste, took his action seriously when he protested the use of actors listed in *Counterattack* in the TV drama they sponsored, "Danger." Johnson wrote Amm-i-dent's manufacturer about plans to create two displays in his supermarkets. One display would be for Amm-i-dent's competitor Chlorodent Toothpaste. The sign on this display would thank Chlorodent for sponsoring programs with pro-American artists. The other display would be for Amm-i-dent, with a sign, to be written by the company, explaining why the sponsor selected subversives as actors. A copy of the letter was sent to CBS. This and later letters sent sponsors and broadcasters scurrying to review copies of *Red Channels*. Thank-you notes were sent to Johnson from TV sponsors including Borden Milk Company, Kraft Foods, and General Ice Cream Corporation. The Red Scare sent a pall of fear over the broadcast industry.[74]

Maintaining family values was part of CBS' censorship efforts. A divorce situation in "The Seeking Heart" for October 9, 1954, was brought into line with the networks standard that "divorce is never treated casually or justifiably."[75] The following were present to the Senate Subcommittee as examples of lines remove from scripts for moral considerations.

Do you remember the first time you made love to me?
And I think about all the wicked things I have done, and about you and me.
She swears she'll be discreet. She doesn't know the meaning of the word.[76]

NBC executives also claimed to present images of an ideal family life to the American public. Joseph Hefferman, vice president of NBC, told the Senate Subcommittee that NBC's children's shows were designed "to convey the commonly accepted moral, social, and ethical ideals characteristic of American life; to reflect respect for parents, good morals, and honorable behavior; to foster healthy personality development; and to provide opportunities for cultural growth as well as entertainment."[77]

Comic books were also enlisted in efforts to maintain family values and the American Way. Unlike the Sunday School books of the 19th century, comic books were filled with violence and sexuality. One critic went so far as to call comic books "the marijuana of the nursery." These criticisms eventually led to the comic book industry adopting a self-censorship code similar to the early movie and radio codes. The parallels between industry regulation of comic books and those occurring in the movies and broadcasting were pointed out in a 1954 article in *Christian Century*: "Like movie magnates and radio station operators before them, 24 of the 27 leading publishers of these often lurid picture-pulps [comic books] are trying to still cries for censorship by promising to censor themselves."[78]

Some American leaders thought comic books were a direct threat to the American way of life. After their development in the 1930s, comic books became a major part of the American publishing industry. In 1940, there were 150 comic book titles generating an annual revenue of $20 million. By 1950, there were 300 comic book titles, with annual revenues of $41 million. Between 1950 and 1953, the number of titles jumped to over 650, and revenues leaped to $90 million a year.[79]

What set off the hue and cry about this new form of children's literature was the appearance of crime and horror comics between 1945 and 1954. Unlike TV executives, comic book publishers defended the use of crime and gore. In 1954, when the Senate Subcommittee on Juvenile Delinquency opened hearings on comic books, Senator Estes Kefauver confronted William Gaines, president of the Entertaining Comics Group, with a cover of one of his company's comic books, *Shock Suspense Stories*, depicting an ax-wielding man holding the severed head of a blonde woman. Gaines responded by saying that the cover would only be in bad taste if the head were held "a little high so the neck would show with the blood dripping from it." Kefauver shot back, "You've got blood dripping from the mouth."[80]

In fact, horror and crime comic books of the early 1950s depicted criminal acts, maimed and tortured individuals, and suggestive sexual scenes. At the New York City hearings of the Senate Subcommittee on Juvenile Delinquency, a variety of comic books were introduced to illustrate possible harmful effects on children. In one example, "Bottoms Up," from *Story Comics*, an alcoholic father was responsible for the accidental death of his son while obtaining liquor from a bootlegger. The mother is shown taking revenge in the final four panels of the story by proceeding to kill and hack her spouse to pieces with an ax. The first panel shows her swinging the ax and burying its blade in her husband's skull. Blood spurts from the open wound, and the husband is shown with an expression of agony. . . . She then cuts his body into smaller pieces and disposes of it by placing the various pieces in the bottles of liquor her husband had purchased. She then returns the liquor to the bootlegger and obtains a refund. Another example provided by the subcommittee was from "Frisco Mary" from *Ace Comics*. One scene in this story showed Mary standing over a police officer pouring machine gun bullets into his back while other gang members urge her to stop shooting and flee. In "With Knife in Hand" from *Atlas Comics*, a young surgeon ruins his career by being forced by the spendthrift habits of his wife to treat criminals. In the final scenes of this story, a criminal brings in his

Comic books and censorship

wounded girlfriend to be treated by the doctor. The doctor discovers that the girl is his own wife. The next panel shows the doctor committing suicide by plunging a scalpel into his own abdomen. His wife, gasping for help, dies on the operating table for lack of medical attention. The last scene shows her staring into space, arms dangling over the sides of the operating table. The doctor is sprawled on the floor, his hand still clutching the knife handle protruding from his bloody abdomen. There is a leer on his face and he is winking at the reader, displaying satisfaction at having wrought revenge on his unfaithful spouse. One comic book was described as ending with the victim "lying dead on the bed with a gaping hole in his chest, a rib protruding, blood flowing over the bed onto the floor, his face fixed in a death mask as he stares at the reader."[81]

Following the pattern of movies and broadcasting, the comic book industry needed a profamily code. Wanting to avoid continued community protest and the threat of censorship laws, comic book publishers organized to create and impose their own standards. Their first attempt was the 1948 formation of the Association of Comics Magazine Publishers and its adoption of a six-point code. A seal was to be attached to comic books to indicate conformity to the code. Like other codes, there was an emphasis on issues involving sex, crime, language, the family, and attacks on religious and racial groups. This early code proved ineffective, with only 12 of the 34 major publishers of comic books belonging to the comic book association. With increased pressure from government and private organizations, a new organization, Comics Magazine Association of America, was formed in 1954 with a membership of 28 of the then 31 major publishers of comic books. This association appointed New York City magistrate Charles Murphy to enforce a comic book code. The words *horror* and *terror* were not allowed in titles. Crime comics were to be screened to exclude methods of committing crimes. No sympathy was to be given for criminals, and nothing should "create disrespect for established authority." In addition, the code banned "profanity, obscenity, smut, vulgarity, ridicule of racial or religious groups."[82]

In keeping with the belief that the sanctity of family was necessary for protection of the American way of life and to prevent juvenile delinquency, the code ensured protection of the sanctity of marriage and the value of the home. In addition, "divorce was not to be shown as desirable."[83] Beginning in 1955, a seal was placed on the front of comics as proof that these values were being protected. It was estimated that the code was enforced on 75% of the estimated 60 million comic books published each month in the United States.[84] Dell Comics, one of the three publishers that did not belong to the Comics Magazine Association of America and publisher of approximately 20% of the comic books in the United States, did not join the association because it already had its own code of ethics. In any case, Dell primarily published comics based on adventure stories and Walt Disney characters. It was known in the trade as having a *wholesome approach.* One of the other nonmembers was Classics Illustrated, which adapted classic novels, such as Charles Dickens' *Oliver Twist,* to a comic book format. William Gaines, the originator of horror comics and another nonmember, announced that he would cease publishing all horror and terror magazines. Thus, comic books joined in the media chorus protecting the American way of life.[85]

TEXTBOOKS AND THE CONSUMER FAMILY

Idealized images of American women and men were part of the American way of life. The ideal American female and male were ardent patriots protecting traditional American values. In general, the idealized 1950s' American woman sought her identity in the home through the upbringing of children and the consumption of home products. Reflecting lingering Puritanical fears that consumption would lead to hedonism, according to May, "Family centered spending reassured Americans that affluence would strengthen the American way of life. The goods purchased by middle-class consumers, like a modern refrigerator or a house in the suburbs, were intended to foster traditional values."[86]

The idealized male sought his identity in his job and family life. The male earned the money to be used to buy products that protected traditional values. His realm of consumption usually included automobiles and products used to maintain the interior and exterior of the home. His province was the yard, garage, and home workshop. Reflecting the traditional sense that outdoors was male territory, he was usually given the responsibility for outdoor barbequing.

These gender roles were represented in school textbooks read by all children regardless of their geographical location or race. In 1954, Frank Tannenbaum published a survey of 10 years of primers and first-, second-, and third-grade reading texts entitled "Family Living in Textbook Town." Tannenbaum noted that all the texts depicted the same type of suburban neighborhood with

> rows of brightly polished little cottages, fronted by neatly manicured lawns, all suggesting an atmosphere of order and cheerfulness. In this sunny neighborhood setting, children have lots of room for out-of-doors play, and families are able to enjoy their living space with the kind of "elbowroom" that is not possible in the more thickly populated cities. The reader gets to know these

"Textbook Town"
idealized
Family + gender roles

picturesque surroundings quite intimately, for much of the action in the stories takes place there.[87]

Textbooks portrayed fathers with their favorite easy chairs and workshops and mothers in well-equipped kitchens. The father was usually slim and handsome, often depicted arriving home from work dressed in a neat suit in the family car. Only when making minor home repairs was the father shown in work clothes. The mother had no occupation outside of housework, devoting her time to caring for her family. She was usually young, attractive, and well dressed. The only time she was seen outside of the house was shopping and on family recreation trips.

Children in Textbook Town were all happy and well adjusted. They spent their time playing and doing minor chores with their parents. They were well behaved and never fought with their siblings or parents. In Tannenbaum's words, "Nothing is ever allowed to interfere seriously with the spirit of joy, security, and cooperativeness that dominates family living in Textbook Town."[88] Everyone in Textbook Town was White. No people of color or with distinctive ethnic characteristics lived in Textbook Town, and no one in Textbook Town was poor.

THE MALE WARRIOR PROTECTS THE AMERICAN WAY

Males could escape from Textbook Town through media-created images of the cowboy and war hero. For women, the only media escapes were through the life of glamorous actresses, insanity, or adopting the role of male delinquents. As Wini Breines stated in her study of female delinquents of the 1950s, "Middle-class white girls who rejected dominant values had little choice but to utilize and adapt male versions of rebellion and disaffection. . . . There were few female models."[89]

The screen image of John Wayne provided men with an escape from the humdrum corporate and suburban life. On the screen, Wayne fought for the American Way and values. For White adults and boys, John Wayne represented the ideal of rugged American masculinity in the tradition of Theodore Roosevelt. Even as late as 1995, 16 years after his death, he was still ranked as America's favorite movie star by a Harris Poll.[90] Wayne's movie career encompassed the 1930s' movie code, Hollywood's active World War II cooperation with the government, and the purge of so-called *communists* after the War. During the 1930s, Wayne rose to stardom as primarily an actor in cowboy movies. In these movies, he portrayed the independent and tough cowboy who fought to protect traditional values.[91] During World War II, the U.S. Government's Office of War Information worked actively with the movie studios to produce propaganda films that would stimulate the war effort, boost morale, and fire up a sense of patriotism.[92] Wayne contributed to this effort by starring in important war films, including *Flying Tigers* (1942), *The Fighting Seabees* (1943), and *Back to Bataan* (1945). His portrayal of patriotic war heroes continued after the end of the conflict with *Sands of Iwo Jima* (1949) and *Flying Leathernecks* (1951). He also made the first war movie about Viet Nam called *The Green Berets* (1968). As a sign of his personal patriotism, Wayne struggled to find a studio that would make the movie because of the controversy surrounding the war. Regarding *The Green Berets*, Wayne stated, "I want to show the folks back home just what they're [U.S. troops in Viet Nam] up against out there, their heroism against tremendous odds."[93]

Wayne's screen images of cowboy and patriotic warrior were often mistaken for reality. His biographer, Ronald Doris, reported the following incident that occurred shortly after World War II: "You know," a woman said to screenwriter Edmund Hartmann, "our most decorated soldier is John Wayne." "I think you're wrong," Hartmann replied. "Wayne was never in the army. He never fired a gun in earnest in his life. John Wayne never shot anybody who didn't get up and go for coffee afterwards."[94] After the destruction of the World Trade Center on September 11, 2002, I was surprised to find a life-size cardboard replica of John Wayne wearing a cowboy outfit and holding a rifle among the flowers and memorial signs for the tragedy's victims in Union Square Park in New York City. Across his chest someone had pasted a sign reading, "God Bless America."

During and after World War II, John Wayne joined others in trying to purge communists from the movie industry. In 1944, he worked with Ayn Rand, Walt Disney, Cecil B. DeMille, and Gary Cooper to form the Motion Picture Alliance for the Preservation of American Ideals. The Alliance declared, "In our special field of motion pictures, we resent the growing impression that this industry is made up of, and dominated by, Communists, radicals and crackpots." The organization gave its promise to the American people "to fight, with every means at our organized command, any effort of any group or individual to divert the loyalty of the screen from the free America that gave it birth."[95]

Writer Ayn Rand wrote the organization's movie code to ensure that movies protected the American way of life. The code included the precepts:

Don't *Smear* the Free Enterprise System
Don't Glorify the Collective
Don't Glorify Failure
Don't Smear Success
Don't Smear Industrialists

> It is the moral (no, not just political but moral) duty of every decent man in
> the motion picture industry to throw into the ashcan where it belongs, every
> story that smears industrialists as such.[96]

Wayne also associated himself with the American Legion's efforts to purge un-Americanism from movies, schools, and TV. At a 1951 Legion convention, General MacArthur declared to Wayne, despite that Wayne had never served in the armed forces, "You represent the American serviceman better than the American serviceman himself."[97]

John Wayne's screen image was the direct opposite of that of the corporate-suburban family man. However, both images protected against communism and supported American values. The suburban man gave up his individualism to corporate life, whereas John Wayne stood for individualism and independence. "All I'm for," Wayne claimed, "is the liberty of the individual."[98] Yet the corporate man protected the American Way by maintaining the family and providing the income to consume. John Wayne's importance was his role in the fantasy life of Americans and not the reality of his being. Actress Maureen O'Hara said to a congressional subcommittee shortly before Wayne's death, "To the people of the world John Wayne is the United States of America."[99] Commenting on Wayne's role in public fantasies, screenwriter Huggins said, "People actually thought of Wayne as a great hero and, of course, John Wayne was just an actor. He was never in any armed service, never saw a war, never even saw a gun fired that actually had lead in it. . . . It says something about the confusion in the American people between reality and myth."[100]

The John Wayne image found its way into advertising as the Marlboro Man. The story of the Marlboro Man highlights the appeal of the cowboy in 20th century. In the 1920s, Marlboro cigarettes were marketed to women with a red paper beauty tip to conceal lipstick. In the 1950s, it was decided to change marketing strategies and sell the product to men. The Marlboro Man appeared in 1955 dressed in a cowboy outfit sitting on a horse or relaxing by a campfire. All it required was a change in gender image to sell the cigarette to men. As advertising historian Juliann Sivulka wrote, "Cowboys symbolized the most masculine type of man, and . . . [the] ads evoked memorable imagery of real men in a man's world. The campaign became one of the all-time greats in advertising history."[101]

Fantasies about John Wayne and the Marlboro Man's independence and action-filled life might have psychologically relieved the reality of suburban man's dependence on corporate life and completing the mundane tasks of lawn mowing and car washing. In the arena of patriotism, the internalization of the American myths of the cowboy and battlefield added potency to an anticommunism being fought on the front lines of consumerism.

Washing their cars in their suburban driveways, the organization man could envision charging into battle to protect the American way of life.

TRAPPED IN TEXTBOOK AND CONSUMER TOWN: WOMEN AND THE LACK OF INDEPENDENT MEDIA IMAGES

For White women, the screen offered escape into the fantasy images of the ultimate consumer, the Hollywood star. Otherwise the screen was dominated by women treated as sex objects or insane. Women of the 1950s disliked Marilyn Monroe, the era's major sex symbol. This attitude would change in later years. In *From Reverence to Rape: The Treatment of Women in the Movies*, Molly Haskell wrote, "Women, particularly, have become contrite over their previous hostility to Monroe, canonizing her as a martyr to male chauvinism, which in most ways she was."[102]

According to Haskell, men rarely played the role of an actor in movies, whereas women often performed in actress roles. As Haskell suggested, there were two major movie roles for women that paralleled how they might be forced to act in normal life—namely, prostitution and role-playing. The actress role on screen allowed female viewers to image living the life of a glamorous movie star. Haskell wrote, "The actress legend took various forms: the mystique of the actress, the myth of the movie star, the mystique of the actress versus the myth of the movie star."[103] There were a few alternatives to the glamorized sex object and actress role, but nothing that matched the power of the John Wayne image for men. Haskell argued that Grace Kelly and Audrey Hepburn provided screen models for the independent woman: "They never swallowed their pride, exploited their sexuality, or made fools of themselves over men."[104]

Lacking female fantasy role models, female rebels frequently modeled themselves after male media images. Wini Breines found that many women who rejected the life of Textbook Town identified with the male characters in Jack Kerouac's novel, *On the Road*, although they were macho and sexist.[105] On the screen, young women were attracted to Marlon Brando in *The Wild One* and James Dean in *Rebel without a Cause*. Breines argued, "Widespread interest in Dean, Elvis [Presley], the Beats, and young men from the 'other side of the tracks' suggests an attraction to a life that was 'dramatic, unpredictable, possibly dangerous,' the antithesis of white middle-class life in postwar America."[106]

Television reinforced the female roles represented in Textbook Town. Daytime TV, which was programmed for the housewife, intentionally educated women about consumption for the suburban home. When the major networks began daytime broadcasting in the early 1950s, their first project was teaching the housewife how to watch TV while working. For instance, a 1955 NBC ad showed a housewife wearing an apron and holding a feather duster exclaiming, "Where did the morning go?" Surrounding her were TV screens with scenes from NBC's daytime TV programming. The ad's text read, "Time for lunch already? Where did the morning go? The chores are done, the house is tidy . . . but it hasn't *seemed* like a terribly tiring morning." Her morning was portrayed as opening with family breakfast while watching the "Today Show." After breakfast she tidied up while her daughter watched the "Ding Dong School." Then she rested while watching the soap opera serial "Way of the World" and began ironing during the "Sheila Graham Show." The rest of the morning, as depicted in the ad, followed this combination of work and TV.[107]

Some of the programming followed a magazine format that integrated "housework, consumerism, and TV entertainment."[108] In these programs, entertainment was surrounded with advice on shopping and products along with fashion and cleaning tips. Lynn Spigel quoted a production handbook: "The theory is that the housewife will be more likely to take time from her household duties if she feels that her television viewing will make her housekeeping more efficient and help her provide more gracious living for her family."[109]

Plus there were products the woman consumer could buy to make TV viewing more efficient, including snack trays, TV trays, and TV frozen dinners. Dishwashers were advertised as freeing the housewife from the kitchen to join the family before the TV. A 1950 Hotpoint ad showed a housewife washing dishes while in the next room the rest of the family was watching TV. In large print, the ad pleaded, "PLEASE . . . LET YOUR WIFE COME INTO THE LIVING ROOM!" This was followed in smaller type with: "Don't let dirty dishes make your wife a kitchen exile!" In the lower right-hand corner of the ad was a dishwasher with the statement, "No martyr banished to kitchen, she never misses television programs. Lunch, dinner dishes are in an electric dishwasher."[110]

Media provided the housewife few role models for escaping from Textbook Town. The male could dream of being a cowboy or warrior and the woman could imagine escaping into the glamor of Hollywood or latching onto a rebellious male who could free her from her mundane world. Consumption fantasies left her trapped in Textbook Town with men who dreamt of being warriors in defense of the American Way.

CONCLUSION: THE AMERICAN WAY

I really enjoyed writing this chapter because I could pull together similar public images that were emerging from schools and media as a result of consumerism and anticommunism. Most striking were those excluded from this public image—namely, non-Whites, gays, lesbians, and those rejecting the life of Textbook Town. Of course media did present images of beatniks, delinquents, the insane, and the criminal, but these were always constructed as deviant to the American way of life and Textbook Town.

An important development during this period was the growing awareness by private groups of the importance of controlling public opinion, particularly controlling the filters or preconceptions used to interpret world events. This development was highlighted by the NAM's use of public relations in the American Way campaign to create in the public mind an immediate association among democracy, free enterprise, consumerism, and Americanism. Anticommunist groups aided this effort by attempting to eradicate from media and schools anything that might question the value of free enterprise.

The other important event was the interrelationship among schools, advertising, and media in creating a national teenager culture. Advertising would continue to play a role in defining images of differing parts of the public. Because African Americans, Latinos, Asians, gays, and lesbians were recognized as important consumers, advertisers and media would increasingly gear ads and programs to these groups. The result was an interrelationship between group images projected by ads and media and self-identification. Of course this would not be a one-way road. There would be a constant feedback, as there was with teen culture, between the group, as measured by market research and consumer spending, and media and advertisers. This feedback was not static. Often it would be hard to tell whether a public group dressed according to ad and media campaigns or whether ad and media campaigns reflected the dress of the group.

The importance of the general public image continued despite the development of specific images for particular publics, such as teens, older people, African Americans, and so on. The American Way images of democracy, free enterprise, suburbia, and consumption existed side by side with a national teen culture. Although White teens developed their own national cultural, clothing, and media styles, there was still an effort by schools and media to connect teen minds to a more general public mind that valued the American Way.

The problem was that the American Way image did not include all Americans. The poor, composed of Whites, African Americans, Native Americans, and Asian Americans, were not full participants in consumerism. Their images were not in Textbook Town or reflected in national advertising. In part, the great civil rights movement of the 1950s and 1960s reflected a desire to join the consumerist culture. I am not discounting the major political victories of the civil rights movement, such as the end of segregation and the achievement of voting rights. However, I would argue that the civil rights movement's economic goals were primarily to gain full participation of all groups in consumerist culture.

In the next chapter, I discuss the implication of the civil rights movement for consumerism and the American Way. In addition, the civil rights movement occurred as major changes were occurring in marketing, creation of consumer desires, and food processing—namely, the development of shopping malls, the expansion of fast-food chains, the building of Disneyland, and the establishment of Wal-Mart, which is now the world leader in retailing.

Chapter 6

Participating in the
American Dream

A goal of the civil rights movement was inclusion of all people's images in textbooks, advertising, and media as equal participants in the American dream. African Americans, Native Americans, Mexican Americans, Asian Americans, women, and people with disabilities hoped that the struggle for equal social and political rights would also result in the projection of positive images of them in textbooks, media, and advertising. Also the civil rights movement's pursuit of equality of opportunity promised a chance for all to participate in consumerism. The women's movement wanted to replace the image of Textbook Town's housewife with one emphasizing women's career options and personal freedoms. Inevitably, these goals were integrated into advertising copy to expand consumerism to all groups.

THE COLORING OF TEXTBOOK TOWN

A 1964 California State Department of Education report on "The Negro in American History Textbooks" declared that "[Ralph Ellison's novel, *Invisible Man*] demonstrates whites frequently do not 'see' Negroes. But Negroes are Americans. . . . They need to be 'seen' in textbooks."[1] The report was issued by a distinguished panel of University of California historians headed by Kenneth Stampp. The panel had been organized in 1963 by the Berkeley, California, chapter of the Congress on Racial Equality (CORE) to analyze American history textbooks adopted for use in Grades 5 and 8 and two textbooks used in the state's high schools. The panel's report was important because the California State Board of Education selected textbooks that were adopted by local state school systems. Given the large number of sales involved, the textbook industry was attuned to the desires of the California State Board of Education. The State Board of Education distributed the report to interested groups, including textbook publishers, and in 1966 it played an important role in the deliberations of the U.S. House of Representatives' investigation of the treatment of minority groups in textbooks, which reprinted it in its proceedings.[2] Intensifying discussions about racial images in textbooks was the news that New York City's African-American elementary school students were drawing White faces when asked to complete self-portraits.[3]

CORE's panel of academic historians found almost total neglect of African-American history. One textbook failed to mention African Americans. One did not refer to slavery during the colonial period, whereas others did not discuss anything about African Americans after the Civil War. The report complained, "The greatest defect in the textbooks we have examined is the virtual omission of the Negro."[4] The panel criticized the unrealistic treatment of the relationships between Whites and African Americans. When discussed at all in the textbooks, interracial contacts were portrayed as harmonious. The history of racial violence was seldom mentioned in textbooks. "In their blandness and amoral optimism," the panel's analysis concluded, "these books deny the obvious deprivations suffered by Negroes. In several places they go further, implying approval for the repression of Negroes or patronizing them as being unqualified for life in a free society."[5] The report recommended full treatment of African-American history. The historians on the panel suggested that books begin with the early importation and treatment of slaves and conclude with the recent history of the civil rights movement. The report also urged, the "Gains that have been made should be described realistically and not as an ode to the inevitable justice and progress of the democratic system."[6]

The National Association for the Advancement of Colored People (NAACP) and the editors of *Ebony Magazine* were also concerned about textbooks. Since the NAACP's demonstrations against the movie *Birth of a Nation* in 1915, the organization had paid vigilant attention to public images of African Americans. In 1966, the organization issued a guide to integrated textbooks that stated, "in the crucial effort to guarantee to all our children, white and black, a curriculum that makes sense in a multi-racial society, such a listing is long overdue."[7] After studying textbooks for 5 years, senior editor of *Ebony*, Lerone Bennett, concluded that, "The use of textbooks filled with half-truths, evasions and distortions is disastrous to both white and black Americans . . . [and] white oriented textbooks tend to inoculate white Americans with the virus of racism. . . ." Bennett called on the federal government to provide the resources and power to solve the textbook problem.[8]

Bennett warned, in testimony before the 1966 House Subcommittee investigating textbooks' racial and cultural content, that "segregated textbooks . . . are as dangerous to the internal peace of America as segregated schools and residential areas." In fact, he argued that if all schools and neighborhoods were immediately integrated without integrating textbooks, then all schools and neighborhoods would soon become segregated again. Bennett found it ironic that the largest race riots had occurred in Chicago, which was originally founded by African-American Jean Baptiste Pointe Du Sable. "And it seems to me," he declared, "that a solution to our current crisis depends to a great extent on the opening of our minds and our textbooks to all the Du Sables and the excluded range of American life and culture that they personified."[9]

Publishers expressed their concerns about racial integration of textbooks through their trade association the American Textbook Publishers Institute (ATPI), which represented 110 publishers of textbooks and other educational materials. The organization scheduled a 1965 joint conference with the Urban League to determine "the needs of the Negro child and the kinds of materials which would help him relate to the total American society."[10] The executive director of the National Urban League, Whitney Young, Jr., told the meeting, "You publishers want the respect of generations born and generations yet unborn. We live together as brothers, or we die together as fools." Another member of the Urban League, Edwin Berry, insisted that publishers do more than just integrate textbooks with pictures of differing ethnic groups. He argued, they should also provide a realistic view of society by including "tall people, short people, fat and slim people, people with glasses, balding men and pregnant women."[11]

Meeting in 1965 with the Great Cities Research Council, the ATPI agreed to collect urban—by this time, *urban* was a code word for poor and non-White students—educational materials in cooperation with the U.S. Office of Education. The ATPI organized itself as a clearinghouse for new research on urban education. To further aid the objectives of publishers, the joint conference arranged visits by teams of publishers to meet with educators in member school systems. Also before congressional investigators, ATPI's McCaffrey described how publishers were being pressured by local school systems to produce multiracial textbooks: "I think 2 or 3 years ago a number of principal cities in the country passed resolutions in their boards of education that it was the policy of these cities to purchase only books that had a fair representation of minorities."[12]

Publishers claimed federal money made it possible to produce multiracial texts. A senior vice-president of McGraw-Hill, Robert W. Locke, told the House Subcommittee, "Purchases of new textbooks and other instructional materials have risen sharply this year because of ESEA, and part of the gap has been closed between what should be done for schoolchildren and what is being done." In fact, Locke indicated that federal money was the most important element in the expansion of the textbook publishing industry in the early 1960s; he told the subcommittee: "My guess is that something like 30 or 40 percent of our increase in sales this year at the elementary and secondary level will be a result of . . . [federal] funds."[13] Publishers sought more federal funds when ATPI and Scott, Foresman & Co.'s president, Darrel Peterson, told the House Subcommittee, "I would like to offer strong endorsement for the Government's efforts to improve the quantity and quality of educational materials available to students in our schools. . . . These Federal investments in libraries and instructional materials in general are eminently worthwhile."[14]

Responding to federal actions, McGraw-Hill published texts depicting multiethnic urban settings. In 1965, the company issued the *Skyline* reading series for Grades 2 through 4, which contained stories about people living in multiethnic cities. For example, one story, "The Hidden Lookout," was about Rosita's search for a place of her own in a city with millions of people. Eventually she builds a box house on an apartment roof. The *Skyline* series was only one of several related series published by McGraw-Hill in 1965. That year it also published a series called *Americans All*, with specific titles on "The American Negro," "Our Oriental Americans," "Our Citizens From the Caribbean," and "Latin Americans of the Southwest." In 1965, the company published a high school textbook focusing on civil liberties, *Heritage of Liberty*.[15]

However, publishers were accused of shady practices by publishing special editions for the Southern market. Harcourt, Brace & World, Inc. issued textbook editions that were free of multiracial pictures. In 1965, Southern states approved sight-unseen new editions of the company's elementary school grammar and composition texts. Southern school districts complained about books containing illustrations of White and African-American children playing together. Harcourt's vice-president, Cameron S. Moseley, explained to the House Subcommittee, "There was an unofficial, implied threat to cancel all our contracts." Consequently, the company printed a special edition that deintegrated the illustrations by showing only White children.[16]

In a similar situation, in 1965 Scott, Foresman published three new multiethnic series in reading, health, and social studies. "These books," the company's president Peterson stated, "which are multiethnic in character, present all kinds of children in natural situations and, where appropriate, contribute to the positive imagery of the diversified composition of American society."[17] However, Scott, Foresman continued printing its 1962 all-White edition of the reading series. When questioned about the all-White series, Peterson claimed that the company was not producing a series just for the South because both series were being sold throughout the country.

All school districts in the country had a choice between the multiethnic and all-White versions. The increased cost of publishing two editions, he explained, was balanced by the bigger volume of business.[18]

Illustrations were the major difference between the all-White and multiethnic editions. In describing its new urban social studies program, the executive vice-president of Holt, Rinehart & Winston, Ross Sackett, emphasized that, "Dramatic photographs capture the interaction between individuals and groups in an actual multicultural, multiracial community."[19] Publishers described books by the number of multiracial illustrations. For example, Craig Senft, president of Silver Burdett Co., proudly described a new first-grade textbook, *Families and Their Needs,* as identifying "facts that determine just how the needs of families from a variety of physical environments and cultures are met. It so happens that of the 54 photographs illustrating some aspect of American families, 18 show minority group families or individuals." He emphasized, "We intentionally chose photographs that included minority groups to show as many ethnic and socioeconomic strains as were needed to portray the differences that give our society its variety and richness."[20]

The process of adding African Americans to pictures was sometimes referred to as giving textbook characters a *sunburn.* There were several techniques involved in this process. One created integrated drawings by using different mechanical color separations or simply two colors. Simple black and white line drawings showed ethnically vague features that could be filled in by the reader's imagination. Photographs of integrated groups were frequently used in popular settings such as stores, playgrounds, neighborhood streets, and homes. Relying on changes in illustrations, textbook publishers could claim integration of a wide variety of texts, including those in science and mathematics. McGraw-Hill's representative Locke considered their elementary school science program, "Experiences in Science," as integrated because, in his words to the House Subcommittee, "we have taken great care to include minority-group children in the illustrations."[21] He also included an arithmetic filmstrip because its frames included both White and non-White groups.

In the new Textbook Town, multiracial images resided in a world of social harmony. In textbook scenes, African Americans and Whites worked and played together despite continued discrimination and racial violence in society. No longer invisible in textbooks, African Americans were catapulted to a world of equality and racial harmony. Integrated textbook stories also conveyed a message of racial harmony. Although illustrations were the easiest and most popular method for publishers to integrate textbooks, multiracial and multiethnic stories were placed in readers. "Galumph," the opening story of Houghton-Mifflin's second-grade reader, was about a cat who divided its time among an African-American child, an Italian baker, a

Hispanic girl, and a sick White child. Another story, "Traffic Policeman," was about a White child cooperating with an African-American policeman. "A Penny for a Jack Rabbit" was the unlikely tale—given the racial tension and housing discrimination in the society at that time—of suburban African-American and White children playing together at a party.[22]

Therefore, the setting and population of Textbook Town changed without disturbing the basic message of harmony and happiness. Political pressures and government funding added an urban dimension and a multiracial and multiethnic population to Textbook Town. Textbook Town now included apartment buildings as well as suburban bungalows, where happy groups of multiracial children played together. History textbooks contained sections on slavery and the civil rights movement. Yet an integrated Textbook Town still seemed out of touch with the reality of racial violence and discrimination.

BEAUTY IN THE PUBLIC MIND

In the 1950s, Black Power advocates condemned the use of skin whiteners and hair straighteners because they reflected beauty standards of the White community. Traditionally, ads for these hair and skin lotions were the richest source of advertising for the African-American press.[23] Black pride was part of a general movement, which also included Indians and Chicanos, to embrace beauty standards based on racial self-esteem. Among these groups, traditional dress, jewelry, and hair styles became a symbol of rebellion against White images in textbooks, ads, and media. African-American pride championed natural beauty fashioned by Afro hair styles and acceptance of natural skin color. The result was a decline in the use of traditional African-American hair and cosmetic products. A study of ads in *Ebony* magazine between 1949 and 1972 found a rapid decline in ads for hair straighteners and skin whiteners and the appearance of ads for Afro hairstyles.[24]

This beauty trend resulted in the growth of new African-American-owned cosmetic companies. In 1965, the Flori Roberts Company began marketing African-American cosmetic products originally developed for African-American models. This was followed by Fashion Fair Cosmetics, which was a product line marketed by *Ebony*. In 1973, Johnson Products became the first African-American-owned company to be listed on a major stock exchange as a result of its wildly popular Afro-Sheen products.[25]

A new magazine, *Essence*, promoted products and new beauty standards to African-American women. Clarence Smith, *Essence*'s publisher, defined his marketing strategy as an outgrowth of the rebellion against dominant White images. Smith wrote, "They [marketers] don't see how much Black women are competing with White women to prove they are as good or

better. Since childhood they have been inundated with media images of
beauty as the White woman."[26] Marketing strategies, Smith contended,
should be cast in the framework of African-American pride. He wrote,
"They [black women] want to be as attractive as possible and show the Black
man that her beauty is fine. Marketers should see that she is overcompen-
sating in buying products to dispel negative stereotypes."[27]

Robert E. Weems, Jr., noted that the revolution in African-American female identity was not accompanied by the same loyalty to African-American
businesses as had existed in the past. Eventually, as they recognized the
spending power of the African-American community, White-owned businesses controlled the African-American cosmetic market. In 1991, the Maybelline Company introduced Shades of You cosmetics for African-American women. At the time its major competitor in the general cosmetic's
market was Çover Girl. Industry consultant Allan Motus said Maybelline's
introduction of Shades of You was a smart move: "Instead of going eyeball
to eyeball with Cover Girl, they can go for a specific segment for incremen-
tal market share."[28] Also in 1991, Estee Lauder began marketing Prescrip-
tives for All Skins with 100 makeup shades. The product line attracted
50,000 African-American buyers in its first year.[29]

Ironically, the Black pride movement integrated African Americans into
the general consumer market while undermining traditional African-
American businesses. For some African Americans, the civil rights movement meant equal opportunity to pursue the American dream within the
framework of a specific racial identity. Freedom to consume did not mean
having to take on a White identity. For many African Americans, equality of
educational opportunity and equality of opportunity meant an equal
chance to earn and consume.

INTEGRATING CONSUMER MARKETS:
AFRICAN-AMERICAN SPORT STARS
REPLACE WHITE COWBOYS

The recognition by White-owned companies of an African-American consumer market prompted changes in the traditional use of degrading racial
images in ads, and it provided an opportunity for the establishment of African-American-owned ad agencies. Prior to the influence of the civil rights
movement, African-American ad images were usually as cooks and butlers
to White families, such as Aunt Jemima, Cream of Wheat's Chef Rustus, and
Hiram Walker's butler. Clearly these images were not going to sell products
to the African-American community.

Vince Culler's was the first African-American-owned ad agency when it
opened in Chicago in 1956. At first Culler did ads for African-American-
owned companies such Johnson Products. Culler's ads were successful in

promoting Johnson's Afro-Sheen products. A 1960s ad by Culler's agency for Afro-Sheen showed the heads of African-American men and women sporting Afro hair styles. Reflecting the emphasis on Black pride and rejection of attempts to look White, the ad proclaimed that these were "People who wear the natural as a proud symbol of beautiful blackness."[30] Culler's agency eventually garnered non-African-American owned company accounts such as Kellogg and Pizza Hut.[31]

An important advertising goal was creating images that would synthesize or integrate the consumer market. By this I mean the creation of ad images designed to appeal to all racial audiences. This step, I would argue, established a certain level of interracial camaraderie about consumer products. According to Bernice Kanner, the author of *New York* magazine's column "On Madison Avenue," one of the best 100 all-time TV ads showed African-American football player Mean Joe Greene drinking a bottle of Coca-Cola. The first thing to note about the ad was that, by the 1970s, the football player had replaced the cowboy as the primary macho image. The vice-president of marketing for Coca-Cola, Bill Van, commented about the ad, in the words of Bernice Kanner, "Just as Marlboro owned macho cowboys, Coca-Cola thought it could own the world of smiling Americans . . . Coke spots featured product as hero, causing the smile."[32]

Made in 1979 by the McCann–Erickson Worldwide agency, the ad opened with Mean Joe Green limping down a stadium tunnel appearing battered from a big game. A little boy admiringly told the player, "I just want you to know, I think you're the best." After the unsmiling player grunted an unfriendly response, the boy offered his Coke. As Mean Joe Green lifted the bottle to his lips, music and lyrics proclaimed, "A Coke and a smile, makes me feel good, makes me feel nice." Revived by the drink, the player smiled and thanked the boy by tossing him his dirty jersey. After the boy shouted, "Wow! Thanks Mean Joe!", a voice-over proclaimed, "Have a Coke and a smile. Coke adds life."[33]

Another example of synthesizing or integrating the consumer market was Pepsi-Cola's ad for the macho symbol of Americanism—the Super Bowl. This 1990 TV ad by the Batten, Barton, Durstine & Osborne featured African-American singer Ray Charles who, in the opening scene, was rehearsing "You Know When Its Right."

> You know when you feel it, baby.
> You hold it. You hear it. You taste it. It's right.
> Diet Pepsi.[34]

The scene shifts to a performance with dancing chorus girls and Ray Charles singing praises to Pepsi-Cola. The final line by Charles was: "You know when it's right. You know when you taste it!" followed by a voice-over, "You got the right one, baby, Uh, Huh, Diet Pepsi."[35]

Another example of the effort to synthesize or integrate the consumer market was a 1993 ad for McDonald's—the same desire to integrate the consumer market. The ad was clearly designed to appeal to White and African-American consumers who might envision eating together at McDonald's. The ad included basketball player Michael Jordan who would eventually become a worldwide consumer symbol for Nike shoes. Also included was White basketball player Larry Bird. Produced by the Leo Burnett agency, the ad was called "Showdown Combo" and portrayed Bird and Jordan competing for a Big Mac and bag of fries. Making impossible shots, the final scene shows them on top of Chicago's John Hancock building trying a shot that would be "off the expressway, over the river, off the billboard, through the window, off the wall . . . nothin' but net. . . ." The voice-over concluded, "McDonald's. What you want is what you get . . . and, The ball goes in, nothin' but net."[36]

The importance of Michael Jordan as a global consumer symbol cannot be overstated. In her market survey of global teens, Elissa Moses found that the icon for the Chicago Bulls' basketball team was the 10th most widely recognized brand name in the world. In her words, "Michael Jordan's superstar status elevated the Bulls, in tenth place, higher than the NBA [National Basketball Association], which came in thirteenth."[37] The recognition of both the Bulls' icon and the NBA resulted from a global media effort by the NBA. Moses argued that Nike's use of Jordan in ads made the Nike icon the fourth most recognized among global teens. In her words, Jordan "embodies the essence of far-reaching greatness that is synonymous with the athletic footwear's 'Just Do It' positioning. Utilizing the world wide recognition and admiration of Michael Jordan leverages a core unifier for the brand's growth and continued success."[38]

Advertising columnist for the *Village Voice*, Leslie Savan, argued that White males were attracted to Nike's African-American advertising images out of a desire to be hip. In reference to the concept of "aspiring white Negroes," she wrote, that it could be used as a "label for the whiter hipsters who . . . strive to imitate black male athletes (Nike says 87 percent of its domestic athletic shoes are sold to whites), sneakers tease all men with the possibility of making hipless out of nothingness."[39] Does being hip also mean incorporating fantasizes of African-American male sexuality?

The transformation of America's macho symbol from the White cowboy to the African-American sports star confirms both the integration of the consumer market and the strange perversions of American images. Nineteenth-century White males would not accept an African-American sports star as an image of ideal masculinity. In *Manliness and Civilization*, Gail Bederman described the reaction of White men to African-American boxer Jack Johnson winning the heavyweight boxing championship in 1908. Similar to the emotions that spurred the lynching of African-American men to protect White womanhood, White men reacted as if the triumph of Johnson was a threat to White masculinity. Recognizing this reaction, Johnson made his penis look larger under his boxing trunks by wrapping it in cloth before stepping into the ring. He also found companionship with White women. The question in White men's minds at the time was, according to Bederman, "Did Johnson's success with white women prove him a superior specimen of manhood?"[40] At the time, White men turned to the macho image of Theodore Roosevelt as cowboy and hunter conquering the primitive Indian and demonstrating to Africans his supposed superiority at hunting.

In the later part of the 20th century, as the cowboy image of manhood disappeared from media, the African-American sports star became the new White model of masculinity. One wonders whether this change resulted from White men capitulating to their fantasizes of superior African-American masculinity and sexual prowess. Rather than being threatened by the myth of African-American male superiority, White men now wanted to embody it in their own beings. This could now be done by buying consumer products. Nike ads promised buyers that they could be like Michael Jordan.

MAKING SHOPPING MASCULINE

A dilemma in men's marketing was the early 20th-century public image of women as consumers and men as producers. Men interested in shopping and fashion were considered effeminate. *Esquire* and *Playboy* magazines remedied this situation by combining ads targeted to males with erotic images of women. Supposedly the objectification of women's bodies provided an aura of masculinity to the accompanying shopping ads. By tying sex directly to consumption, the magazines literally wanted to teach men to love shopping.

Esquire pioneered eroticized male consumption. First published in 1933, the core concept of the magazine was articulated by its editor Arnold Gingrich:

> It is our belief, in offering *Esquire* to the American male, that we are only getting around at last to a job that should have been done a long time ago. . . . The general magazines, in the mad scramble to increase the woman readership that seems to be so highly prized by national advertisers, have bent over backwards in catering . . . to the feminine audience.[41]

The founders believed a magazine targeted to the right male demographics would attract national advertisers. Also in the words of historian Kenon Breazeale, "*Esquire's* founders were fearful that their magazine's interest in apparel, food, decor, and so on might make it appear to be targeted at homosexuals."[42]

Designed for upper middle-class males, columns included advice to men on food, drink, gardening, and etiquette. All columns followed an editorial formula supporting the idea that males were actually better than women at cooking, mixing drinks, gardening, and hosting parties. One result was the magazine's success in attracting ads from the beer, wine, and liquor industries. Also the magazine garnered a large number of ads for men's apparel.

To avoid being seen as a magazine for homosexuals, the magazine featured eroticized female images. However, this had to be done in a manner that did not appear pornographic and offend upper middle-class readers. This was accomplished with pinups and centerfolds of illustrations by George Petty, which became known as "Petty Girls." Petty Girls were White women with erotically proportioned large breasts, long slender legs, and small waists and buttocks. In a similar fashion, *Esquire's* covers were noted in the industry for linking "heterosexual social life . . . [with] female anatomy."[43] *Esquire's* cartoons focused on erotic themes with unsuspecting nude women being chanced on by plumbers, burglars, firefighters, and window washers. The favorite, according to Breazeale, was the artist and nude female model where the artist is more interested in leering than painting.[44] Cartoons additionally featured two female types. The gold digger was willing to sell sex, whereas the African-American domestic freely gave it away.

First published in 1953, *Playboy* elaborated on *Esquire's* techniques by incorporating serious fiction and nonfiction with centerfolds, pinups, and advice on cooking, mixing drinks, and male etiquette. Based on *Esquire's* history, Breazeale rejected the often repeated crediting of *Playboy* "with first organizing and exploiting consuming masculine ideological work."[45] After the 1970s, *Playboy* would be accused of exploiting women's bodies for the purpose of stimulating male consumer desires. However, by this time, advertisers were freely targeting male consumers. *Esquire* and *Playboy* paved the way for including men in the advertised consumer's market.

Esquire and *Playboy* provided an alternative fantasy world to that of the cowboy and warrior. Certainly less violent, the *Playboy* man could fantasize mixing drinks for a beautiful woman in a luxury urban apartment, or he could dream of gliding into a nightclub dressed in the height of fashion with a Petty Girl on his arm. He could imagine sipping champagne while soaking in a hot tub filled with nude women. For the suburban male washing his car, there was now the option of escaping through images of the macho cowboy, the warrior, or the debonair womanizer and consumer.

LIBERATING THE TEXTBOOK TOWN HOUSEWIFE
FOR MORE CONSUMPTION

As the color and setting changed in Textbook Town, women's textbook images changed from being a dependent housewife to include personal freedom outside the home. In its 1966 founding statement, the National Orga-

women's History Project 1970s

nization for Women (NOW) emphasized that public schools were "the key to effective participation in today's economy . . . [and they should educate women] to her full potential of human ability."[46] The organization engaged in a variety of tactics to change women's education ranging from equal treatment in sports programs to eliminating bias in college admissions. Working actively for the passage of Title IX of the 1972 Higher Education Act, NOW could claim an important role in ensuring equal treatment for women in vocational education, athletic programs, textbooks, and the curriculum. The 1976 Educational Equity Act authorized development of a nonsexist curricula for the public schools. Also in the 1970s, the National Women's History Project pressured publishers to include more women's history in public school textbooks.[47]

Besides changes in public school textbooks that resulted in depicting women in a variety of occupations, schools encouraged women's sports and gender-integrated vocational courses. Media responded with movies and TV programs depicting women as professionals, workers, living as independent singles, and divorced. The public images found in the 1950s' Textbook Town became a thing of the past.

New feminist images were used by the advertising industry. Maidenform bra ads showing political buttons on women's chests resulted in double-digit sales increases. The buttons proclaimed, "No Means No," "My Body My Choice," and "Right to Life." The accompanying ad line read, "Isn't it great when a woman's mind gets as much support as her body?"[48] Nike increased its sales to women by 40% in the 1990s with ads designed to make women feel empowered.[49] In contrast to 1920s ads that promised women weight reduction by smoking, Virginia Slims' cigarette ads of the 1970s declared, "You've Come a Long Way, Baby!"[50]

Products originally marketed with dependent and submissive female images were now targeted to independent women. For instance, a 1988 ad for Revlon's Charlie perfume showed the back of a woman and man dressed in business clothes with both carrying briefcases. The woman's hand was shown patting the man's buttock with the caption reading, "She's Very Charlie."[51] In the 1930s, Tampax pioneered independent women's ads by showing a woman diving off a swimming board with the caption, "In 1936, Tampax invented a little something for women who had things to do."[52] In 1990, Tampax ads associated the product with female political activism as represented by environmentalism. The ad featured the Helen Reddy song "I am Woman" with the line, "I am woman, hear me roar, in numbers too big to ignore." The ad opened with newsreel clips of WWII's Women's Air Force. The ad moved to a 1990s scene emphasizing that Tampax was biodegradable. In it a young woman romped in a field of green as a voice-over proclaimed, "We thought you'd feel good knowing that more women trust their bodies to the tampon that's very, very kind to the earth."[53]

The 1950s housewife was reborn in the 1990s as *Good Housekeeping* magazine's "The New Traditionalist," which was described as a "reaffirmation of family values unmatched in recent history."[54] The ad language supporting the concept emphasized the ever-present word *choice*. Regarding the issue of work versus staying home, Carl Casselman, creative director of Jordan, McGrath, Case & Taylor, said, "We're saying they have a choice."[55] Supposedly the Yankelovich market research firm discovered the New Traditionalist and described it as a combination of family values of the 1940s and 1950s and personal choice values of the 1960s and 1970s.[56] In ads, personal choice meant consumer choice.

The real meaning of the new educational feminism for advertising and consumerism was exemplified by Parker Pen's 1974 TV ad "Finishing School." Listed by Kanner as one of the top 100 TV ads, the ad opened in a British finishing school where obviously wealthy students were being prepared for a final lesson on "how to spend Daddy's lovely money." The teacher commanded, "Checkbooks open, girls. Pens at the ready." When a student pulled out an unacceptable pen, the teacher warned her that she should not shop with a poor quality pen. The teacher gave the girl a Parker Pen in white rolled gold and declared that it was easy to write a check while shopping with "a pen with style, a pen with elan. A Parker lady in white rolled gold. Words just seem to roll from its tip. Signatures just flow with a flourish. Now, then, altogether girls."[57] In this manner, the educational reforms promising greater independence for women merged in the advertising world with the consumer market.

MOVIES AND THE RACIAL INTEGRATION
OF CAPITALISM

It was the movie industry that actually pioneered the idea of integrating previously excluded racial groups into the general consumer economy. Corresponding with the efforts of the American Way campaign to gain access for probusiness messages in the media, Eric Johnston, president of the U.S. Chamber, replaced Will Hays, who resigned in 1945, as head of the Motion Picture Producers and Distributors of America. Johnston quickly changed the name of the organization to the Motion Picture Association of America. Previous to this appointed, Johnston had proclaimed that "All Americans are capitalist."[58]

Eric Johnston believed that integration of all racial groups into the American consumer market was necessary for the United States to gain economic superiority over the Soviet Union. Johnston brought to Hollywood an economic vision formed during his years as businessman and president of the U.S. Chamber of Commerce. Born in 1896 in Spokane, Washington,

Johnston organized a successful electrical supply company in Spokane and became active in local civic affairs. In 1931, he became president of the Spokane Chamber of Commerce and in 1942 president of the U.S. Chamber of Commerce. His economic views were explained in his 1944 book, *America Unlimited: The Case for a People's Capitalism.*

Similar to the American Way public relations campaign, Johnston advocated greater cooperation between local Chambers of Commerce and school systems to ensure that educational programs served the needs of American business. Johnston believed economic prosperity required some collaboration between business and government. Johnston wrote, "Americans will accept collective action through their government but only to achieve purposes which cannot be achieved by private capital."[59]

Ending racism was part of Johnston's economic agenda. A member of the NAACP, he proclaimed racism a destructive economic force because it kept businesses from adequately using human resources because they could not hire the best workers. In the book's conclusion, he used the image of blending metals to describe the importance of developing racial and cultural tolerance in American society. He wrote, "It is thus with the American, who fuses in his blood and his spirit the virtues and vitalities of many races, creeds, and cultures-giving us an amalgam that is new, unique, and immeasurably strong. That is why tolerance is necessarily and rightly a supreme American characteristic." Johnston claimed it was only "crackpots and psychopaths . . . who teach race hatreds."[60]

In a 1945 speech to the Writers' War Board, Johnston tied the theme of intolerance to the management of public opinion. Linking prejudice and intolerance to the quality of the American economy, he called on the gathered writers and their colleagues in the movies, theater, radio, and the press to use their influence to fight racism. "You are the people with direct access to the mind," he told the writers, "and what is more important, to the heart and emotions of the American people." He urged them to work cooperatively to eliminate racism. "Surely," he told the writers, "the businessman and the artist share responsibility in eradicating the myth of group or class superiority." Again he stressed the importance of eliminating intolerance for economic development: "Wherever we erect barriers on the grounds of race and religion, or of occupational or professional status, we hamper the fullest expansion of our economic society. Intolerance is destructive. Prejudice produces no wealth. Discrimination is a fool's economy."[61]

During Johnston's early years in Hollywood, major studios were willing to explore racial themes. Two important films produced by Darryl Zanuck, *Gentleman's Agreement (1947)* and *Pinky (1949),* dealt with the issue of prejudice. *Pinky* created a stir in Southern states in its portrayal of a White-skinned but partly African-American nurse who traveled from the North to Mississippi.

Another movie, *Lost Boundaries,* was banned in Memphis, Tennessee, because it dealt with "social equality between whites and Negroes in a way that we do not have in the South."[62] The movie portrayed the problems of an African-American physician who passes as White. In *1949,* the Supreme Court of Tennessee upheld the right of the Memphis censorship board to ban the movie *Curley* because it showed, according to the chair of the censorship board, "little negroes [mixed with whites in a classroom], as the South does not permit negroes in white schools nor recognize social equality between the races even in children."[63] Eric Johnston reacted to the Curley decision with the vow that the MPA "intends to meet the issue of political censorship head-on in the highest court."[64]

It was the U.S. Supreme Court's ruling on *Pinky* that finally resolved the issue of municipal and state censorship boards prohibiting the showing of films dealing with racial issues. In 1952, the U.S. Supreme Court overturned the conviction of a Texas theater owner for showing *Pinky.* The *Pinky* case limited the ability of Southern censors to ban movies containing racial themes. The decision dealt with the denial by the censors in Marshall, Texas, to license a showing of *Pinky* because the film was "of such character to be prejudicial to the best interests of the people of said City." The theater owner ignored the ban and was convicted of violating the local censorship law. The U.S. Supreme Court dismissed the conviction as a violation of the First Amendment. This court decision supported Johnston's hopes of achieving racially integrated capitalism with movies that dealt realistically with racial issues.[65]

ADDING COLOR TO TV

It was not just a matter of racial inclusion. It was also a matter of racial stereotypes. This was the major issue over the representation of people of color on TV. For instance, when "Amos 'n' Andy" made its debut on CBS in 1951 with an all African-American cast, the NAACP immediately campaigned to get it off the air. CBS founder William Paley recalled, "Five days after the first broadcast, the National Association for the Advancement of Colored People denounced the show as insulting to blacks. The television show, under attack by black leaders for its entire life, left the network after two seasons."[66] The protest, according to Historian Thomas Cripps, came from the African-American middle class because they worried that the program left audiences with the impression that all African Americans were ignorant and rowdy. According to Cripps, the African-American community was divided over the program. African-American actors saw the program opening doors to employment, whereas other African Americans enjoyed the program and questioned the charge of racism. The sponsor of the program, Blatz Beer, released a poll showing that 77% of African-American New Yorkers liked the program.[67]

Ebony's editors and the NAACP, according to Cripps, led "the black middle class in challeng[ing] what they took to be a parody of their historical struggle for social mobility in a hostile society."[68] In fact, the NAACP was not successful in convincing all African Americans that the show was their enemy. Cripps concluded that Blatz withdrew its sponsorship for a more prestigious show, the "Four Star Playhouse," and not because of the objections of the NAACP.[69] In the light of Cripps' argument, it would be difficult to claim a major victory for the NAACP, but one could assume that the organization's protest played some role in Blatz's decision to end its sponsorship.

Television advertisers and programmers were caught between potential objections from civil rights groups representing non-White racial groups and racist White viewers. As civil rights activities increased in the 1950s, many advertisers refused to sponsor programs that might give the impression of supporting civil rights. One of the first victims of these fears was a 1957–1958 miniseries on the Civil War called "The Gray Ghost." The series presented a romantic portrayal of Confederate Colonel John Singleton Mosby and his band of raiders. It premiered in September 1957 when the civil rights confrontations occurred at Central High School in Little Rock, Arkansas. Fearing entanglement in civil rights issues, advertisers withdrew support from the program. Another source of problems were TV broadcasts of movies. In 1957, many Southern stations refused to air the African-American musical *Cabin in the Sky*. Broadcasts of the movies *Go, Man, Go*, about the Harlem Globetrotters, and *The Jackie Robinson Story* met with Southern resistance. In the early 1960s, Monitor South was organized to coordinate the denial network programming involving racial themes and social equality.[70]

Networks tried to balance these conflicting pressures by, as NBC named its policy in the 1950s, *integration without identification*. This meant the avoidance of racial themes on TV, but the use of African-American actors in minor parts. In 1957, an NBC official stated: "It is so easy, really, in casting for sympathetically portrayed roles to hire actors whose racial derivation is apparent . . . I hope you have noticed here and there everything from taxidrivers to newspapermen, from doctors to social workers, played by competent Negro actors or actors of other racial minority derivation."[71]

These slight gains did not appease civil rights organizations. Under continued criticism, CBS announced in 1962 a policy of "no discrimination because of race, creed, religion, or national origin." In 1963, the American Federation of Television and Radio Artists issued a declaration of nonbias. Yet these pronouncements seemed to have little effect on the actual images in TV programming. A survey in 1963 found that a New York City viewer on an average evening would see three African Americans, only one of these for longer than 1 minute. An editorial in the *Daily Defender* on June 11, 1963, complained that "the TV industry as a whole is still perpetuating a picture of lily-white America on video in keeping with the 'boob tube' concept."[72]

The pressure of political events forced a revolution in African-American TV images. The 1963 March on Washington set the stage for a number of TV documentaries. ABC produced a five-part series, "Crucial Summer," presenting African Americans in a heroic struggle to overcome segregation and prejudice. Featured on the series were Roy Wilkins and Martin Luther King, Jr. An NBC special, "The American Revolution of '63," devoted 5½ hours over 5 weeks to examining the civil rights movement.[73]

A 1966 U.S. Court of Appeals' decision forced Southern TV stations to show programs with racial themes. The case involved TV station WLBT in Jackson, Mississippi. The first complaints against the station were made in 1955 to the Federal Communications Commission (FCC) when a network program on race relations featuring the General Counsel of the NAACP was cut off and replaced by a sign flashing "Sorry, Cable Trouble." Complaints were again lodged in 1957 for the broadcast of a program urging racial segregation, and the subsequent refusals by the station to broadcast opposing viewpoints. Similar charges regarding the presentation of only one viewpoint were filed in 1962 after the outbreak of civil rights demonstrations at the University of Mississippi.[74]

The U.S. Court of Appeals considered the case after the FCC granted a 1-year license renewal over petitioners' protests. The Court's ruling made it possible for organized groups to directly influence the broadcasting industry. Five years after the decision, the journal *Broadcasting* summarized the impact of the decision:

> The case did more than establish the right of the public to participate in a station's license renewal hearing. It did even more than encourage minority groups around the country to assert themselves in broadcast matters at a time when unrest was growing and blacks were becoming more activist. It provided practical lessons in how pressure could be brought, in how the broadcast establishment could be challenged.[75]

Greater public participation made it easier to challenge images disseminated by TV. Media advocacy groups were formed representing African Americans, women, homosexuals, and others. The TV industry now confronted a variety of organizations concerned about the image of their constituents on TV.

Besides the NAACP and CORE, groups such as NOW set up special media task forces. In 1970, NOW announced its intention to change "the derogatory, demeaning and stereotyped images of women presented by

broadcast programming and advertising."[76] Other groups organized to protect their TV images, including the National Black Media Coalition, the
Italian-American League to Combat Defamation, the German-American
Anti-Defamation League, the Polish-American Guardian Society, the Tribal
Indian Land Rights Association, and the Gay Media Task Force. Tom Ker-
sey, an ABC vice-president, estimated at the time that "any challenge to a
station would be an enormous threat. [And] one of our stations was worth
between $35 and $40 million."[77]

The result was an interplay between the desires of advocacy groups to
manage TV images and the needs of the TV industry to control the power
of the advocacy groups. In *Target: Prime Time: Advocacy Groups and the Struggle over Entertainment Television*, Kathryn Montgomery traced the history of
strategies developed by the networks for controlling advocacy groups. For
instance, Mexican Americans protested TV characters showing Mexican
Americans as meek and hat in hand. The advocacy group Justicia demanded TV networks put aside $10 million for shows portraying Chicano
characters in a positive manner. In 1971, Justicia launched challenges to all
California TV licenses. Justicia was joined by the Mexican-American Anti-
Defamation Committee, the League of United Latino Citizens, and the National Latino Media Coalition to drive two well-known Mexican-American
characters off the TV screen. One was the "Frito Bandito" used in commercials for Frito Corn Chips. The cartoon character was charged with creating
a racist image of Mexican Americans as sneaky thieves. Another was "Jose
Jimenez," who, it was charged, created the image of Mexican Americans being happy go lucky and not very bright. In response, ABC began hiring
technical consultants from advocacy groups. ABC invited leaders from
Justicia to review scripts containing Mexican-American characters. This policy did not stop criticism of networks' failure to include Mexican-American
characters in programs. In addition, advocacy groups were invited to
prescreen programs, and networks began to hire minorities into their departments of standards and practices.[78]

Which group represented a particular community? For instance, should
Mexican Americans be represented by Justicia or the Mexican-American
Anti-Defamation Committee? This question was answered by the one-voice
concept, where a network identified a single organization to represent a
whole group. Of course TV networks worked with the most moderate organizations. In the case of Mexican Americans, the networks finally decided
to work closely with the Nosotros, an advocacy group for Latino actors,
rather than more politically active groups. Summarizing the evolution of
network management of advocacy groups, Montgomery concluded that advocacy groups "would encounter a team of experts within the networks,
equipped with a sophisticated set of skills and strategies designed to mini-
mize disruption and maximize friendly, cooperative relationships."[79]

According to Montgomery, gay activists groups were the most effective in changing network policies. One reason was the large number of gays employed by the industry. Many of these insiders supplied information to outside organizations. For instance, a script for an upcoming episode of "Marcus Welby, M.D." was smuggled out of ABC in 1973 and given to the Gay Activist Alliance (GAA). In the episode, Marcus Welby advises a married man concerned about his homosexual tendencies that he would not fail as a husband and father if he suppressed his gay tendencies. The smuggled script caused angry members of the GAA to descend on network offices. Afterward networks consulted regularly with gay activists about any scripts dealing with homosexuality.[80]

An integrated TV market occurred with the program "All in the Family." The genius of the program was its appeal to both White racist and non-White groups. The main character was the racist and bigoted Archie Bunker. Norman Lear, the program's producer, consciously sought to fight racism and bigotry by having Archie use words such as *spades, spics, spooks, schwartzes, coons, coloreds,* and *chinks*. The program broke all the traditional TV taboos by dealing with issues such as homosexuality, race, female equality, and birth control. A spin-off program, "Maude," caused a storm of protest the following year when it dealt with the issue of abortion. *Time* magazine noted in 1972 that in the wake of "All in the Family" there were 20 new series dealing with controversial themes.[81]

Although "All in the Family" dealt with White racism, the majority of TV shows presented non-White characters as assimilated into White culture or as unrealistic cultural images. During what media historian J. Fred MacDonald called "The Golden Age of Blacks in Television: The Late 1960s," there were over two dozen programs featuring African Americans as leading characters. In addition, there were 19 TV series with supporting African-American characters. Programs with leading roles played by African Americans ranged from "I Spy" and "Mission Impossible" to "The Bill Cosby Show" and "The Young Lawyers." MacDonald contended that "I Spy" had the greatest effect. The show was the first network dramatic series to feature an African-American actor, Bill Cosby. Cosby's character projected a new image of African Americans to White TV audiences. He was equal to White characters in his encounters with foreign spies, women, government leaders, and criminals. In an early episode, he committed the revolutionary act, at least for TV, of kissing a Japanese woman. Cosby's character broke the unspoken TV taboo against showing African Americans kissing and demonstrating affection.[82]

Television images were integrated without any major changes in content. Cosby's part on "I Spy" could have been played by a White without any noticeable change in the character. Certainly, Cosby was not playing a part that would have required an African American. No major African-American themes or issues were raised by the program. In fact, "The Bill Cosby Show," which by the 1990s was the most popular program on TV, featured an African-American family that could have been easily interchanged with any White upper middle-class family.

The major complaints about TV programs featuring African Americans was their depiction, or lack of depiction, of African-American culture. After reviewing the history of African-American sitcoms in the 20th century, Angela Nelson wrote, "Black sitcoms are not 'Black' in that they exhibit an African American world view or a Black philosophy of life. Rather, they are 'Black' because the performers are Black and their characters are supposedly dealing with their sitcom situations from a 'Black' perspective."[83] She argued that the TV shows "Julia" and "The Bill Cosby Show" in the late 1960s presented African-American characters as fully integrated into White culture. In the 1970s, TV introduced a form of assimilated hybrid minstrelsy or coon characters in the programs "The Jeffersons" and "Sanford and Son." In the 1980s and 1990s, the most popular African-American TV show was Bill Cosby's "The Cosby Show." Although it avoided *coon characters*, the program portrayed the life of an upper middle-class African-American family that was fully assimilated into White culture.[84]

The transformation of Native American characters was the most unrealistic integration of positive non-White images. Traditionally, Indians in movies and TV programs were portrayed, except for those who were subservient to Whites such as Tonto in "The Lone Ranger" radio and TV series, as blood-thirsty savages fighting against the expansion of the noble White settlers and cowboys into the West. After the civil rights movement, Native American images were pacified and portrayed as protectors of nature and the environment. Suddenly Native American rituals became popular spiritual events rather than pagan affronts to Christianity. The romanticization of Native American life, like the portrayal of African Americans assimilated into White culture, provided images that were unrealistic and characterized Indians as the exotic other.[85]

This transition in Native American images was exemplified by an ad selected by Kanner as one of the top 100. Research found that the ad was the most recognized in the 1970s. Entitled "Keep America Beautiful: Crying Indian," the 1970 TV ad opened with Cherokee Iron Eyes Cody paddling a canoe past smokestacks onto a littered beach. A voice-over complained, "Some people have a deep, abiding respect for the beauty that was once this country. And some people don't." Then an unfinished fast-food meal was tossed from a passing car landing at Cody's feet. The announcer concluded, "People start pollution; people can stop it."[86]

Highlighting the transition in Native American images was that fact that Iron Eyes Cody originally acted in many cowboy movies opposite John Wayne. The ad was paid for by Keep America Beautiful advocacy group and, according to Kanner, "it has amassed 24 billion-plus household impressions, more than any other single TV spot—both commercial and public—in the history of television. Research showed that during the 1970s, 94 percent of viewers recognized the ad."[87] The ad campaign's printed posters showed Cody's head and braids with an overlaid title "Pollution: It's a crying Shame."[88]

Civil rights, advocacy groups, and market research changed TV programming. There appeared positive TV images, and sometimes overromanticized images, of all racial groups. Watching TV, all groups could now feel part of the American dream. Of particular importance were TV ads that brought all people together in the same consumer market.

THE UNDERCLASS AND BIG BIRD: THE GROWTH OF A COMMON MEDIA AND CONSUMER EXPERIENCE

Originally "Sesame Street" was targeted at underclass children, but it eventually became a common media and consumer experience for many American children. It exemplified the integration of Textbook Town by showing children engaged in interracial and intercultural play, singing, and acting. As in Textbook Town, people were generally happy in "Sesame Street."

"Sesame Street" was and is important as a common cultural experience that created common cultural icons in the public mind such as Big Bird, Bert and Ernie, Oscar the Grouch, and Elmo. Most college students raised in the United States respond "yes" when I ask, "Did you learn the alphabet and numbers while watching 'Sesame Street'." Besides being a common educational experience, the program became a common consumer experience with brand-name product spin-offs including dolls, videos, and games.

Intended as an educational program for underclass children, "Sesame Street" was inspired by a belief that TV could be both an educator and a social reformer. The program was first shown in 1969 when race riots were occurring across the country. Originally it was thought of as an educational tool that would break the cycle of poverty. The program was created by the Children's Television Workshop with funding from the Carnegie Corporation and the Ford Foundation. The development of educational children's TV programs was considered necessary, in the words of one federal official, Lee Loevinger, because commercial TV was "the literature of the illiterate; the culture of the lowbrow; the wealth of the poor; the privilege of the underprivileged; the exclusive club of the excluded masses . . . a golden goose that lays scrambled eggs."[89]

In the 1960s, there was strong criticism of the 1950s' image of the housewife using TV as a babysitter, particularly in low-income families. Television was considered a source of intellectual pap for the masses. In the 1960s, Arthur Schlesinger, Jr., historian and advisor to Senator Adlai Stevenson and President John F. Kennedy, worried that TV was breeding disrespect for intellectuals and destroying the quality of American life. "I cannot repress my feelings," he wrote, "that in the main, television has been a great bust." He urged government to improve the quality of TV "because there seems no other way to rescue television from the downward spiral of competitive debasement."[90] Child-care advocate Dr. Benjamin Spock wrote President Kennedy that instead of TV instilling virtue in the citizen, "there is the constant search for the commonest level of taste in passive entertainment . . . used, in turn, to sell goods, in a manner which breeds insincerity and cynicism, and which appeals always to more gratification."[91] Writing in the *Saturday Review*, critic Robert Lewis Shayon expressed disgust at a *1958* episode of "Leave It to Beaver" where the main character was upset at a school IQ text that accidentally classified him as a genius. Beaver was portrayed as shunning the title of *genius*. For Shayon, this was another example of TV appealing to the masses by deprecating the intellect.[92]

The Carnegie Corporation, a major funder of "Sesame Street," sponsored the Carnegie Commission on Educational Television, which issued reports criticizing children's TV. The president of the Carnegie Corporation, Alan Pifer, was concerned with both poverty and the quality of TV. He believed the Carnegie Corporation should support "four basic principles: the right to a job for anyone who needs to or wants to work; equal opportunity and fair rewards for everyone in all sectors of employment; development and utilization of the abilities of every citizen; and maximum flexibility for each person in the organization of his or her own pattern of life."[93] Reflecting in 1982 on the activities of the Carnegie Corporation, Pifer wrote that without programs of social justice and welfare,

> there lies nothing but increasing hardship for ever-growing numbers, a mounting possibility of severe social unrest, and the consequent development among the upper classes and the business community of fear for the survival of our capitalist economic system. Just as we built the general welfare state in the 1930s and expanded it in the 1960s as a safety valve for the easing of social tension, so will we do it again in the 1980s. Any other path is simply too risky.[94]

In the minds of all those involved in "Sesame Street," TV was the third educational institution along with the family and public schools. Also there was the hope that TV would be a better educator than the public schools and save the entire educational system. This utopian vision included the time-honored belief from the 19th century that education could end poverty by preparing students for equal participation in competition for jobs— or in other words, equality of opportunity. In 1967, the Carnegie Corporation's Commission on Educational Television recommended that TV be used for the promotion of social justice and education. In reference to the educational potential of TV, the Commission's report stated, "Important as this can be for adults, the informal educational potential of Public Television is greatest of all for children."[95] The Commission suggested that TV focus on preparing preschool children for formal education. "Public Television programs," the report stated, "should give great attention to the informal educational needs of preschool children, particularly to interest and help children whose intellectual and cultural preparation might otherwise be less than adequate."[96]

Lloyd Morrisett played a leading role in "Sesame Street's" creation. He believed TV could be a substitute for the national shortage of kindergarten and nursery schools. Believing preschool education was important for the cognitive development of children, he worried that preschool programs "would slowly, if at all, reach many of the children who needed them, particularly underprivileged children for whom preschool facilities might not be available."[97] The answer to this problem, he felt, lay in the ability of TV to reach enormous numbers of preschool children. As Morrisett conceptualized the project, TV could be a partner with public schools in the general education of children. It would be the third educator. "The real answer to problems of early education," Morrisett wrote, "is for the total culture of childhood, including television as an important element, to work in harmony with the family and later the school."[98]

In 1968, the Children's Television Workshop was organized, and on November 10, 1969, the first production of "Sesame Street" was broadcast. The chief advisor and chairman to the Board of Advisors was Gerald Lesser, Bigelow Professor of Education and Developmental Psychology at Harvard. Lesser was the guiding hand in developing educational goals for "Sesame Street." Unlike many others, Lesser felt education was limited in its role in solving the world's problems. He wrote that, "Educators cannot remedy the injustices to minorities in our society or create new life styles or new communities to replace deteriorating ones. Yet they sometimes act as if they think they can." This attitude tempered the original focus on helping children of the poor.[99] Although Lesser saw a limited educational role in social reform, he did believe that something drastic should be done about educational problems in the United States. Writing about the $50 billion that was spent on a "massive educational superstructure which holds captive over fifty million children," he complained, "we are failing to educate our children, either disastrously or to a degree no worse than the failures of other social and political institutions, is almost beyond dispute."[100]

Lesser hoped TV would rescue the entire educational system from failure. He believed TV instruction could be superior to public school instruction. Public schooling, he maintained, depended on control of the student by others, public humiliation, and the continuous threat of failure. Television contained none of these elements. In front of the TV, Lesser argued, the child learned without fear of a teacher and threats of humiliation. The TV set could not punish the child. In addition, the child could control the learning process by controlling the TV set. Therefore, Lesser believed that TV was an ideal educator because it was not punitive and provided a shelter from the emotional stress of society. "We may regret the conditions in our society that make sanctuaries necessary and must guard against a child's permanent retreat into them," Lesser wrote, "but sanctuaries are needed, and television is one of the few shelters children have."[101]

Lesser believed TV was a superior teacher because it could be entertaining. He argued that traditional educators separated entertainment from education. In fact, many believed that entertainment would contaminate education. Lesser referred to this as a *lunatic* view of education and thought TV was an ideal vehicle for educating through entertainment.

Besides lauding the potential educational value of TV, Lesser was impressed by the statistics on TV viewing. Using calculations made in 1967, Lesser estimated that in homes with preschool children the TV was on 54 hours per week. On the average, a high school graduate spent 12,000 hours in school and 15,000 hours watching TV. In fact, the high school graduate spent more time watching TV than was spent at any other activity.

The use of TV as an educator seemed to contradict charges that TV viewing was a passive and mind-numbing experiencing. Lesser argued that a great deal of learning takes place through modeling. Children do not need to interact to learn, according to Lesser; they can model themselves after TV characters. In fact, modeling fit Lesser's concept of a nonpunitive form of education. "The child," Lesser wrote, "imitates the model without being induced or compelled to do so. . . . By watching televised models, children learn both socially desirable and undesirable behaviors."[102] Television, Lesser argued, could provide models that demonstrated acceptable behaviors.

In addition to modeling behavior, Lesser believed TV could create myths to guide children's actions. In Lesser's words, TV could provide "a vision of the world as it might be." These myths were created by the presentation of what Lesser called *simple goodness*. He believed that children did not learn from preaching. Considering TV's role in presenting life's tensions and deprivations, Lesser reasoned, "Surely it can create others that help them toward a more humane vision of life."[103]

The decision was made to present urban life as "a vision of the world as it might be" and not reality. "Sesame Street" joined Textbook Town in presenting scenes of a harmonious world. Lesser believed that little could be gained in showing to the child living in an urban ghetto the harsh realities of life. As program planning evolved, there was a drift toward presenting the sweeter side of life. In giving only the positive side, they realized that they might be accused of presenting a sugar-coated world. This approach was by a program designed to show children how an urban bus driver and passengers acted on a trip around the city. "Now, we all know that a bus driver is often not our best example of someone who is courteous and civil," Lesser wrote. "But on the 'Sesame Street' bus trip, the driver responds to his passengers' hellos and thank-yous, tells a child who cannot locate his money, 'That's all right, you can pay me tomorrow,' and upon seeing a young woman running after his bus just as it has left the curb, actually stops to let her on." Lesser referred to this as an "outrageous misrepresentation" of most urban transportation systems, but he justified it as presenting a model of behavior that would guide children to a better world. Lesser maintained, "We wanted to show the child what the world is like when people treat each other with decency and consideration. Our act of faith . . . was that young children will learn such attitudes if we take the trouble to show them some examples, even if we stretch familiar reality a bit in order to do so."[104]

Given the desire to present a model of an idealized world, "Sesame Street" was harmoniously and racially integrated. Like the new Textbook Town of the 1960s, this presentation sugar-coated the harsh realities of racial conflict in American society. A criticism that Lesser recognized was that the program taught "minority-group children to accept quietly middle class America's corrupt demands to subjugate themselves."[105]

Although doubting the ability of educational TV to end poverty, Lesser did believe TV was the key to reforming the educational system. He wanted to create a program for all children. In Lesser's words, "To succeed, a national television series must attract as large a national audience as possible, including children from all social classes and cultural groups and from all geographic regions."[106] The decision to seek a national audience resulted in "Sesame Street" becoming a common cultural experience. Yet this also created a fear that the program might increase the educational gap between poor and rich children. Lesser wrote, "We hoped that poor children would learn as much and that the gap would not be widened, despite the fact that almost all comparisons of educational progress show middle-class children proceeding more rapidly."[107] The solution he offered was to make the series appealing to low-income children and to encourage viewing in low-income families. Although Lesser felt negatively about public schooling, he argued that the only realistic goal was to emphasize an education that would prepare children to enter school. This approach tied the program directly to the needs of formal schooling.

Preparing children for school and helping low-income children determined the basic shape of "Sesame Street." The staff believed that low-income parents wanted their children to achieve in the basic subjects of reading, writing, and arithmetic. The major complaint of these parents, the

Sesame Street

staff understood, was the failure of the school to teach these subjects. Therefore, the staff concluded that the program should focus on preparation for learning these subjects in school. According to Lesser, teaching the alphabet was the most controversial decision on preparation for school. This created "howls of repugnance . . . over . . . use of the new technology to teach what appears to be an arbitrary and useless skill."[108] Yet, it was argued that the alphabet was essential for early reading. What TV could accomplish was to make memorizing the alphabet a form of entertainment.

During its early years, "Sesame Street" scored a major success in reaching low-income children. During its first year, almost 50% of the potential preschool audience was estimated to have watched the program, including children in day care and other prekindergarten programs serving poor children. The program was watched by 91% of the at-home children in low-income Bedford-Stuyvesant and Harlem sections of New York City. Eighty-eight percent of low-income families interviewed in Chicago tuned their sets to "Sesame Street."[109]

Similar to advertising efforts to convince housewives to watch daytime TV and use it as a babysitter, advertising campaigns were used to attract viewers to "Sesame Street." This advertising effort included "Sesame Street" clubs, door-to-door solicitation of viewers, a *Sesame Street Magazine,* and announcements in libraries, schools, and community organizations. In Chicago, 120 mothers in low-income areas conducted "Sesame Street" viewing sessions. A similar project was conducted in the Mexican-American section of Los Angeles. The Children's Television Workshop ran a Neighborhood Youth Corps Project that involved adolescents from poor families in teaching preschool children and focused on viewing "Sesame Street." During the first year, 240 adolescents worked in viewing centers with 1,500 children. The following year, the numbers increased to 1,200 adolescents helping 15,000 low-income children of the poor in 13 different cities. By 1972, there were 10,000 tutors helping 100,000 preschool children in viewing centers.[110]

Even in the 21st century, "Sesame Street" was marketed as an educational package for caregivers, including preschool programs, babysitters, and parents. On its 2002 Web site, Big Bird was shown standing next to a range of caregivers with the message, "Just like you, part of our work is to find new ways to reach and teach children . . . we want to meet the needs of our 2- and 4-year-old viewers by appealing to the way they think, learn, and explore."[111] In keeping with its idealized world, the Web site announced four new programs designed to help children cope with the September 11, 2002, destruction of the World Trade Center. "The season's premiere episode," the Web site stated, "features a group of heroes from Ground Zero. New York City firefighters arrive on Sesame Street after Alan extinguishes a fire at Hooper's Store. Elmo is frightened at first, but feels much safer after spending time with the firefighters, who take him—and viewers—on a tour of a working firehouse."[111]

Also by the 21st century, the program had created a new consumer market. Elmo, Ernie, Bert, Big Bird, and the Cookie Monster became national icons to sell brand-named products. As icons associated with an educational TV program, they could give brand-named products an aura of educational value.

As caregivers seated their charges in front of the TV to watch "Sesame Street," the were preparing preschoolers for product recognition of toys manufactured by Mattel, Fisher-Price, and Arco. Elmo served as a product figure for Mattel's *Elmo's Dance and Learn Game,* whereas other "Sesame Street" figures were used to sell their puzzles *Puzzle* and *Puzzle: "What's Wrong with this Picture."* Arco toys offered *Sesame Street Games: Electronic Cookie Monster's Kitchen Game* and *Elmo's Count & Pop Balloon Game.* These were only a few of the games and puzzles offered with "Sesame Street" icons, others included *Cookie Monster Wood Board, Sesame Street 24-piece, Big Bird Wood Board,* and *Ernie Wood Board.*[112]

The games and puzzles might be educational, but it would be a stretch of the imagination to label as educational the top-selling "Sesame Street" products. In May 2002, the Amazon Web site listed as the top-selling "Sesame Street" spin-offs an Elmo doll called *Let's Pretend Elmo* and in second place the *Talk With Elmo Cell Phone.* The third and fourth places were occupied by the Fisher-Price's *Sesame Street 11" Baby Tickle Me Big Bird Doll* and *Rock 'N Roll Elmo* (an Elmo doll holding a guitar).[113]

I recognize that commercial children's TV is more exploitive than "Sesame Street." However, "Sesame Street" is packaged as an educational program and promoted for use in day-care centers, preschool programs, and home care. It also has a reputation for promoting cultural and racial harmony and positive gender role models for girls and boys. Also it deals with issues affecting children from low-income families.

"Sesame Street" serves as a good example of the marriage of education, advertising, and consumerism in creating common cultural and consumer knowledge among America's children. "Sesame Street" teaches consumerism by creating brand loyalty or, in this case, loyalty to brand icons. The benign atmosphere created by the educational aspects of the program act as a soft sell. Both children and parents learn to trust characters such as Elmo and Big Bird as they entertain, teach, and provide models of good behavior and a happy world. Those exposed to "Sesame Street" recognize Fisher-Price, Mattel, and Arco toys using "Sesame Street" icons or figures. The trust in the "Sesame Street" figure is transferred from the program to the toy. In this manner, generations of preschoolers learn to trust and shop for familiar brands.

CONCLUSION: ALL PEOPLE CAN CONSUME

An important accomplishment of the civil rights movement was an integration of the consumer market. Positive, if sometimes distorted, images of non-White groups now appeared in textbooks, advertising, movies, and TV. The 1950s suburban-housewife image was replaced with a multitasking woman who could make a choice among being a housewife, an independent-living careerist, or married with a job. The struggle for consumer equality reached preschool children through "Sesame Street." In all cases, equality often meant equality of opportunity to consume.

Consumerism was able to absorb social justice issues and turn them into marketing opportunities. The next stage in consumerism's triumph over the public mind was the themed environment. Beginning with Disneyland and McDonald's in the 1950s, theming quickly spilled over into public spaces with naming rights for sports stadiums, parks, and other public sites being sold to the highest bidders. Every place, including schools, became a marketing opportunity. Consumerism found every opportunity to slip into the public mind as brand loyalty offered certainty in a rapidly changing world.

Chapter 7

Sonya's Choice:
Fast-Food Education

Repeating Sonya's declaration in *Salome of the Tenements*, "Talk about democracy. . . . All I want is to be able to wear silk stockings and Paris hats the same as Mrs. Astorbilt, and then it wouldn't bother me if we have Bolshevism or Capitalism, or if the democrats or the republicans win."[1] To describe is not to criticize. Sonya's choice seems to fulfill the wishes of large numbers of the world's population. Many rush to the integrated life of production, schools, advertising, media, and commodified leisure. Brand loyalty is global and provides a level of certainty in a transient and fluid global society. People relate through the brands they wear, drive, and eat. The world's consumer economy fulfills Simon Patten's vision of consumption spurring humans to work harder for increased production and consumption. People seek entry into national economies that promise greater access to goods resulting in migrations that uproot families and result in cultural conflicts. For many, the modern consumer society is desirable.

This book's goal is to describe the history of the interrelationship among schools, advertising, and media in the evolution of U.S. consumer society. Of primary concern is understanding how future citizens—namely, children—learn to be consumer-citizens. "Sesame Street" exemplifies the marriage of preschool education and media in consumer training and sustains the goal of TV executives in the 1950s of using daytime TV as a babysitter. There are, of course, earlier examples of media and babysitting, such as in the 1930s when students spent after-school hours listening to advertising jingles accompanying their favorite radio programs. Schools remain important sites for consumer education, with advertising invading school buildings, students wearing clothes sporting designer logo, and corporate materials being used in classroom instruction. The early 20th-century dream of women escaping the drudgery of cooking is now realized in the plentiful availability of processed foods and in quick trips to fast-food franchises that also serve as an entertainment spot for children. Commodified entertainment, theme parks, and fast-food establishments seduce children into buying product spin-offs from movies and TV programs.

In this concluding chapter, I examine the education of consumer-citizens in schools and in desiring communities such as theme parks and fast-food establishments. All of these sites in some manner bring together education, advertising, and media in the promotion of a consumerist ideology.

EDUCATING FOR CONSUMPTION

Education is now a form of consumerism. College education is marketed through paid advertising. Textbooks are peddled to local school districts and state departments of education. The importance of the prom declined during the anticonsumerism period of the 1970s, but was reborn in the 1990s as an important element in graduating a full-fledge shopper.[2] Even standardized testing is a consumer item with organizations such as the Educational Testing Service buying advertising space to proclaim that Americans "are united-by race, ethnicity, age, income level, and political persuasion—in the belief that increased resources [for education] and increased accountability [testing] go together."[3] Appearing in the *New York Times*, and possibly other newspapers, the ad was a response to the impression created by newspaper headlines "that," according to the president of Educational Testing Service, Kurt Landgraf, "Americans are sick and tired of standardized tests in schools."[4] In the ad, Landgraf tries to assure readers that these protests are the actions of marginal groups.

Schools are consumer sites. Alex Molnar, author of the best-selling book, *Giving Kids the Business: The Commercialization of America's Schools* and head of the University of Wisconsin's Center for the Analysis of Commercialism in Education, details the extremes that companies, such as Coca-Cola and Pepsi-Cola, use to advertise and sell their products in schools.[5] On September 14, 2000, the U.S. General Accounting Office released a report on the commercialization of U.S. schools. The report stated,

> In-school marketing has become a growing industry. Some marketing professionals are increasingly targeting children in schools, companies are becoming known for their success in negotiating contracts between school districts and beverage companies, and both educators and corporate managers are attending conferences to learn how to increase revenue from in-school marketing for their schools and companies.[6]

The General Accounting Office found the following:

1. About 25% of the nation's middle and high schools now show Channel One, a broadcast of news features and commercials.
2. Two hundred school districts signed exclusive contracts with soft-drink companies to sell their beverages in schools.
3. Students using computers in classrooms are being offered incentives to enter personal data—names, addresses, information on personal habits—which is then sold to advertisers.[7]

Other examples abound including, as I discuss later, the involvement of the fast-food industry in education. In "Education and Commercialization: Raising Awareness and Making Wise Decisions," Lynn Schrum provides other instances of advertising in schools:

1. Eli Lilly representatives discuss Prozac to high school students in Washington, DC.
2. Procter & Gamble sponsors oral hygiene classes in elementary school in return for distributing samples of Crest.
3. National Soft Drink Association provides a poster entitled, "Soft Drinks and Nutrition."
4. M&M candy company declares nutritional value in their products.
5. McGraw-Hill's math book, *Mathematics: Applications and Connections*, currently in use by sixth-, seventh-, and eight-grade students in at least 16 states, inserts products such as Barbie dolls, Big Macs, and Oreo cookies right into math problems. For example, "Will is saving his allowance to buy a pair of Nike shoes that cost $68.25. If Will earns $3.25 per week, how many weeks will Will need to save?"[8]

TEXTBOOKS: ENVIRONMENTALISM AS THE NEW ENEMY

(replaces communism)

Since the disappearance of Russian communism in the 1990s, the primary enemy of consumerism has become environmentalism. A threat to consumerism is seen in calls for reduction of air pollution; increased mileage standards for cars; criticisms of the mass production of sports utility vehicles (SUVS); demands for more stringent controls on pesticides and herbicides; restrictions on the use of snowmobiles, jet skis, all-terrain vehicles, and motor bikes in public parks and recreational sites; reductions in the use of packaging material for consumer items; protests against the building of mega-discount stores; and protection of green spaces in urban and suburban development. For supporters of consumerism, these demands are a threat to the American way of life.

At the 2002 hearings of the Texas State Board of Education, science textbooks were condemned for saying that there was a scientific consensus that the earth's climate was changing because of global warming. This claim was labeled as "anti-technology," "anti-Christian," and "anti-American."[9] Textbook approval by the Texas Board was important because it was only one of two states, the other being California, in which approval occurred at the state level. The Board rejected Jane L. Person's *Environmental Science: How the World Works and Your Place in It* because of statements such as, "Destruction of the tropical rain forest could affect weather over the entire planet" and "Most experts on global warming feel that immediate action should be taken to curb global warming."[10] To gain acceptance by the Texas Board, the statements were changed to: "Tropical rain forest ecosystems impact weather over the entire planet" and "In the past, the earth has been much warmer than it is now, and fossils of sea creatures show us that the sea level was much higher than it is today. So does it really matter if the world gets warmer?"[11]

In 2001, the Texas Board singled out for censorship Daniel Chiras' *Environmental Science: Creating a Sustainable Future*. The book opened with phrases such as, "Things can't go on as they have been," "We must change our ways," "throwaway mentality," and "obsession with growth." The Board attacked the text for using the "oft-used falsehood that over 100 million Americans are breathing unhealthy air."[12]

One text that did win approval was financed by a consortium of mining companies. Entitled *Global Science: Energy, Resources, Environment,* the book was praised before the Texas Board by Duggan Flanakin, formerly of the U.S. Bureau of Mines and currently a member of the Texas Policy Foundation. The book was also commended by Ms. Shore, chair of the Texas Board and co-owner of TEC Well Service. TEC is a producer of gas and oil and repairs and deepens oil wells. From Ms. Shore's perspective, the oil and gas industries "always get a raw deal" in environmental science textbooks.[13] Although environmental science courses threatened rampant consumerism, home economics courses embraced consumerism under the new name Family and Consumer Sciences.

CONSUMER EDUCATION

Floating candles in a hotel's pool to symbolize the new spirit of home economics, organizational leaders adopted the 1993 "Scottsdale Initiative" and changed the field's name to "Family and Consumer Sciences." The term *consumer* in the new name "was viewed not as a subject matter or content area but as recognition that individuals are both family members and consumers."[14] The Scottsdale Initiative officially recognized students as consumers to be trained for future consumption. Translated into middle and high school Family and Consumer Sciences courses, the outcome goal for students was: "Functioning effectively as providers and consumers of goods and services."[15] Besides being a site for advertising and marketing, schools were now engaged in the specific task of teaching consumerism and careers in consumer industries.

The historic role of home economics courses was transformed from teaching women to be scientific producers of food and clothing in the home to preparation for almost complete reliance on consumer products and for work in the food and textile industries. Of course home economics courses had always taught how to be a good shopper through household management of the budget. What was different was the abandonment of home production for complete reliance on the consumption of products. Despite this change, some patterns remained the same. For instance, fashion shows and learning to shop wisely for ready-to-wear clothes were regular features of 1920s' home economics courses. In the 1990s, this instruction continued under the title "Apparel Shopping on the Web."[16]

In 1994, the American Home Economics Association officially changed its name to the American Association of Family and Consumer Sciences. The core values of the newly named organization included preserving the family as the fundamental social unit, supporting diversity and human rights, and protecting the environment. Regarding consumerism, the core values included:

- holistic, interdisciplinary, integrative, and preventive perspectives in addressing the issues of individuals and families as consumers.
- both global and community perspectives when addressing issues of individuals and families as consumers.[17]

In addition, organizational goals included leadership in "impacting the development, delivery and evaluation of consumer goods and services."[18]

The professional organization for middle and secondary school teachers changed its name in 1995 from the Home Economics Education Association to Family and Consumer Sciences Education Association. This newly named organization issued national standards for Family and Consumer Sciences courses.[19] Unlike the early days when home economics courses focused on teaching cooking, sewing, and household management to girls, the new national standards were directed at teaching both females and males about career, family, and consumer roles. In the new standards, cooking classes were replaced with the study of "careers in food production and services" and "careers in food science dietetics, and nutrition." In the early

20th century, the goals of cooking classes for young women were to Americanize immigrants, reform home diets, and turn the housewives into scientific workers. These new standards were geared toward training workers for production of processed and packaged foods. Unlike early sewing instruction, the new standards were strictly geared to careers in the ready-to-wear and related industries or, in the word of the national standards, "careers in textiles and apparels." Whereas early home economics courses sometimes focused on family leisure time activities, the new standards focused on commodified forms of leisure by introducing students to "careers in hospitality, tourism, and recreation." Finally, household management became a study of "careers in housing, interiors, and furnishing."[20]

Changing instruction from how to do something in the home, such as sewing and cooking, to information on possible careers in food and textile production conveys the consumer message that households should rely on prepared food and ready-to-wear clothing. In addition, informing students about careers in tourism and recreation prepares students to think about leisure time activities as a consumer commodity. Consumer science standards reinforce these attitudes. For instance, under the national standard for "Consumer and Family Resources," the goal is: "Demonstrate management of individual and family resources including food, clothing, shelter, health care, recreation, and transportation."[21] This goal simply means learning to budget for the purchase of these items through reasonable use of consumer credit.

There is a critical edge to these national standards. Ideally, courses are not limited to teaching how to shop and use credit. Students are also to be taught the "relationship of the environment to family and consumer resources" and "support consumer rights and responsibilities."[22] Taken to its critical limits, the implementation of these goals would teach students about the potential detrimental effect of consumerism through environmental pollution and the depletion of natural resources. In addition, education about consumer rights could result in consumer activists concerned about the quality and safety of products. In either case, the goal is to educate a responsible consumer-citizen.

The commitment of these new Family and Consumer Sciences to consumerism is highlighted in the national standards' goal: "Analyze interrelationship between the economic system and consumer actions."[23] This represents the triumph of Simon Patten's economic views. It suggests that the economy should be examined from the standpoint of consumer actions, such as consumer confidence and spending. For instance, students learn why retailers and economists worry about holiday purchases, future consumer spending, and measures of consumer confidence. This view of the economy supports public attitudes that measure the success of a Christmas season by consumer spending.

The national standards also reinforce the importance of consumerism in students' minds by informing them of "careers in consumer services." The term *consumer services* suggests activities directly supporting a consumer-based economy. Students are to "Demonstrate skills needed for product development, testing, and presentation."[24] Also under consumer services is "developing a long-term financial management plan." Reflecting the critical edge in Family and Consumer Sciences courses, consumer services also includes analyzing "consumer advocacy" and "resource consumption for conservation and waste management practices."

While schools are teaching consumerism through conveying the message that education is a form of consumption, in-school ads, and consumerism-oriented courses, the school's most important contribution is creating a peer group of teens who relate through brand names and consumerism-oriented activities. The next section examines how the teen cohort of shoppers is now a global phenomenon.

SCHOOLING CREATES A GLOBAL TEEN MARKET

Mass secondary education created a teenage culture discovered by advertisers in the 1940s and 1950s and incarnated in the pages of *Seventeen* magazine. That teen culture is now a global market. Calling them the "new world teens," market researcher Elissa Moses argued, "Teens who speak different languages all speak the same language of global brand consumption. . . . Teens love brands. . . . Brands are passports to global culture." Asking teens worldwide to identify 75 brand icons, she found the five most popular, in order, were Coca-Cola, Sony, Adidas, Nike, and Kodak.[25]

"Unabashed consumerism" is the number one unifier of global teen culture according to Elissa Moses' advertising study, *The $100 Billion Allowance: Accessing the Global Teen Market.* In the upbeat language of advertising, she wrote, "In an age of abundance for much of the world's growing middle class, teens see consumer products as one of the limitless joys of life." Moses' background in marketing provided her with important background knowledge for the survey. Her clients have been The Coca-Cola Company, Calvin Klein, MTV, General Motors, Levi Strauss, Nike, Burger King, Kodak, and the National Basketball Association. Marketers have found the study useful in selling to teens. "Insights from *The $100 Billion Allowance,*" the president of Royal Philips Electronics, Car Boonstra, claimed, "have already helped Philips better connect to global youth."[26] Representing an icon of global teen jeans, Levi Strauss' Presence and Publicity Director, Ray Edmondson, hailed the study for providing "clever tips and very clear steps to help any marketer find the way through to the hearts and minds of today's youth population."[27] The Worldwide Director of Brand Futures Group,

Marian Salzman says, "the best job I've ever seen of breaking down, bite by bite, a look at teen culture in a range of countries and across a range of industries. A bible for anyone doing business targeting global youth."[28] Despite these claims, it is important to note that the Teen World Survey was limited to lower middle and upper middle-class youth and that only two African nations were presented—South Africa and Nigeria. Although the poorest of the poor were not included in the survey, one wonders if their dreams also include consumption of the world's brand-name products.

The existence of a global teen market suggests that most countries have, through schooling and other institutionalized arrangements, separated youth as a distinct cohort group from children and adults. By indirectly creating a segregated cohort group, secondary schools have allowed for specific marketing techniques to be directed at the global adolescent. Moses suggested that there is a relationship between the unstable period of adolescence and brand affiliation. Brands promise a reliable and standard product. They provide an anchor in an uncertain world of adolescence. Faced with an array of products, a brand name provides guidance. The purchase of Coca-Cola, the world's most recognized brand, in any country promises the consumer the same standardized taste. In addition, Moses' study demonstrates that youth culture, particularly youth consumer culture, varies according to local traditions and economic circumstances. Yes, there is a global teen market, but it is not the same in every nation. Yes, youth consumer groups are transnational. With the rapid movement of the world's population, youth consumers born in one nation might find themselves coming of age in another nation.

Other unifiers of global youth culture sometimes reinforce consumerism. These other unifiers include desires for new technology, entertainment, endless experience, mobility, sports participation and observation, respect for global icons, "humanism," "hope," and "self-navigation."[29] Interest in technology primarily involves the endless purchase of upgraded computers, portable compact disk and tape players, video games, digital cameras, high-definition TV sets, and cell phones. Entertainment is commodified through recordings and videos and world music tours. The search for new experiences and mobility are aided by cheap airline, rail, and bus tickets, which send hordes of backpacking youth across the global landscape. The role of sports in unifying youth is spurred by massive ad campaigns and media. For instance, the American-invented game of basketball is now an international sport because, in part, of the global advertising efforts of the National Basketball League.[30] Of course respect for brand icons is a form of *unabashed consumerism* that unifies youth.

In Moses' study, world teens are divided into six main categories. There are the "Resigned" who believe their futures are decided and that it is futile to engage in any political debate or to keep abreast with the unfolding of human events. In Moses' words, "The resigned have very low expectations for their futures. At an early age, they perceive that their lot in the world has already been determined . . . the resigned are alienated from society and very pessimistic about their chances for economic success."[31] They drop out of secondary schools or scrape by with minimal effort. College is clearly not a destination for this group. They are not interested in political participation.

The marketing segment, "World Savers," are identified closely with participation in political dialogues about alternatives to the good life and, at the same time, are considered avid consumers. "Whether the goal is to combat racism," Moses' summary of the survey data states, "rain forest, or curtail warming, the world saver are marching at the forefront, trying to effect some positive change."[32] Again it should be emphasized that these politically active youth are important world consumers. The marketing strategy for this group contains a cynical edge with the suggestion that a "marketer can piggyback a promotion with a worthwhile cause, and have world savers respond positively to that message."[33]

Targeting "World Savers" results in the commodification of social justice, which is an interesting addition to Simon Patten's earlier pronouncements on consumerism. Recognizing that World Savers are avid consumers, Benetton, the Italian clothing manufacturer, has advertised its clothes with accompanying themes of racial harmony and social justice. For instance, during the late 20th-century civil war in Bosnia, Benetton ads entitled "The Known Soldier" showed "blood-soaked T-shirt and the pants of a Croatian soldier."[34] Another ad showed two handcuffed men, a priest kissing a nun, and an arm tattooed "HIV positive."[35] Turning social and environmental causes into marketing opportunities demonstrates the power of the profit motive to envelop all aspects of life. Nothing can escape the grasp of branding and consumerism.

Along with the "Resigned," the other four teenage groups seem little interested in engaging in rational public discourse about political and economic issues. However, they definitely have strong consumer interests. The "Thrills-and-Chills" are described as "devil-may-care, trying to become independent hedonist . . . who love to buy stuff . . . and . . . do not mind paying the price for expensive items."[36] Coming from middle-class and affluent homes, this group is an important target for marketers. With intellects that are relatively empty of political and social concerns, they can fill their minds with brand icons. Moses wrote, "Spending and shopping are normal activities, and they develop loyalties to those brands that speak their languages."[37]

"Bootstrappers" could almost be described as "Thrills and Chills" wannabes wanting to work hard to achieve affluence and purchasing power. "Bootstrappers," according to Moses, "are young yuppies in training." Similar to the thrills-and-chills crowd, this group fills its minds with brand icons and loyalties as opposed to political and economic interests. "Bootstrappers," the world teen survey concludes, "are . . . on the lookout for goods and services that will help them get ahead . . . [they] stay plugged into the world of media and culture for insights that will give them a competitive edge."[38] Similar to the "Bootstrappers," "Quiet Achievers" work hard for success. The major distinction between the two groups is the degree of conformity. Quiet Achievers are conformists who avoid any type of political or social rebellion and remain tightly linked to their families. Consequently, they are more often followers of political and social rules rather than desiring to make the rules. Although politically inactive, they are active consumers who are concerned with investigating the quality and benefits of a product. "Upholders" are also described as conformists interested in following the rules. In contrast to "Quiet Achievers," this group is not focused on academic and economic success. "Upholders," Moses stated, "do not want to set the world on fire, nor are they into controversy." In the minds of this groups, sports statistics and the names of teams and players often crowd out political and economic issues. Like the other groups, this group is interested in consumption. They want products for their "risk-free quality, value, and reliability."[39]

The classification of global youth into these six categories seems reasonable as long as it is recognized that these groups overlap and that any individual might be a blend of several group characteristics. Moses pointed out that the "Resigned" sometimes act like the "Thrills and Chills" group, but without the same amount of money to spend. Yet I am skeptical of the accuracy of the study's statistical measures. However, they do provide an interesting bases for discussion about the percentage of youth engaged in different forms of consumerism. The following is the study's report on the global distribution of these youth groups. Again, it must be emphasized that most of Africa and the poorest of the poor in other countries are excluded from this survey.

Percentage Distribution of Global Youth Groups

Segment of Global Youth	*Percentage Distribution Worldwide*
Thrills and Chills	18
Upholders	16
Quiet Achievers	15
Resigned	14
Bootstrappers	14
World Savers	12
Unclassified	11

Source: Adapted from Elissa Moses, *The $100 Billion Allowance: Accessing the Global Teen Market* (New York: John Wiley & Sons, Inc. 2000), p. 82.

For those hoping for a politically active youth, the 12% figure for World Savers must be disappointing. Moses evaluated these figures according to national conditions. She wrote, "This analysis sheds light on why teens in Amsterdam pierce body parts, why youth in Brazil are worried about AIDS, why Japanese you are approaching the edge of rebellion, and why U.S. teens seem so motivated to achieve."[40] According to her study, youth groups are clustered around certain nations.

Segment of Global Youth	Countries with High Concentrations of Segment
Thrills and Chills	Germany, England, Lithuania, Greece, South Africa, Netherlands, United States, Australia
Upholders	Vietnam, Indonesia, Taiwan, China, Italy, Peru, Venezuela, Puerto Rico
Quiet Achievers	Thailand, China, Hong Kong, Ukraine
Resigned	Denmark, Sweden, Korea, Japan, Norway, Germany, Belgium, Netherlands
Bootstrappers	Nigeria, Mexico, United States, India, Chile, Puerto Rico, Australia
World Savers	Hungary, Philippines, Venezuela, Brazil, Spain, Colombia, Belgium, Argentina, Russia, Singapore

Source: Adapted from Elissa Moses, *The $100 Billion Allowance: Accessing the Global Teen Market* (New York: John Wiley & Sons, Inc. 2000), p. 82.

It is important to note that the two world leaders in consumerism—Japan and the United States—lack a high percentage of World Savers. In Japan, only 4% of the teen population is identified as World Savers, whereas the majority are either "Resigned" (38%) or "Thrills and Chills" (24%). Sixty percent of Japanese youth love shopping, compared with 42% worldwide.[41] In the United States, only 9% of the teen population is identified as World Savers, whereas the majority are either "Thrills and Chills" (28%) or "Bootstrappers" (26%).[42]

Have the majority of Japanese and U.S. youth made Sonya's choice? Except for the "World Savers" and "Resigned," global teens are fulfilling Simon Patten's dream that consumerism spur people to work harder. Even with the "World Savers," marketers are trying to commodify movements for social justice. The "Resigned" seemed destined to be nourished by fast-food and alienating music. This is not a pretty picture for those interested in rational public discourse on issues of social justice.

Although schools have created a teen cohort group linked by patterns of consumption, children are being seduced by new palaces of consumption interconnected to media and schooling. Media and architecture merge in theme parks and fast-food establishments designed to lure the child and the entire family.

THE SEDUCTION OF CHILDHOOD

Children are often seduced into consumerism by architecturally themed amusement parks and restaurants linked to media and product spin-offs. This phenomenon is an outgrowth of several trends, including 19th-century consumer-oriented architectural designs, advertising directed at children, the growth of media empires, and the inclusion of educational concepts in commercial enterprises. Regarding architectural designs, chapter 1 discussed architectural designs intended to arouse consumer desires and symbolize forms of consumption. Primarily directed at adults, these consumer themes were embodied in department stores and Coney Island theme parks. In the 1950s, this architectural style was broadened to include children and families with the founding of Disneyland and McDonald's. Coney Island was planned as a commodified respite from the tedium of corporate and industrial, while Disneyland included the same goal along with the preservation an imagined set of traditional values associated with the American family. McDonald's embodied the early home economist's dream of inexpensive fast food that could free the housewife from household slavery. Like Disneyland, McDonald's Golden Arches theme was to represent a haven for family values. These themed architectural forms intended to attract consumers and act as brand icons became familiar parts of the American landscape.

These themed environments were rooted in early advertising efforts to teach children how to consume. In 1904, the advertising manager of the *Atlantic Monthly* wrote that the far-sighted advertiser begins with the female child so that the brand name follows her "to school, thrusts its self upon her as she travels, and all unconsciously engraves it self upon her memory." The result is that when the child grows up and goes on her first shopping trip as a wife: "She orders Pears' Soap, White Label Soup, Pearline, Walter Baker's Cocoa, and Knox's Gelatine, because she knows and remembers the names, and does not realize that she has chosen in every instance an article made familiar to her, perhaps, by advertising only."[43] Advertising competitions were a popular technique for interesting children in brand names. In 1911, Colgate toothpaste launched a contest in a children's magazine that offered monetary prizes for writing the best ad copy. The ads instructed participants: "Just imagine that you're writing a short letter to one of your schoolmates telling how important it is to take proper care of the teeth and how [Colgate] Ribbon Dental Cream is not only the best cleansers but besides is so delicious in flavor that its use is a real treat. . . . And remember, the more you believe it the easier it will be to write it and the better the advertisement."[44] In a 1904 ad in *McClure's* magazine, an 8-year-old boy sits on the floor surrounded by opened magazines. Looking at this mother, he tells her, "Mamma, you know magazines are very useful. They tell you what you want, and where to get it."[45]

Product spin-offs turn children into demanding consumers and serve as marketing tools for media giants such as the Disney Corporation. Early ads utilized cartoon figures marketed to children as dolls. Through these dolls, which were also sources of revenue, children gained brand loyalty. In the early 20th century, Jell-O ads utilized cute little Kewpie figures that were nude infant shapes with pointed hairdos that performed tasks beyond their years. Kewpies appeared on Jell-O packages and Jell-O recipe books. One early recipe book showed a little girl pouring hot water into a container of Jell-O while one Kewpie pointed at the Jell-O box and another held up a Jell-O mold. Campbell Soup ads used Campbell Kids' characters in a similar fashion. Both Kewpies and Campbell Kids were marketed as dolls for children's play.[46]

It was the business genius of Walt Disney's brother Roy that led to product spin-offs of media characters. The Disney Corporation's first product spin-off was Mickey Mouse. Walt Disney created the Mickey Mouse character in 1928 and in the same year produced three animated Mickey Mouse cartoons including the sound cartoon, *Steamboat Willie*.[47] After the opening of *Steamboat Willie*, Walt Disney recalled, "Right after Mickey Mouse hit, I was in New York and we needed money. A fellow kept hanging around the hotel with three hundred dollars cash waving at me, and I finally signed a deal to put Mickey Mouse on these big cheap [writing] tablet type things. It was the first deal ever signed."[48] Roy Disney decided to copywrite the Mickey Mouse character and sell products using Mickey's characters and those of other Disney's cartoon figures. In 1930, Roy began a campaign to adorn products with these figures and signed a contract with George Borgfeldt to make toys and other objects using Mickey and Minnie Mouse.[49]

The marketing of these products were tied to Disney movies, syndicated newspaper comic strips, and newly formed Mickey Mouse Clubs. Roy Disney explained the company's merchandising techniques:

Mickey Mouse [newspaper cartoon strip] is now being handled . . . through King Features syndicate, who are rapidly placing the strip in many leading newspapers . . . Borgfeldt & Co. of New York have taken the world rights to manufacture toys and novelties . . . Villa Moret, Inc. . . . are publishing the Mickey Mouse song, used in the pictures. . . . Also in connection with our pictures we have launched a campaign for the formation of Micky Mouse Clubs in theaters where the cartoons are shown. . . . The idea is meeting with astonishing success.[50]

In 1932, the Disney brothers realized that there was a two-way relationship between the promotion of Disney movies and the earnings from merchandise bearing Disney logos. Walt was contacted by an advertising man who convinced him the Mickey could be promoted through merchandising. The Disney brothers agreed and a first spin-off was the now famous collector's item, the Mickey Mouse watch. Lionel Toys, which was having difficulty selling model trains during the Depression, joined the promotion effort. Regarding Lionel Toys, Walt recalled, "During the Depression, it was just bad for the toy business. They made this little windup Mickey Mouse that ran around a track. It was a big item. It sold everywhere."[51]

With the advent of TV, Mickey Mouse Clubs became an important part of marketing strategy for movies, products, and theme parks. On October 3, 1955, shortly after the opening of the Disneyland theme park, "The Mickey Mouse Club" children's TV program premiered on ABC. The most famous merchandise sold through the show was a cap with mouse ears. Children around the country would don their mouse ear caps to sing the programs opening song, which began "M-I-C-K-E-Y M-O-U-S-E, Mickey Mouse." "The Mickey Mouse Club" program proved a bonanza for other Disney products. Constantly plugged through the first programs were Disneyland and two recent Disney movies *20,000 Leagues Under the Sea* and *Lady and the Tramp*. It was believed that both were box office successes because of the plugs they received on the TV program.[52]

In the same year as the premier of the "Mickey Mouse Club," Disney launched another TV series called "Disneyland." The first 90-minute show was devoted to the Disneyland theme park. This marked the beginning of the TV infomercial where an entire program was devoted to information about a product. Many subsequent programs were about Disney movies, including one about the making of *20,000 Leagues Under the Sea*. A program devoted to Davy Crockett tied a Disney movie to Disneyland and a variety of product spin-offs. Davy Crockett was linked to the Disneyland attraction Frontierland. In addition, Disney studios released the movie, *Davy Crockett, King of the Wild Frontier*. The movie's theme song proved a hit among children and Disney-licensed products bearing Crockett's name, including coonskin hats, soaps, lamps, dolls, and a host of other children's products.[53]

When Disneyland opened on July 17, 1955, it had received publicity through Disney's TV infomercial and the "Mickey Mouse Club." Every child who donned the mouse-ear cap or wore Crockett's coonskin hat knew about Disneyland. Its success spawned a new generation of theme parks designed to organize and sell leisure time activities to families. Other theme parks included Dolly Parton's Appalachian family park Dollywood, the beer producer Anheuser-Busch's Busch Gardens, the Hershey Corporation's Hershey Park, the Auto World Theme Park in Flint, Michigan, and United Studios. The number of theme parks increased almost daily. By 2002, the Six Flags Corporation was operating 28 theme parks, including Six Flags Over Georgia, Six Flags Kentucky Kingdom, Six Flags AstroWorld, Six Flags Marine World, and Six Flags Wild Waves/Enchanted Village. Similar to Disney, Six Flags Corporation operated overseas theme parks in Holland, Bel-

gium, Germany, France, Spain, and Mexico. The Six Flags Corporation offered this exciting description of its German Movie World theme park
created in cooperation with Warner Bros. Movie studios:

> Warner Bros. Movie World Germany is Europe's unique movie and entertain-
> ment park located near Dusseldorf. The magical world of Hollywood be-
> comes reality. Five themed areas offer an exciting variety of more than 40 at-
> tractions, shows and rides, each of them based on famous Warner Bros. films
> and successful German productions, that guarantee an unforgettable day.
> This year, Warner Bros. Movie World presents Eraser - The Ride, a new roller
> coaster based thematically on the 1996 action film, "The Eraser - The Ride".
> Eraser - The Ride is a suspended looping coaster making 85 km/h one of the
> most exhilarating experiences in Europe. Warner Bros. Movie World Ger-
> many is open April through October.[54]

In addition, Disneyland Paris and Tokyo represented the exporting of the
theme park concept.

In contrast to Fred Thompson's plans for Luna Park in Coney Island,
Walt Disney made clear that his goal was clean middle-class fun for the entire family. While riding around the Disneyland construction site, Walt Disney commented to his biographer Bob Thomas, "Disneyland isn't designed
just for children. . . . I believe the right kind of entertainment can appeal to
all persons, young or old. I want Disneyland to be a place where parents can
bring their children—or come by themselves and still have a good time."[55]
On another occasion, Disney commented,

> We gotta charge people to get in. If we don't, we'll get all kinds of drunks and
> molesters; they'll be grabbing girls in the dark. You'll get a better class of peo-
> ple if you charge them to enter. . . . One of the things I hated about carnivals
> and piers was all the crap that was everywhere. You're stepping on chewing
> gum and ice cream cones. I think people want clean amusement parks.[56]

The Disneyland model, adopted by other theme park franchises, promised fenced-in security against the world's brutality. First, there was the
process of self-selection through the admission charge. In 2002, admission
tickets for Disneyland were $43 for those over 9 years old, $33 for children 3
to 9, and free for those under 3.[57] The cost was even higher for out-of-town
travelers. According to Disney's online reservation site in 2002, a complete
two-night package for two adults and two children in a standard view room
at Disney's Grand Californian Hotel with a "Resort Magic Package," and "4-
day Ultimate Park Hopper Ticket" was $1,152.90.[58] Air fare or costs for
other forms of travel and food made this an expensive family trip. Cost, as
Disney planned, kept out the riffraff, whereas tight security controlled the
crowds within. One could argue that the combination of security measures

and enclosed space made Disneyland into a model for a totalitarian state of pleasure.

With his background in movie production, Disney planned the park as an integrated experience flowing through scenes beginning with the Town Square and leading down Main Street to Fantasyland, Frontierland, Adventureland, and Tomorrowland. Unlike other amusement parks that had several entrances to ease congestion, Disney insisted on only one entrance to ensure a standardized experience. He wanted the Town Square to set the mood, similar to the opening of a movie, with visitors being greeted by brass bands, balloons, flowers, a fire wagon, a horse-drawn trolley, and surreys. Looking from Town Square down Main Street, visitors could see Sleeping Beauty's Castle.[59]

Walt Disney called the view of the Castle a *wienie*, which acted as a lure to draw visitors down Main Street. The use of the term *wienie* suggests all sorts of Freudian interpretations. According to his biographer, Disney frequently used wienie to refer to something that would seduce viewers into following the lines of a movie plot. Again Freudian interpretations are possible because the main wienies at Disneyland were Snow White's Castle and the towering Rocket in Tomorrowland. From this perspective, Disney's planning did have an eroticized dimension. However, Disney borrowed the term *wienie* from dog trainers who used frankfurters to induce dogs to perform tricks.[60]

Disneyland's Main Street was designed to evoke memories of small-town America, similar to the world in which Disney grew up in Marceline, Missouri, when things were simpler than the complex metropolitan world of Los Angeles that surrounded Disneyland. Walt Disney even had his father's name and business displayed on Disneyland's Main Street: "Elias Disney, Contractor, Est. 1895." Other parts of Disneyland were related to America's past and present. Frontierland offered a distorted view of the U.S. government's expansion into the West and the conquest of Native Americans and Mexicans. Adventureland, with its ersatz African jungle experience, suggested the inferiority of Africans and it was related to U.S. and European imperialism around the globe. The cold war's technological and military race between the United States and the Soviet Union was symbolized by the towering space rocket in Tomorrowland. Of course Fantasyland represented American domination of movies and TV and the cluttering of global minds with images of Disney characters.

Disneyland is a worldwide model for themed and commodified leisure. No sophisticated level of interpretation is required to explain brilliance of the Disneyland plan. The Disney Web site, *http://disneyland.disney.go.com*, describes the genius of the park's intermixture of consumption, fantasy, leisure, and nostalgia. Despite the entrance fee, there is still money to be spent inside. Consider how nostalgia and shopping are described on Disney's Web site for Main Street, U.S.A.: "Walt Disney once said, 'I love the nostalgic myself. I hope we never lose some of the things of the past.' So he created Main Street, U.S.A. to make sure we could always embrace those wonderful feelings of days gone by. From the decor in the old-time speciality shops to the music in Central Plaza to the taste of the ice cream sundaes, Main Street is pure Americana."[61] On Main Street, shoppers can find themed snack shops and stores, such as the Candy Palace with "mouth watering caramel apples, fudge, and other yummy delicacies [made] before your eyes"; and the China Closet with "Disney-themed china pieces"; along with the New Century Jewelry, the Mad Hatter, the New Century Times Pieces, the Silhouette Studio, and the Penny Arcade. This is a truly brilliant plan where you charge people to enter a street lined with other opportunities to spend money.

Other parts of Disneyland offer a similar combination of entertainment, shopping, and dining experiences. Disney's Web site describes Adventureland as "the perfect playground—whether you're cruising through the African jungles, avoiding poison darts and snakes while searching for ancient artifacts, or *simply sampling the topical faire in the village shops*" (italics added).[62] The themed stores include Tropical Imports, South Seas Traders, and Indiana Jones Adventure Outpost. The Bengal Barbecue offers kebabs of beef, chicken, and vegetables; the Indy Fruit Cart offers fresh fruit and bottled water; and the Tike Juice Bar provides a "pineapple lover's dream."[63]

With "western-themed shows, shops and eateries . . . [which] celebrate the spirit and strength of the American pioneer," Frontierland provides the Western shopping experience at Pioneer Mercantile, Westward Ho Trading Company, and Bonanza Outfitters and the Western eating experience at Rancho del Zocalo, River Belle Terrace, and Golden Horseshoe Stage. Fantasyland, "where dreams really do come true," offers Tinker Bell Toy Shoppe along with six other shopping opportunities. Diners can partake of Mousekemeals at the Pinocchio-themed Village Haus or hot dogs and pizzas at Troubadour Treats. Tomorrowland, billed as "a tribute to the power of the human mind," offers four shopping opportunities with Autopia Winner's Circle and Star Trader at the top of the list. Themed eating experiences include Redd Rockett's Pizza Port with "Starfire Chicken Pizza, Celestial Caesar Salad, and Mars-inara Pasta," and Club Buzz-Lightyear's Above the Rest with an "out-of-this-world food menu."[64]

Compared to early department stores, Disneyland is a major advance in consumerism. Departments stores sparked consumer desires through displays of merchandise and environments that turned shopping into a leisure time activity. Department stores did not earn money by charging an entrance fee. In department stores, shoppers could receive a day's worth of entertainment without spending any money. During their shopping adventure, consumers could leave the store and eat at some nearby restaurant.

Disney's brilliant ensemble of entertainment and consumer products is replicated at Dolly Parton's Dollywood near Knoxville, Tennessee. Mark Gottdiener wrote, "The park features folksy, down home, country attractions pumped up by marketing and promotional techniques perfected by the Disney Corporation, including Disney-style regulation of customers— 'no litter, no alcohol, no bare feet on young'uns'."[65] When the park opened in 1986, the focus was Appalachian culture and Dolly Parton's rise from rural poverty to global fame. Eventually Dollywood became known for performances by country bands. The result is a theme park that emphasizes a combination of Appalachian mountain culture and country music. These themes appear in the park's amusement rides, craft demonstrations and museums, restaurants, and stores.

Similar to Disneyland, Dollywood represents a new form of merchandising that combines the model of Coney Island theme parks with the department store sales techniques advocated by L. Frank Baum in *The Show Window*. In fusing consumerism with commodified leisure, Disneyland and Dollywood borrow the smoke and mirror methods used by the Wizard of Oz in the Emerald City. At Dollywood, themed restaurants offer various forms of country cooking. Aunt Granny's, the park's first restaurant, advertises food cooked according to Dolly Parton's country recipes. Country fare is also offered at Grannie Ogle's Ham'n Beans located in Dollywood's "Craftsman's Valley."[66] Among Dollywood's many themed stores in Lid'l Dolly's Handcrafted Children's Dresses. The shop's Web site tempts buyers with a photo of a little girl in a hand-made dress called "Easter Bunny Town." The store also offers the Original Southern Belle's dress, which is described as "Grandma's favorite."[67]

Dollywood's Mission Statement is: "Create Memories Worth Repeating." Both Disneyland and Dollywood play with human memories and imagination. Both parks draw on historical memories based in fantasy rather than reality. Few visitors have actually experienced an early 20th-century main street or Appalachian mountain living. However, history books, movies, songs, and other media have implanted feelings and images of these places in people's minds. Walking down Disneyland's Main Street evokes feelings and memories that are learned rather than experienced. A similar response occurs when visiting the Dollywood Craft Preservation School or Dollywood Crafts. Through media, people learn to associate feelings of peace, security, and happy times with mythical pasts. However, the actual experience of Appalachia's past might include exploitation in coal mines, poverty, malnutrition, and lung disease. At Disneyland, the visitor can leave Main Street for Frontierland where nostalgic feelings of the winning of the West seem to contradict the actual Western experience of the expansion of slavery into Texas, the government-sponsored slaughter of buffalo, and the genocide and genital mutilation of Native Americans.

MEMORIES AND CRITICAL HISTORY

In *The Mouse that Roared: Disney and the End of Innocence,* Henry Giroux criticizes Disney for removing any critical elements from its portrayal of history.[68] Similar to proposals by early advocates of the Public Relations, Disney enterprises fabricates memories to add to the enchantment of the consumer experience. There is no room for critical history when it is used to sell products. At Disneyland, Frontierland's Rancho del Zocalo ties the consumption of food to nostalgic memories of happy Mexican cowboy's strumming guitars. Diners are not reminded of Mexico's attempts at the Alamo to keep Americans from extending slavery into Texas or the U.S. government's unprovoked conquest of Mexico's Northern Territories. Diners at Rancho Del Zocalo are not treated to the memory taught to Mexico City residents at the entrance to Chapultepec Park where a large memorial honors the three children killed by U.S. Marines during the 1846 invasion. Nor are diners at Dollywood's Grannie Ogle's Ham'n Beans reminded of the thin-boned emaciation of country people. Nor are shoppers at Lid'l Dolly's Handcrafted Children's Dresses reminded that in the past the store's clothing could only be afforded by the families that owned and managed Appalachia's coal mines.

Just as historical memories can be used to merchandise food and other products, education can be integrated into themed environments and marketing. In chapter 6, "Sesame Street" exemplified a strong relationship between education and consumerism. When Florida's Disney World opened, Walt Disney focused on the educational experience provided at its Epcot Center. Celebration, the Disney corporation's attempt to create model U.S. communities, involved the company directly in the operation of a school system. To inflate their images of being child- and family-friendly, fast-food chains directly support educational programs. In all these cases, education serves as a medium for selling other products.

In 1996, the Walt Disney Company signed a marketing agreement with the king of fast-food restaurants, McDonald's. The global agreement allows Disney to market its films at McDonald's restaurants while giving McDonald's rights to use Disney videos and characters to sell its products.[69] For instance, in 2002, McDonald's so-called Happy Meal was sold with characters from Disney's film, *The Many Adventures of Winnie the Pooh.* This mutual marketing of a movie and food involved toys representing six Winnie the Pooh characters and advertised as "Pooh and Friends! Toys that Bend!" At the same time, McDonald's was offering teachers and public schools a "Black History" curriculum.[70]

FAST-FOOD EDUCATION

Fast-food franchises are a continuation of the American cuisine developed in the 1890s when home economists embraced Jell-O and packaged and prepared foods and attempted to standardize American tastes in school cafeterias and hospital kitchens. Most franchises were born in the 1950s when the automobile and suburban living created a mobile population looking for a quick meal. To a certain extent, fast food realized home economist Ellen Richard's dream of community kitchens and conveyance food that freed women from cooking.

Fast food's involvement in education was a logical outgrowth of efforts, similar to those of Disney, to project an impression of being friendly and clean places for children and families to eat. Also educational involvement served as a public relations method to create a positive community image. Beginning shortly before the opening of Disneyland, themed fast-food designs and logos served to identify their establishments to passing motorists and attract children and families. For instance, McDonald's, founded in 1953, changed the "M" representing the name McDonald into the Golden Arches symbol, which is now recognized around the world. In 1960, a Washington, DC, McDonald's sponsored the children's TV program "Bozo's Circus," and Bozo appeared at the restaurant attracting large crowds. When the TV program was canceled, an ad agency created a new clown called Ronald McDonald.[71] Adding to the kid-friendly image created by Ronald McDonald was the introduction of indoor play areas for children. With its own line of children's videos, McDonald's has wedded advertising and entertainment in one video starring Ronald McDonald, *The Wacky Adventures of Ronald McDonald.*[72] In the early 21st century, it was estimated that at least once a month 90% of U.S. children between 3 and 9 visit a McDonald's.[73]

McDonald's Black History curriculum confirms Henry Giroux's contention that media—in this case, a fast-food chain—strips history of its critical element. McDonald's Black History curriculum includes a list of "Little Known Black History Facts." These facts contain little or no mention of the history of slavery, lynching, race riots, Jim Crow laws, or violent White reaction to the civil rights movement. The following is a list of the first five Black History Facts provided in the curriculum. Each of these facts is followed by an explanation. I am only presenting the boldly printed first lines of the facts as examples of uncritical historical material.

1. Issac Murphy: The First Jockey to win the Kentucky Derby Three Times

2. The Black Lifesavers: A Band of Unsung Heroes on Pea Island, North Carolina

3. The Red Ball Express: Legendary Operation That Provided Vital Supplies to the Front Lines During World War II

4. William Cooper Nell: The First African American to Hold a Federal Position

5. Alexander Lucius Twilight: The First African American to Graduate From an American College[74]

Critical historical questions are absent from the eight-page teacher guide accompanying the facts list. The listed sources for McDonald's teacher guide are from major professional organizations, including the National Council for the Social Studies, the National Council of Teachers of English, and the International Reading Association. The guide is divided into three columns entitled "Objective," "Curriculum Connections," and "Standards." The first of two objectives, which reflects the racial uplift quality of the facts list, is: "Students will discuss the importance of being the 'first' to accomplish something. . . ." and "Students will discuss the importance of leadership. . . ." The last objective could raise critical issues: "Students will discuss the many obstacles that African Americans (and others) must overcome. . . ."[75] The objectives page is followed by a "Welcome Teachers" page, which opens, "McDonald's is pleased to bring you 'Little Known Black History Facts.' The following lessons rely on simple memorization skills without any critical questions. For instance, there is a list of questions requiring memorization, such as 'Who became the first African American to publish a novel?' "[76]

Similar to McDonald's birth in the 1950s' suburban-car age, McDonald's rival Burger King was founded in Daytona, Florida, in 1953 by Keith Cramer after he visited and studied the newly opened McDonald's in California.[77] Like McDonald's, Burger King uses themed architecture including playgrounds. Also Burger King exploits media connections such as a 2002 marketing agreement with Dreamworks film studio to distribute by Virtual Vision Scopes for the studio's showing of *Spirit: Stallion of the Cimarron*. In another media connection, Burger King has an agreement with the Nickelodeon TV network to cooperate in reviewing and showing TV videos submitted by children.[78]

Burger King goes beyond McDonald's educational and community efforts by operating Burger King Academies and is involved in welfare reform. Jumping on the charter school bandwagon, Burger King in cooperation with Communities in Schools, Inc. (CIS) has opened 24 CIS/Burger King Academies across the nation for students facing problems of "poor school attendance, illiteracy, teen pregnancy, drug and alcohol abuse, school violence, and lack of self-esteem."[79] The Burger King Academies, serving as both advertising for the franchise and public relations, work with local service groups, public schools, and universities. Local Burger King franchises also establish partnerships with local school systems to provide mentors and tutors, and they team up with local newspapers to sell newspapers with part of the proceeds going to Burger King Academies.[80] Bearing the appellation Burger King Scholars, needy students can attend college or postsecondary vocational schools with scholarships from the Burger King/ Lahore Foundation's North American Scholarship Program, which in 2001 provided $1,082,000 in awards.[81]

In his 1997 State of the Union address, President Bill Clinton named Burger King as one of five companies working with the federal government on welfare reform. Obviously serving its own needs for low-paid workers, Burger King Corporation was a founding member of the Welfare to Work Partnership. By December 2001, the franchise had hired 35,000 former welfare recipients. For Burger King there was a clear advantage in hiring from welfare roles. Not only did it ensure low-paid workers, but it provided a more stable workforce. According to the Burger King Corporation, "The industry employee turnover rate for quick service restaurants is approximately 300%. Burger King employees hired off public assistance roles have 45% higher retention rates than the turnover rate for all other employees in the industry."[82] Burger King has effectively used media ties, Burger King Academies and Scholarships, and government welfare programs for advertising, building community relations, and providing more reliable and low-cost workers.

The company most involved in education is YUM Brands corporation, which over the years acquired Taco Bell, A&W, KFC, Long John Silver's, and Pizza Hut. When YUM Brands acquired A&W and Long John Silver's in 2002, the company proudly announced that, "The acquisition allows us to accelerate our multi branding strategy and . . . to be expanded international leaders . . . in chicken, pizza, Mexican and seafood." The company's motto is, "Our passion is to put YUM on our customer's faces all over the world."[83] YUM Brands is now a leader in the construction and operation of themed environments. For instance, in 1922, the A&W logo was created by Roy Allen and Frank Wright to represent their two last names. Opening in Lodi, California, the men constructed an outdoor stand that looked like a root beer barrel. In 1923, A&W developed the first car-hop service initiating the spread of drive-in restaurants. Later restaurants relied on the logo rather than the barrel design for name recognition.[84] Opening in 1968, Long John Silver's new "exteriors," as described by the company, sported "a stronger retail identity with bolder colors, accent stripes, illuminated canopies on drive-thrus, and a new roof design."[85]

Three of the five YUM franchises—Taco Bell, Pizza Hut, and KFC—are directly involved in educational activities. In 1999, for the first time, all three franchises were linked to a media event when they gained exclusive rights as global restaurant partners for Star Wars Episode I.[86] Taco Bell's educational projects overshadow those of McDonald's. Taco Bell began the same year and in the same town as McDonald's when Glen Bell opened the Bell Taco stand in San Bernardino, California. Bell experimented with food processing and developed a processed method for producing tacos. The name changed to Taco Bell, and it adopted the logo of the ringing mission bell.[87]

As sponsor of the Discovery Science Center in Santa Ana, California, Taco Bell provides science programs aligned to the requirements of California State Science Content Standards. One program is "Dynamic Earth" program while another is "Astronomy—Avoiding Misconceptions." Both programs are free and done in cooperation with NASA. Also free are science exhibits and a three-dimensional theater with science shows. In cooperation with the Bank of America, the Discovery Center provides a free open house to teachers along with free field trips for students.[88] Taco Bell Foundation, in partnership with Boys & Girls Clubs of America, operates TEENSupreme programs throughout the United States and on worldwide military installations. According to the official statement of Taco Bell, the programs are "designed to develop leadership skills, values, and a voice among our nation's youth to prepare them to become successful adults and productive leaders." To build a public awareness of their sponsorship of TEENSupreme, Taco Bell has in-store canisters so that patrons can make donations to support the program.[89]

In 1988, President Ronald Reagan awarded Pizza Hut's president, Art Gunter, a Private Initiative Citation for its educational program BOOK IT![90] The first Pizza Hut opened in 1958 in Wichita, Kansas, and its first franchise opened in Topeka the following year. In 1965, its first TV commercial featured the musical jingle, "Putt-Putt to Pizza Hut." In 1967, it gained global recognition for baking the world's largest pizza (6 feet in diameter). In 1975, it promoted itself through product placement by being featured in the movie *The Bad News Bears*.[91] In 1982, it linked itself to the movie *ET* by distributing ET glasses at its franchises.

Pizza Hut's BOOK IT! national reading incentive program began in 1984 with an enrollment of 200,000 elementary school students across the nation. By the 1998–1999 school year, 22 million children in 895,000 classrooms were enrolled. The program serves as a public relations project, as advertising gimmick, and indirectly sells extra pizzas to parents of student winners. As advertisers suggested in the early 20th century, it is important to implant brand names in children to establish adult preferences. Under the program, children who achieve their monthly reading goals are rewarded with a Personal Pan Pizza and a button from the manager of the local Pizza Hut restaurant. Achieving 6-month goals earns an All-Star Medallion at a local Pizza Hut restaurant. In 1998, the BOOK IT! BEGINNERS PROGRAM started for preschool and kindergarten students with a monthly Personal Pan Pizza award. In 1999, this beginners program was active in 20,000 kindergarten classrooms and day-care centers around the country.[92]

BOOK IT is a win–win program. Children, particularly preschoolers and kindergartners, are usually escorted by their parents to the local Pizza Hut restaurant. Do the parents simply sit and watch their child eat a Personal Pan Pizza or do they also buy the child a drink and pizzas and drinks for themselves? It is possible that the parents might spend more than the cost of the award. In fact, Pizza Hut might actually make money by giving the award while implanting their brand name in the child's mind. In addition, Pizza Hut gets free help for their advertising campaign from the local school system. Principals and teachers enroll the students in the program, and teachers set monthly goals, verify completion of reading assignments, and mark wall charts to monitor children's progress toward their Personal Pan Pizza.

YUM Brands' Kentucky Fried Chicken (KFC) franchises focus on early childhood education. The original KFC started in 1930 when Harland Sanders began cooking and serving food at his service station in Corbin, Kentucky. Developing his Kentucky Fried Chicken recipe using a "secret blend" of 11 herbs and spices, he moved from his service station to a restaurant across the street. In 1935, Kentucky's governor, Ruby Laffoon, officially named Harland Sanders a "Kentucky Colonel" for his contribution to the state's cuisine. In the early 1950s, the new interstate highway system doomed his restaurant as travelers bypassed Corbin. In 1952, he decided to franchise his chicken recipe by traveling from restaurant to restaurant across the nation offering samples and franchises. By 1964, there were 600 KFC franchises. Similar to other fast-food outlets, KFC used theme architecture with Colonel Sanders serving as its logo. In fact, many KFC franchises placed likenesses of the Colonel sitting on a bench outside their restaurants.[93]

KFC has entered education in a big way. While Burger King Academies serve high school students, KFC has entered the day-care business for infants and preschool children. On August 4, 2001, the nation's first Colonel's Kids Child Care Center opened in Columbus Junction, Iowa, with the center initially offering for children 2 weeks to 12 years old infant care, day care, crisis care, before and after-school care, and summer recreational programs.[94] The company's program is called *The Colonel's Kids Charity*. In the promotion piece the company asks, "Did you know more than 29 million children have no place to go while their parents work?"[95] KFC defines the child-care crisis in the following words.

There is a child-care crisis in the United States. Every state reports shortages in child care. Consider this:

- Nearly two thirds of parents (65%) juggle multiple child-care arrangements.
- More than 15 million people work during nontraditional hours and are in need of child care.
- Nine out of 10 adults agree that finding affordable quality child care is difficult for most American families.

It is fitting to end this brief review of fast-food education with KFC's support of day-care centers. It could be suggested that the need for Colonel's Kids Child Care Centers and Burger King Academies for troubled adolescents is a product of the mobile and frantic family life that made fast food successful. Contrary to the 1950's myth of the traditional family, the harried lives of two wage earner households creates dependence on fast food. It is a distortion of home economist Ellen Richard's dream of saving time from cooking so that women could have more freedom. Would she have approved of a quick and cheap family dinner at McDonald's or Burger King so that the kids could use the franchise's playgrounds?

Interestingly, the evolution of American cuisine has mapped out a whole set of public spaces beyond the school cafeteria and hospital kitchen. The cuisine created a marriage among education, advertising, and media. Obviously fast-food franchises' connection to media and education is a form of advertising and is used to build a public image of being family friendly. The range of fast-food educational projects is amazing when one considers they include a Black History curriculum, college scholarships, cooperative reading programs with public schools, a science center using state educational standards, science programs, day-care centers, teenage programs, and charter schools. In and out of school, children and teenagers consume American cuisine as food and brand names.

CONCLUSION: GETTING COCA-COLA
INTO THE CLASSROOM

This chapter and book conclude with the now famous 1997 story of the overzealous efforts of Colorado Springs School District administrator John Bushey to have students consume more Coca-Cola. The tale provides an important view of historical change. As the reader may recall from chapter 1, Coca-Cola was created in the 19th century as brain tonic for the weary businessman. In the late 1890s, it was transformed and sold as a general beverage and advertised as simply "Delicious and Refreshing." Advertising and marketing eventually made Coca-Cola the most recognized brand symbol among global youth. At the same time that Coca-Cola was being repackaged, the school cafeteria was born with the promise of providing students with a healthy American cuisine. Jell-O made it into the school cafeteria, but not Coca-Cola. However, by the early 21st century, fast food and so-called *junk food* were becoming standard school items, with Taco Bell, Pizza Hut, and McDonald's supplying school cafeterias.

John Bushey's deal with Coca-Cola to increase school consumption of their products was, in part, a result of a defined teenage market created in the 1930s and 1940s as an outcome of mass secondary education. By the 1990s, advertisers were interested in placing ads in high schools to capture the market. Dan DeRose's DD Marketing pioneered the effort after DeRose, as athletic director at the University of Southern Colorado, was able to raise $250,000 in corporate sponsorship for his sports teams. His first deal after organizing DD Marketing was negotiating a $3.4 million partnership between Dr. Pepper and Grapevine–Colleyville school district in Texas. Dr. Pepper's advertising campaign within the school district included placing ads on school rooftops to be seen by passengers flying in and out of the Dallas–Fort Worth Airport. One of his other accomplishments was opening in the Derby, Kansas, school district a Pepsi GenerationNext Resource Center.[96]

It seems fitting that school sports as a symbol of masculinity and as the 1920s' solution for channeling adolescent male sexuality would become a target of advertising agencies. In Pueblo, Colorado, DD Marketing worked out an agreement between the school district and Burger King to provide for ads throughout the school, including stadium banners and an ad over the stadium's public-address system. Corporate sponsorship of new high school scoreboards bearing the corporate name or logo became common.[97]

Bushey's push for increased soft drink sales was part of a Coca-Cola marketing plan to increase consumption by children and teenagers.[98] Bushey's school district signed an agreement with the company to sell 21,000 cases of Coke products. Bushey's administrative memo urged principals to increase sales of Coke products by allowing students to drink them in classrooms. He suggested placing Coke machines closer to classrooms for easier access. Bushey went on to become principal of the high school in Disney's planned community Celebration.[99]

Not only is the distinctiveness of American cuisine represented by Taco Bell in the school cafeteria and Coca-Cola in the classroom, but also America's marriage of education, advertising, and media. The wedding of these three resulted from efforts to redefine femininity and masculinity in the corporate age, reform the American family, control American youth, resolve the conflict between the schools and media over the control of national culture, sell the American way of life as a product of consumerism and capitalism, use media and schools as part of national defense in the cold war, create efficiency in food production, and maintain consumerism. The ideology of consumerism makes increased production dependent on increased consumption. Within this framework, increased consumption requires motivating consumer desires through advertising. Advertising becomes the driving force of the economy. Every space, including public spaces, becomes an advertising opportunity. The promise of increased levels of schooling is not greater happiness, but increased levels of consumption. Equality of opportunity means equality of opportunity to consume. Schools are now training grounds for consumer-citizens. America's cuisine, advertising, and media are its most important contributions to world culture.

Notes

CHAPTER 1

1. Eric Schlooser, *Fast Food Nation: The Dark Side of the All-American Meal* (Boston: Houghton Mifflin Company, 2001), p. 4.

2. Matthew Purdy, "A Chance to Live, and Then Describe, Her Own American Dream," *New York Times on the Web* (24 June 2001).

3. The dilemmas presented to Americans by industrial and agricultural abundance are explored by Jackson Lears in *Fables of Abundance: A Cultural History of Advertising in America* (New York: Basic Books, 1994).

4. Simon N. Patten, *The New Basis of Civilization* (Cambridge: Harvard University Press, 1968), p. 215.

5. Ibid., p. 141.

6. Patten, p. 137.

7. Anzia Yezierska, *Salome of the Tenements* (Urbana: University of Illinois Press, 1995), p. 27.

8. My review of these civilizational differences can be found in Joel Spring, *Globalization and Educational Rights: An Intercivilizational Analysis* (Mahwah, New Jersey: Lawrence Erlbaum Associates, 2001).

9. Lears, p. 20.

10. Thomas Jefferson, "To the Chiefs of the Cherokee Nation. Washington, January 10, 1806," in *The Life and Selected Writings of Thomas Jefferson*, edited by Adrienne Koch and William Peden (New York: The Modern Library, 1944), p. 578.

11. William G. McLoughlin, *Cherokees and Missionaries 1789–1839* (New Haven: Yale University Press, 1984), p. 61.

12. "President Jackson on Indian Removal, December 8, 1829" in Francis Paul Prucha, ed., *Documents of United States Indian Policy, Second Edition* (Lincoln: University of Nebraska Press, 1990), pp. 47–48.

13. See John Sugde, *Tecumseh: A Life* (New York: Henry Holt & Company, 1998).

14. Ibid., pp. 118–119.

15. J. R. Pole, *The Pursuit of Equality in American History* (Berkeley: University of California Press, 1993), p. 37.

16. Ibid., p. 37.

17. Ibid., p. 151.

18. Harry Warfel, *Noah Webster: Schoolmaster to America* (New York: Macmillan, 1936), pp. 71–75.

19. Pole, p. 138.

20. Ibid., p. 152.

21. Carl F. Kaestle, *Pillars of the Republic: Common Schools and American Society 1780–1860* (New York: Hill & Wang, 1983), p. 90.

22. Roland Marchand, *Advertising the American Dream: Making Way for Modernity 1920–1940* (Berkeley: University of California Press, 1985), pp. 32–38.

23. See David Tyack and Elisabeth Hansot, *Managers of Virtue: Public School Leadership in America 1820–1980* (New York: Basic Books, 1990).

24. Footnote Protestant reformers.

25. Richard Mosier, *Making the American Mind: Social and Moral Ideas in the McGuffey Readers* (New York: Russell & Russell, 1965), pp. 167–170; Harvey C. Minnich, *William Holmes McGuffey and His Readers* (New York: American Book Company, 1936), pp. 30–89.

26. Stephen Rachman, "Shaping the Values of Youth: Sunday School Books in the 19th Century America, *http://memory.loc.gov/ammem/award99/miemhtml/svyhome.html*, pp. 11–12. This essay accompanies the digitization of 19th-century Sunday School books as part of the Library of Congress' National Digital Library Program. I will be using material from this collection in my discussion of the content of Sunday School books. The digitized books are accompanied by the following statement: "This collection presents 163 Sunday school books published in America between 1815 and 1865, drawn from the collections of Michigan State University Libraries and the Clarke Historical Library at Central Michigan University Libraries. They document the culture of religious instruction of youth in America during the Antebellum era. They also illustrate a number of thematic divisions that preoccupied 19th century America, including sacred and secular, natural and divine, civilized and savage, rural and industrial, adult and child. Among the topics featured are history, holidays, slavery, African Americans, Native Americans, travel and missionary accounts, death and dying, poverty, temperance, immigrants, and advice.

27. Mosier, p. 161.

28. William H. McGuffey, *McGuffey's Newly Revised Eclectic Second Reader* (Cincinnati: Winthrop B. Smith, 1843), pp. 47–48.

29. Ibid., pp. 48–50.

30. By A. Lady, *The Factory Boy, or The Child of Providence* (Philadelphia: American Baptist Publication Society, 1839), pp. 8–9 (numbering is based on digitalized version, see endnote 44).

31. Ibid, p. 23.

32. Ibid., p. 49.

33. E. M. Sheldon, *"I Wish I Was Poor"* (New York: American Tract Society, 1864), pp. 1–2.

34. Ibid., p. 3.

35. Ibid., p. 10.

36. Ibid., pp. 10–11.

37. Ibid., p. 12.

38. Ibid., p. 13.

39. Ibid., p. 13.

40. Author Unknown, "A Ride to the City," *Common Sights in Town & Country. Delineated & Described for Young Children* (Philadelphia: American Sunday-School Union, 18-?), p. 2.

41. Ibid., p. 2.

42. By a Lady, *The Factory Boy*, p. 6.

43. Ibid., p. 6.

44. "The Coal Cart" in *Common Sights in Town & Country* . . . , p. 4.

45. Ibid., p. 4.

46. Ibid., p. 4.

47. Author Unknown, *Frank Harper, or, The Country-Boy in Town* (Philadelphia: American Sunday-School Union, 1847), p. 6.

48. David M. Henkin, *City Reading: Written Words and Public Spaces in Antebellum New York* (New York: Columbia University Press, 1998), p. 12.

49. Ibid., p. 50.

50. Ibid., p. 81.

51. Ibid., p. 84.

52. Quoted in Jackson Lears, *Fables of Abundance: A Cultural History of Advertising America* (New York: Basic Books, 1994), p. 267.

53. Ibid., p. 213.

54. Sivulka, p. 31.

55. Henkin, p. 176.

56. As quoted in Headrick, p. 190.

57. Ibid., p. 190.

58. Ibid., p. 191.

59. Henkin, pp. 105–108.

60. Richard Ohmann, *Selling Culture: Magazines, Markets, and Class at the Turn of the Century* (New York: Verso, 1996), p. 21.

61. Ibid., p. 21.

62. Henkin, p. 103.

63. Ibid., p. 127.

64. See Ralph Henry Gabriel, *Elias Boudinot: Cherokee & His America* (Norman: University of Oklahoma Press, 1941), pp. 108–109 and Grant Foreman, *Sequoyah* (Norman: University of Oklahoma Press, 1938).

65. Quoted in Henkin, p. 115.

66. Ibid., p 117.

67. Stephen Fox, *The Mirror Makers: A History of American Advertising and Its Creators* (Urbana: University of Illinois Press, 1997), p. 65.

68. These ads are reproduced in Sivulka, pp. 76–77.

69. Reproduced in Henkin, p. 120.

70. Ibid.

71. John Lust, *The Herb Book* (New York: Bantam Books, 1974), p. 476.

72. Ibid., pp. 411–412.

73. William Leach, *Land of Desire: Merchants, Power, and the Rise of a New American Culture* (New York: Vintage Books, 1993), pp. 55–60.

74. Quoted by Leach, p. 60.

75. I am relying on Gottdiener, *The Theming of America* . . . , for developing this conceptual framework regarding themed environments.

76. Quoted by William Leach in *Land of Desire: Merchants, Power, and the Rise of a New American Culture* (New York: Vintage Books, 1993), p. 39.

77. Quoted by Leach, p. 60.

78. Quoted by Leach, p. 62.

79. Ibid., p. 64.

80. Quoted in Ibid., p. 65.

81. Ibid., p. 66.

82. Quoted in Ibid., p. 74.

83. Leach's description, p. 77.

84. Woody Register, *Coney Island: Fred Thompson and the Rise of American Amusements* (New York: Oxford University Press, 2001), p. 93.

85. Ibid., p. 151.

86. Ibid., p. 15.

87. Register, pp. 95–99.

88. Register, p. 25.

89. Ibid., pp. 92–93, 152–153.

90. Kathy Peiss, *Cheap Amusements: Working Women and Leisure in Turn-of-the Century New York* (Philadelphia: Temple University Press, 1986), pp. 131–132.

91. Associated Press, "U.N. Study: Americans Work More," *New York Times on the Web*, *www.nytimes.com* (1 September 2001) SEP 01, 2001.

92. Ibid.

93. The statement on compassionate conservativism that influenced President George W. Bush is Marvin Olasky's *Renewing American Compassion: How Compassion for the Needy Can Turn Ordinary Citizens Into Heroes* (Washington, DC: Regenery Publishing, Inc., 1996).

CHAPTER 2

1. For a summary statement of historical interpretations of this transition in domestic roles see, Steven Lubar, "Men/Women/Production/Consumption," in *His and Hers: Gender, Consumption, and Technology* edited by Roger Horowitz and Arwen Mohun (Charlottesville: University Press of Virginia, 1998), pp. 7–37.

2. Susan Strasser, *Never Done: A History of American Housework* (New York: Henry Holt & Company, 1982).

3. See Gail Bederman, *Manliness & Civilization: A Cultural History of Gender and Race in the United States 1880–1917* (Chicago: University of Chicago Press, 1995) and Michael Kimmel, *Manhood in America: A Cultural History* (New York: The Free Press, 1996).

4. Sivulka, p. 64.

5. Susan Strasser, *Satisfaction Guaranteed: The Making of the American Mass Market* (Washington, DC: Smithsonian Institution Press, 1989), p. 52.

6. Quoted from a 1932 advertising brochure by Gary Cross in *An All-Consuming Century: Why Commercialism Won in Modern America* (New York: Columbia University Press, 2000), p. 32.

7. Shapiro, p. 152.

8. Rima D. Apple, "Liberal Arts or Vocational Training? Home Economics Education for Girls," in *Rethinking Home Economics: Women and the History of a Profession* edited by Sarah Stage and Virginia B. Vincenti (Ithaca: Cornell University Press, 1997), p. 85.

9. Laura Shapiro, *Perfection Salad: Women and Cooking at the Turn of the Century* (New York: Random House, 2001), p. 4.

10. Ibid., p. 68.

11. See Carolyn M. Goldstein, "Part of the Package: Home Economists in the Consumer Product Industries, 1920–1940," pp. 271–291; " 'Where Mrs. Homemaker Is Never Forgotten': Lucy Maltby and Home Economics at Corning Glass Works, 1929–1965," pp. 163–181; and "Agents of Modernity: Home Economists and Rural Electrification, 1925–1950," pp. 237–252 in *Rethinking Home Economics.* . . . Also, James C. Williams, "Getting Housewives the Electric Message: Gender and the Energy Marketing in the Early Twentieth Century," *His and Hers* . . . , pp. 95–114.

12. See Lynn Nyhart, "Home Economists in the Hospital, 1900–1930," *Rethinking Home Economics* . . . , pp. 125–144.

13. Announcement quoted by Sarah Stage in "Ellen Richards and the Social Significance of the Home Economics Movement" in *Rethinking Home Economics* . . . , p. 17.

14. Ibid., pp. 21–23.

15. Virginia B. Vicenti, "Chronology of Events and Movements Which Have Defined and Shaped Home Economics," in *Rethinking Home Economics* . . . , p. 322.

16. Quoted in Shapiro, p. 34.

17. Ibid., p. 130.

18. Quoted by Stage, p. 28.

19. Quoted in Shapiro, p. 38.

20. Ibid., p. 39.

21. Ibid., p. 40.

22. Ibid., p. 103.

23. Ibid., p. 109.

24. Ibid., pp. 147–148.

25. Vincenti, p. 322.

26. Shapiro, p. 152.

27. Ibid., pp. 75–76.

28. Ibid., p. 76.

29. Ibid., p. 136.

30. Barbara Ehrenreich and Deirdre English's *For Her Own Good: 150 Years of the Experts' Advice to Women* (New York: Anchor Books, 1978), p. 165.

31. Ruth Schwartz Cowan, *More Work for Mother: The Ironies of Household Technology from the Open Hearth to the Microwave* (New York: Basic Books, 1983), p. 73.

32. Shapiro, p. 161.

33. Quoted in Andrew Heinze, "Jewish Women and the Making of an American Home," in *The Gender and Consumer Culture Reader* edited by Jennifer Scanlon (New York: New York University Press, 2000), p. 22.

34. Marjorie East, "The Life of Caroline Hunt, 1865–1927," in *Caroline Hunt: Philosopher for Home Economics* edited by Marjorie East (College Park: Division of Occupational and Vocational Studies, College of Education, Pennsylvania State University, 2001), pp. 1–33.

35. Caroline Hunt, "Revaluations," *Ibid.*, p. 56.

36. Caroline Hunt, "Home Economics at the University of Wisconsin, A Housekeeper Conference, From the Sixth Lake Placid Conference on Home Economics, 1904, *Ibid.*, p. 71.

37. Caroline Hunt, "Higher Education: Symposium, Eighth Lake Placid Conference on Home Economics, 1906," *Ibid.*, p. 77.

38. Ibid., p. 76.

39. Ibid., p. 76.

40. Ibid., p. 77.

41. Ibid., p. 78.

42. Caroline Hunt, "Woman's Public Work for the Home, Ninth Lake Placid Conference on Home Economics, 1907" in East, pp. 86–92.

43. Ibid., p. 87.

44. Caroline Hunt, "Homes for the Greatest Number," *The Chautauquan* (October 1902) in East, p. 105.

45. Ehrenreich and English, p. 164.

46. Ibid., p. 176.

47. Ibid., p. 176.

48. Quoted in Ibid., p. 177.

49. Caroline Hunt, "Homes for the Greatest Number," p. 90.

50. Caroline Hunt, "More Life for Man," in East, p. 111.

51. Ellen Gruber Garvey, *The Adman in the Parlor: Magazines and the Gendering of Consumer Culture, 1880s to 1910s* (New York: Oxford University Press, 1996), p. 150.

52. Ibid., p. 155.

53. Ad is reproduced in Marchand, p. 113.

54. Ibid.

55. Reproduced in Carolyn Wyman, *Jell-O: A Biography* (New York: Harcourt, Inc., 2001), p. ix.

56. Ibid.

57. Ibid.

58. As quoted in Ibid., p. 21.

59. This process is described in Ibid., p. 1.

60. Ibid., p. 3 and Shapiro, p. 93.

61. Shapiro, p. 94.

62. Wyman, p. 22.

63. Ibid., p. 23.

64. Ibid., p. 23.

65. See Strasser, *Satisfaction Guaranteed* . . . , pp. 3–5.

66. Shapiro, p. 204.

67. Shapiro, p. 203.

68. Strasser, *Satisfaction Guaranteed* . . . , p. 4.

69. Kathy Peiss, *Hope in a Jar: The Making of America's Beauty Culture* (New York: Henry Holt & Company, 1998).

70. Quote by Peiss, p. 95.

71. Ibid., p. 135.

72. Ibid., p. 91.

73. Ibid., pp. 90–94.

74. Jennifer Scanlon, "Advertising Women: The J. Walter Thompson Company Women's Editorial Department," in *The Gender and Consumer Culture Reader* . . . , p. 218.

75. This ad is reproduced in Peiss, p. 138.

76. Ibid.

77. Reproduced in Ibid., p. 146.

78. Reproduced in Marchand, p. 187.

79. Ibid.

80. Reproduced in Peiss, p. 221.

81. Robert E. Weems, Jr., "Consumerism and the Construction of Black Female Identity in Twentieth-Century America," in *The Gender and Consumer Reader* edited by Jennifer Scanlon (New York: New York University Press, 2000), p. 167.

82. Ibid., pp. 167–168.

83. Ibid., p. 169.

84. I discuss the Protestant background of the early advertising industry in Chapter 1. See Roland Marchand, *Advertising the American Dream: Making Way for Modernity 1920–1940* (Berkeley: University of California Press, 1985), pp. 32–38.

85. All of these statistics are taken from Richard Ohmann's *Selling Culture: Magazines, Markets, and Class at the Turn of the Century* (New York: Verso, 1996), p. 49.

86. Ibid., p. 58.

87. Ibid., p. 83.

88. This is Ohmann's central argument regarding the development of a mass consumer culture in the 20th century. He is not alone in advancing this thesis. For instance, John Philip Jones in *What's in a Name? Advertising and the Concept of Brands* (Lexington, MA: D.C. Heath, 1986), p. 23, states, "the driving force in [early] advertising was . . . the simple and pressing need to sell rapidly the burgeoning output of mechanized production."

89. Sivulka, p. 106.

90. Ibid., p. 49.

91. Ibid., p. 109.

92. Ibid., p. 111.

93. Ibid., p. 168.

94. Jackson Lears, *Fables of Abundance: A Cultural History of Advertising in America* (New York: Basic Books, 1994), p. 10.

95. Ibid., p. 10.

96. Reproduced in Ibid., p. 158.

97. Sivulka, p. 67.

98. Reproduced in Ibid., p. 68.

99. Jeffery Steele, "Reduced to Images: American Indians in Nineteenth-Century Advertising" in *The Gender and Consumer Culture Reader* . . . , p. 113.

100. J. Walter Thompson consistently had the highest dollar billings until it was bypassed by Young & Rubicam in 1975. Information on yearly ad agency billings is provided in the appendix of Stephen Fox's *The Mirror Makers: A History of American Advertising & Its Creators* (Urbana: University of Illinois Press, 1997), pp. 331–333.

101. Ibid., p. 81.

102. Ibid., pp. 81–83.

103. Ibid., p. 84.

104. Quoted in Stuart Even, *PR! A Social History of Spin* (New York: Basic Books, 1996), p. 132.

105. Ibid.

106. Ibid., p. 144.

107. Kerry W. Buckley, *Mechanical Man: John Broadus Watson and the Beginnings of Behaviorism* (New York: Guilford Press, 1989), p. 137.

108. Ibid., p. 119.

109. Ibid., pp. 119–120.

110. Ibid., p. 120.

111. Ibid., p. 139.

112. Ad is reproduced in Sivulka, p. 112.

113. Ad reproduced in Ibid., p. 159.

114. Buckley, p. 141.

115. Ad is reproduced in Sivulka, p. 161.

116. Ad reproduced in Marchand, p. 114.

117. Ad is reproduced in Ibid., p. 202.

118. Jenna Weissman Joselit, *A Perfect Fit: Clothes, Character, and the Promise of America* (New York: Henry Holt & Company, 2001), pp. 7–22.

119. Ibid., p. 25.

120. Quoted in Marchand, p. 51.

121. Joselit, p. 29.

122. Ibid., p. 30.

123. Ibid., p. 30.

124. Ibid., p. 39.

125. Ibid., p. 40.

126. Ibid., p. 40.

127. Marchand, p. 156.

128. Cross, pp. 50–51.

129. Ad reproduced in Sivulka, p. 114.

130. Ad reproduced in Cross, p. 51.

131. Marchand, pp. 160–161.

132. See Gay Wilentz, "Introduction," to Anzia Yezierska, *Salome of the Tenements* (Urbana: University of Illinois Press, 1995), pp. ix–xxiv.

133. Ibid., p. 91.

134. Ibid., p. 27.

135. Ibid., p. 157.

136. Ibid., p. 132.

137. Ibid., p. 33.

138. Ibid., p. 37.

139. Ibid., p. 74.

140. Ibid., p. 74.

141. Ibid., p. 75.

142. Ibid, p. 75.

143. Ibid., p. 75.

144. Ibid., p. 134.

145. Ibid., p. 136.

146. Ewen, p. 240.

CHAPTER 3

1. Gail Bederman, *Manliness & Civilization: A Cultural History of Gender and Race in the United States, 1880–1917* (Chicago: University of Chicago Press, 1995), p. 14.

2. Reproduced in Julie Wosk, *Women and the Machine: Representations from the Spinning Wheel to the Electronic Age* (Baltimore: Johns Hopkins Press, 2001), p. 7.

3. Ibid., p. 4.

4. Steven Gelber, "Do-It-Yourself: Constructing, Repairing, and Maintaining Domestic Masculinity," in *The Gender and Consumer Reader* edited by Jennifer Scanlon (New York: New York University Press, 2000), p. 72.

5. Bederman, p. 12.

6. Ibid., p. 14.

7. Michael Kimmel, *Manhood in America: A Cultural History* (New York: The Free Press, 1997), p. 182.

8. For a summary of these arguments regarding school activities and sexuality, see Joel Spring, *The American School 1642–2000* (New York: McGraw-Hill, 2001), pp. 259–273.

9. Mark A Swiencicki, "Consuming Brotherhood: Men's Culture, Style and Recreation as Consumer Culture, 1880–1930," in *Consumer Society in American History: A Reader* edited by Lawrence B. Glickman (Ithaca: Cornell University Press, 1999), p. 233.

10. Bederman, p. 13.

11. Swienciki, p. 214.

12. Jenna Weissman Joselit, *A Perfect Fit: Clothes, Character, and the Promise of America* (New York: Henry Holt & Company, 2001), p. 77.

13. George Chauncey, *Gay New York: Gender, Urban Culture, and the Making of the Gay Male World 1890–1940* (New York: Basic Books, 1994), p. 13.

14. Ibid., p. 13.

15. My description is based on a photo that I took of the statue.

16. Sivulka, p. 279.

17. This ad is reproduced in Sivulka, p. 105.

18. Bederman, p. 22.

19. Susan Porter Benson, "Living on the Margin: Working-Class Marriages and Family Survival Strategies in the United States, 1919–1941," in *The Sex of Things: Gender and Consumption in Historical Perspective* edited by Victoria de Grazia with Ellen Furlough (Berkeley: University of California Press, 1996), p. 214.

20. Ibid.

21. Ibid., pp. 215–220.

22. The title of Chapter 1 of M. E. Melody and Linda M. Peterson's *Teaching America about Sex: Marriage Guides and Sex Manuals from the Late Victorians to Dr. Ruth* (New York: New York University Press, 1999) is "The Late Victorians and Spermatic Political Economy," pp. 20–49.

23. Quoted in Ibid., p. 30.

24. Quoted in Ibid., p. 31.

25. Ibid., p. 23.

26. See Bederman, pp. 170–217 and Kimmel, pp. 181–188.

27. Kimmel, p. 181.

28. Bederman, pp. 180–181.

29. This quote is transcribed from photos I took inside the Roosevelt rotunda.

30. Ibid.

31. Ibid.

32. Bederman stresses the male orientation of Hall's concept of adolescence. Ibid., pp. 103–105.

33. G. Stanley Hall, *Adolescence*, Vol. 1 (Englewood Cliffs, NJ: Prentice-Hall, 1904), p. xv. Also see G. Stanley Hall, "Childhood and Adolescence" in Charles Strickland and Charles Burgess, eds., *Health, Growth, and Heredity* (New York: Teachers College Press, 1965), p. 108.

34. Bederman, p. 77.

35. G. Stanley Hall, *Adolescence*, Vol. 2 (Englewood Cliffs, NJ: Prentice-Hall, 1904), p. 125.

36. Kimmel, caption on photos between pp. 272–273.

37. Rev. W. J. Hunter, "Manhood Wrecked and Rescued," reproduced in Kimmel in photos between pp. 272–273.

38. Ibid.

39. The cover is reproduced in Ibid.

40. This poster is reproduced in John D'Emilio and Estelle Freedman *Intimate Affairs: A History of Sexuality in America* (New York: Harper & Row, 1988) between pp. 274 and 275.

41. "Tentative Report of the Committee on a System of Teaching Morals in Public Schools," *Proceedings of the National Education Association, 1911*, vol. 49 (Ann Arbor, MI: NEA, 1911), p. 360.

42. Irving King, *The High-School Age* (Indianapolis, IN: Bobbs-Merrill, 1914), p. 80.

43. Michael V. O'Shea, *The Trend of the Teens* (Chicago: Drake, 1920), p. 13.

44. Commission on the Reorganization of Secondary Education, National Education Association, *Cardinal Principles of Secondary Education, Bureau of Education Bulletin* (Washington, DC: U.S. Government Printing Office, 1918), p. 111.

45. V. K. Froula, "Extra-Curricular Activities: Their Relation to the Curricular Work of the School," *National Education Association Proceedings (1915)* (Washington, DC: National Education Association, 1915), pp. 738–739.

46. Quoted by E. Anthony Rotundo, *American Manhood: Transformations in Masculinity from the Revolution to the Modern Era* (New York: Basic Books, 1993), p. 240.

47. Ibid., p. 241.

48. Ibid., p. 243.

49. Margaret Lamberts Bendroth, *Fundamentalism and Gender: 1875 to the Present* (New Haven: Yale University Press, 1993), p. 65.

50. D'Emilio and Freedman, pp. 203–208.

51. "Report of the Committee on Character Education of the National Education Association," *Department of the Interior Bureau of Education Bulletin, 1926, no. 7 Character Education* (Washington, DC: U.S. Government Printing Office, 1926), p. 15.

52. Thomas W. Galloway, *Sex and Social Health: A Manual for the Study of Social Hygiene* (New York: Social Hygiene Association, 1924), pp. i–vii.

53. Ibid., p. 51.

54. Ibid., pp. 33–34.

55. Ibid., p. 65.

56. Ibid., pp. 286–287.

57. Ibid., p. 71.

58. Ibid., p. 51.

59. Ibid., p. 134.

60. Ibid., p. 96.

61. Kathy Peiss, *Cheap Amusements: Working Women and Leisure in Turn-of-the Century New York* (Philadelphia: Temple University Press, 1986), p. 88.

62. Ibid., p. 101.

63. Ibid., p. 102.

64. Quoted in Ibid., p. 99.

65. Quoted in Ibid., p. 125.

66. Quoted in Ibid., p. 126.

67. Peiss, pp. 131–132.

68. Ibid., pp. 178–181.

69. John Dewey, "The School As Social Center," *Annual Proceedings of the National Education Association, 1902* (Washington, DC: NEA, 1922), pp. 373–383.

70. T. Bowlker, "Women's Home-Making Function Applied to the Municipality, *American City*, Vol. VI (1912), pp. 863–869.

71. Beth L. Bailey, *From Front Porch to Back Seat: Courtship in Twentieth-Century America* (Baltimore: John Hopkins University Press, 1988), p. 4.

72. Mary McComb, "Rate Your Date: Young Women and the Commodification of Depression Era Courtship," in *Delinquents & Debutantes: Twentieth-Century American Girls' Cultures* (New York: New York University Press, 1998), p. 45.

73. Ibid., p. 45.

74. Quoted in Ibid., p. 45.

75. Ibid., pp. 52–54.

76. Amy L. Best, *Prom Night: Youth, Schools, and Popular Culture* (New York: Routledge, 2000), p. 6.

77. Ibid., p. 10.

78. Ibid., pp. 35–63.

79. Ibid., p. 4.

80. Kelly Schrum, "Teena Means Business: Teenage Girls Culture and Seventeen Magazine, 1944–1950," in *Delinquents & Debutantes: Twentieth-Century American Girls' Cultures* edited by Sherrie A. Inness (New York: New York University Press, 1998), pp. 140–141.

81. "Report of the Committee on Character Education of the National Education Association, *U.S. Department of the Interior Bureau of Education Bulletin, 1926, no. 7: Character Education* (Washington, DC: U.S. Government Printing Office, 1926), p. 6.

82. William Gellerman, *The American Legion as Educator* (New York: Teachers College, Columbia University, 1938), p. 88.

83. Quoted by Stuart Ewen, *PR! A Social History of Spin* (New York: Basic Books, 1996), p. 215.

84. Howard K. Beales, *Are American Teachers Free?* (New York: Scribner's, 1936), pp. 108–109.

85. Ibid., p. 126.

86. Howard K. Beales, *A History of Freedom of Teaching in American School* (New York: Scribner's, 1941), p. 247.

87. Milton Bennion, "Report of the Committee on Citizenship and Character Education," *School and Society*, vol. 14 no. 351 (September 17, 1921), pp. 190–191.

88. "Report of the Committee on Character Education. . . ."

89. Ibid., pp. 5–7.

90. Ibid., p. 6.

91. Gellerman, p. 20.

92. Ibid., pp. 21–39.

93. Russell Cook, "American Legion," *Proceedings of the Annual Meeting of the National Education Association, 1934*, vol. 72 (Washington, DC: NEA, 1934), pp. 111–116.

94. Ibid., p. 111.

95. Gellerman, p. 68.

96. As quoted in Ibid.

97. As quoted in Ibid., pp. 90–91.

98. As quoted in Ibid., pp. 203–204.

99. As quoted in Ibid., p. 206.

100. Mrs. Russell William Magna, "Daughters of the American Revolution," *Proceedings of the NEA, 1934* (Washington, DC: NEA, 1934), pp. 116–121.

101. Gellerman, pp. 206–207.

102. Ibid., pp. 208–214.

103. Beales, *Are American Teachers Free?*, p. 317.

104. These laws are reviewed by Bessie Louise Pierce, *Civic Attitudes in American Schools* (Chicago: University of Chicago Press, 1930), pp. 231–235).

105. Ibid., p. 246.

106. Roland Marchand, *Advertising The American Dream: Making Way for Modernity 1920–1940* (Berkeley: University of California Press, 1985), pp. 188–190.

107. Ibid., p. 190.

108. Richard M. Fried, "Introduction," to Bruce Barton, *The Man Nobody Knows* (Chicago: Ivan R. Dee, 2000), p. vii.

109. Stephen Fox, *The Mirror Makers: A History of American Advertising & Its Creators* (Urbana: University of Illinois Press, 1997), pp. 101–112, 331–333.

110. Barton, p. 23.

111. Ibid., p. 28.

112. Ibid., p. 23.

113. Ibid., p. 77.

114. Ibid., p. 83.

115. Ibid., pp. 61–64.

116. Reproduced in Sivulka, p. 102.

117. Reproduced in Ibid., p. 112.

118. Reproduced in Susan Strasser, *Satisfaction Guaranteed: The Making of the American Mass Market* (Washington, DC: Smithsonian Institution Press, 1989, p. 98.

119. Reproduced in Ibid., p. 99.

120. Ibid.

121. Sivulka, p. 221.

122. Reproduced in Ibid., p. 155.

123. Reproduced in Lendol Calder, *Financing the American Dream: A Cultural History of Consumer Credit* (Princeton: Princeton University Press, 1999), p. 193.

124. Reproduced in Ibid., p. 198.

125. See Ronald L. Davis, *Duke: The Life and Image of John Wayne* (Norman: University of Oklahoma Press, 1998).

126. I have already referenced the major works of Bederman and Kimmel. William Pinar's *The Gender of Racial Politics and Violence in America: Lynching, Prison Rape, & the Crisis of Masculinity* (New York: Peter Lang, 2001) provides the most complete history of these issues from the 19th to the 21st centuries.

127. Alexander Walker, *Rudolph Valentino* (New York: Penguin Books, 1977), p. 47.

128. Ibid., p. 49.

129. Ibid., p. 50.

130. Quoted in Ibid., p. 68.

131. Ibid., p. 69.

132. Photo shown in Ibid., p. 71.

133. Ibid., p. 8.

134. Ibid., p. 113.

135. Ibid., p. 113.

CHAPTER 4

1. Simon N. Patten, *The New Basis of Civilization* edited by Daniel Fox (Cambridge: Harvard University Press, 1907), p. 123.

2. Ibid., p. 123.

3. Ibid., p. 123.

4. Ibid., p. 136.

5. Ibid., p. 137.

6. Herbert Blumer, *Movies and Conduct* (New York: Macmillan, 1933), p. 50.

7. Quoted in Kathy Peiss, *Cheap Amusements: Working Class Women and Leisure in Turn-of-the-Century New York* (Philadelphia: Temple University Press, 1986), p. 153.

8. A standard history of the early development of films is Lewis Jacobs, *The Rise of the American Film: A Critical History* (New York: Teachers College Press, 1967). Figures on movie attendance and description of early audiences can be found in Lary May, *Screening Out the Past: The Birth of Mass Culture and the Motion Picture Industry* (New York: Oxford University Press. 1980), pp. 35–42.

9. "Cheap Theaters," *The Social Evil in Chicago* (Chicago: Chicago Vice Commission, 1911), reprinted in *The Movies in Our Midst*, ed. Gerald Mast (Chicago: University of Chicago Press, 1982), pp. 61–63.

10. May, p. 37.

11. Terry Christensen, *Reel Politics: American Political Movies from Birth of a Nation to Platoon* (New York: Basil Blackwell, 1987), p. 15.

12. Ibid.

13. Richard Randall, *Censorship of the Movies: The Social and Political Control of a Mass Medium* (Madison: University of Wisconsin Press, 1968), pp. 12–13.

14. Will H. Hays, "Motion Pictures and Their Censors, The American Review of Reviews, Vol. 75 (April 1927), pp. 393–398.

15. *Mutual Film Corporation v. Industrial Commission of Ohio* (1915) reprinted in *The Movies in Our Midst*, ed. Gerald Mast (Chicago: University of Chicago Press, 1982), pp. 136–143.

16. Ellis Oberholtzer, "What Are the 'Movies' Making of Our Children?" *World's Work*, vol. 4 (January 1921), pp. 249–263.

17. Ellis Oberholtzer, "The Censor and the Movie 'Menace'," *The North American Review*, vol. 212, no. 780 (November 1920), pp. 641–647.

18. Ibid.

19. May, pp. 53–55.

20. John Collier, "Censorship and the National Board, *The Survey*, vol. 35 (October 1915), pp. 9–14.
21. Ibid., p. 31.
22. John Collier, "A Film Library," *The Survey*, vol. 35 (March 1916), p. 668.
23. "Discussion," *Annual Proceedings of the NEA, 1914*, p. 747.
24. Alfred H. Saunders, "Motion Pictures as an Aid to Education," *Annual Proceedings of the National Education Association, 1914*, vol. 52 (Ann Arbor, MI: NEA, 1914), p. 744.
25. "Discussion," *Annual Proceedings of the NEA, 1914*, p. 746.
26. Ibid.
27. Neal Gabler, *An Empire of Their Own: How the Jews Invented Hollywood* (New York: Crown, 1988).
28. Ibid., p. 277.
29. Norman Zierold, *The Moguls* (New York: Coward-McCann, 1969), p. 287.
30. Ibid., p. 24.
31. May, pp. 169–177.
32. Gabler, pp. 164–165.
33. Raymond Moley, *The Hays Office* (Indianapolis, IN: Bobbs-Merrill, 1945), pp. 135–137.
34. Gabler, pp. 277–278.
35. Ibid.
36. Randall provides a chart categorizing the various censorship laws of state and city governments. See Randall, pp. 88–89.
37. "Film Censors and Other Morons," *The Nation*, vol. 117, no. 3049 (December 12, 1923), pp. 678–679.
38. For surveys of state and municipal censorship boards, see Thomas Leary and J. Roger Noall, "Note: Entertainment: Public Pressures and the Law—Official and Unofficial Control of the Content and Distribution of Motion Pictures and Magazines," Harvard Law Review, vol. 71(1957), pp. 326–367, and Randall, pp. 15–18, 88–89.
39. Lewis Jacobs, *The Rise of the American Film: A Critical History* (New York: Teachers College Press, 1967), p. 23.
40. Will Hays, "Improvement of Moving Pictures," *Annual Proceedings of the National Education Association, 1922*, vol. 60 (Washington, DC: National Education Association, 1922), pp. 252–257.
41. "Education and the Movies," *The Elementary School Journal*, vol. 23 (February 1923), pp. 406–408.
42. This financial support is recounted in Charles Judd, "Report of Committee to Cooperate with the Motion Picture Producers," *Annual Proceedings of the National Education Association, 1923*, vol. 61 (Washington, DC: NEA, 1923), pp. 243–244.
43. Ibid., p. 245.
44. Col. Jason Joy, "Motion Pictures in Their Relation to the School Child," *Proceedings of the National Education Association, 1927*, vol. 65 (Washington, DC: NEA, 1927), pp. 964–969.
45. Ibid., p. 967.
46. Ibid., p. 967.
47. Moley, pp. 77–78.
48. The following is a list of the authors and their research titles. Many of the researchers sponsored by the Payne Fund were in their own disciplines and consequently added to the prestige of the studies.

1. P. W. Holaday, Indianapolis Public Schools, and George Stoddard, Director, Iowa Child Welfare Research Station. "Getting Ideas from the Movies."

2. Ruth C. Peterson and L. L. Thurstone, Department of Psychology, University of Chicago "Motion Pictures and the Social Attitudes of Children."

3. Frank Shuttleworth and Mark May, Institute of Human Relations, Yale University: "The Social Conduct and Attitudes of Movie Fans."

4. W. S. Dysinger and Christian Ruckmick, Department of Psychology, State University of Iowa. "The Emotional Responses of Children to the Motion Picture Situation."

5. Charles Peters, Professor of Education, Pennsylvania State College "Motion Pictures and Standards of Morality."

6. Samuel Renshaw, Vernon L. Miller, and Dorothy Marquis, Department of Psychology, Ohio State University. "Children's Sleep."

7. Herbert Blumer, Department of Sociology. University of Chicago: "Movies and Conduct."

8, 9, and 12. Edgar Dale, Research Associate, Bureau of Educational Research, Ohio State University: "The Content of Motion Pictures," "Children's Attendance at Motion Pictures," and "How to Appreciate Motion Pictures," respectively.

10. Herbert Blumer and Philip Hauser, Department of Sociology, University of Chicago, "Movies, Delinquency, and Crime."

11. Paul Cressey and Frederick Thrasher, New York University "Boys, Movies, and City Streets."

49. Henry James Forman, *Our Movie-Made Children* (New York: Macmillan, 1933).

50. W. W. Charters, *Motion Pictures and Youth: A Summary* (New York: Macmillan, 1933), p. 12.

51. Ibid., p. 13.

52. Ibid., p. 13.

53. Forman, pp. 280–282.

54. John D' Emilio and Estelle Freedman, *Intimate Affairs: A History of Sexuality in America* (New York: Harper & Row, 1988), pp. 256–257.

55. Cited in Lary May, *Screening Out the Past: The Birth of Mass Culture and the Motion Picture Industry* (New York: Oxford University Press, 1980), p. 203.

56. D'Emilio and Freedman, pp. 256, 268.

57. M. E. Melody and Linda M. Peterson, *Teaching America about Sex: Marriage Guides and Sex Manuals from the Late Victorians to Dr. Ruth* (New York: New York University Press, 1999), pp. 59–63.

58. Ibid., pp. 63–65.

59. Ibid., pp. 72–114.

60. Blumer, pp. 45–49.

61. Charles Peters, *Motion Pictures and Standards of Morality* (New York: Macmillan, 1933).

62. The Legion of Decency, *The Commonwealth*, vol. 20 (May 18, 1934), p. 58.

63. The pledge can be found in Ibid.

64. The pledge can be found in Ibid.

65. Moley, pp. 57–58.

66. Martin Quigley, *Decency in Motion Pictures* (New York: Macmillan, 1937).

67. The 1930 movie code can be found in Moley, pp. 241–248, and Mast, pp. 321–333.

68. Ibid.

69. The 1927 Code can be found in Moley, pp. 240–241.

70. The 1930 movie code can be found in Moley, pp. 241–248, and Mast, pp. 321–333.

71. Will H. Hays, "The Motion Picture in Education," *Proceedings of the Annual Meeting of the National Education Association, 1939*, vol. 77 (Washington, DC: NEA, 1939), p. 80.

72. Juliann Sivulka, *Soap, Sex, and Cigarettes: A Cultural History of American Advertising* (Belmont, CA: Wadsworth Publishing, 1998), pp. 211–222.

73. "British vs. American Radio Slant, Debate Theme in 40,000 Schools," *Variety*, vol. 111, no. 12 (August 29, 1933), p. 1.

74. Ibid.

75. See Philip T. Rosen, *The Modern Stentors: Radio Broadcasters and the Federal Government, 1920–1934* (Westport, CT: Greenwood Press, 1980), pp. 128–133, Erik Barnouw, *A Tower in Babel: A History of Broadcasting in the United States to 1933* (New York: Oxford University Press, 1966), pp. 172–179, and E. Frost, *Education's Own Stations: The History of Broadcast Licenses Issued to Educational Institutions* (Chicago: University of Chicago Press, 1937), pp. 1–5.

76. The other members were the National University Extension Association, the Jesuit Educational Association, The Association of Land-Grant Colleges and Universities, and the Association of College and University Broadcasting Stations.

77. "Virtues, Vices of Radio . . . ," pp. 3–10.

78. Joy Elmer Morgan, "A National Culture—By-Product or Objective of National Planning?" Ibid., p. 29.

79. Ibid., p. 30.

80. Merlin H. Aylesworth, "Radio as a Means of Public Enlightenment," *Proceedings of the National Education Association*, 1934, vol. 72, pp. 99–102.

81. William Paley, "Radio as a Cultural Force: These notes on the economic and social philosophy of America's radio industry, as represented by the policies and practices of the Columbia Broadcasting System, Inc., were embodied in a talk on October 17, 1934, before the Federal Communications Commission, in its inquiry into proposals to allot fixed percentages of the nation's radio facilities to non-commercial broadcasting," Located in CBS Reference Library, New York City, pp. 8–9.

82. Ibid., p. 13.

83. Ibid., pp. 13–14.

84. Barnouw, *The Golden Web*, p. 26.

85. Paley, p. 14.

86. Ibid., p. 18.

87. *Variety*, vol. 117, no. 1 (December 18, 1934), p. 34.

88. "St. Paul Meet on Kid Programs Calls Radio Villains Likeable; Suggest Boycott, Probation" *Variety*, vol. 117, no. 2 (December 25, 1934), p. 29.

89. "Air Reformers After Coin," *Variety*, vol. 117, no. 7 (January 29, 1935), pp. 1, 66.

90. Raymond Stedman, *The Serials: Suspense and Drama by Installment* (Norman: University of Oklahoma Press, 1977), pp. 143–191, and Erik Barnouw, *The Golden Web: A History of Broadcasting in the United States, 1933–1953* (New York: Oxford University Press, 1968), pp. 89–108.

91. Stedman, p. 192.

92. Ibid., pp. 194–195.

93. *Radio's Golden Years* (tape recording) (Minneapolis: Cassettes, Inc., 1972).

94. Clara Savage Littledale, "Better Radio Programs for Children," *Parents Magazine*, vol. 18, no. 13 (May 8, 1933).

95. "Boycott MDSE in Air Protest?" *Variety*, vol. 109, no. 12 (February 28, 1933), p. 47.

96. "Cal. Teachers List 'Bad' Programs," *Variety*, vol. 110. no. 8 (May 2, 1933), p. 34.

97. "Mrs. Harold Milligan," *Educational Broadcasting 1937*, ed. C. S. Marsh (Chicago: University of Chicago Press, 1938), pp. 258–261.

98. "Radio: Mothers Chasing the Ether Bogeyman," *Newsweek*, March 11, 1933, p. 30.

99. "Clubwomen Launch Westchester Cowboys," *Variety*, vol. 117, no. 10 (February 20, 1935), p. 39.

100. "Women's Radio Committee Clarifies," *Variety*, vol. 118, no. 10 (May 22, 1935), p. 36.

101. "Mrs. Harold Milligan," p. 259.

102. Ibid., pp. 258–259.

103. Ibid., p. 261.

104. "Squawks Force NBC Move for Less Honor," *Variety*, vol. 109, no. 12 (February 26, 1933), p. 45.

105. "Now Agree Too Much Honor for Kids, Junior Programs Turning to Fantasy, *Variety*, vol. 111, no. 8 (August 1, 1933), p. 41.

106. "Radio Wants Clubwoman Good Will: Offer Transmitters to Gals with Messages—Will Hays Started It," *Variety*, vol. 112, no. 6 (October 17, 1933), p. 37.

107. "Dime Novel Air Stuff Out: Protests Chafe FCC Into Action," *Variety*, vol. 118, no. 3 (April 3, 1935), pp. 1, 58.

108. "Paley in Annual Report Deprecates 'Straightjacket' for Broadcasting; Air Voluntarily Censors Programs," *Variety*, vol. 134, no. 4 (April 5, 1939), p. 23.

109. "NBC Slant on CBS Policy," CBS Reference Library, p. 37.

110. "Sponsor Rights Defined," *Variety*, vol. 134, no. 4 (April 5, 1939), p. 23.

111. Statement by William S. Paley over the Columbia Network, Tuesday, May 14, 1935, CBS Reference Library.

112. Arthur Jersild and Frances Holmes, *Children's Fears* (New York: Teachers College, 1935), pp. 318–335.

113. "New Policies: A Statement to the Public, to Advertisers, and to Advertising Agencies" (May 15, 1935), CBS Reference Library, p. 4.

114. Ibid., p. 5.

115. Ibid., p. 6.

116. "NBC's Tentative Program Code," *Variety*, vol. 134, no. 4 (April 5, 1934), p. 24.

117. Ibid.

118. Ibid.

CHAPTER 5

1. Lendol Calder uses this magazine cover for the cover of his book, *Financing the American Dream: A Cultural History of Consumer Credit* (Princeton: Princeton University Press, 1999). Calder discusses the artist's original intentions on p. 305.

2. Stuart Ewen, *PR! A Social History of Spin* (New York: Basic Books, 1996), p. 147.

3. Edward S. Herman and Noam Chomsky, *Manufacturing Consent: The Political Economy of the Mass Media* (New York: Pantheon, 1988).

4. For a review of these early works on controlling public opinion, including Lippmann's *Public Opinion*, see Ewen, pp. 131–174.

5. Quote by Ewen, p. 149.

6. Ibid., p. 303.

7. Ibid., pp. 322–323.

8. Quoted by Ewen, p. 304.

9. Ibid., p. 167.

10. Ibid., p. 163.

11. Ibid., pp. 297–298.

12. Photos of billboards shown in Ewen, p. 323.

13. Ibid., p. 306.

14. Ibid., p. 314.

15. Ibid., p. 315.

16. Commission on Character Education, Tenth Yearbook, *Character Education* (Washington, DC: Department of Superintendence of the National Education Association, 1932), p. 15.

17. Educational Policies Commission, *Learning the Ways of Democracy: A Case Book of Civic Education* (Washington, DC: NEA, 1940), pp. 63–64.

18. Ibid., p. 65.

19. Ibid., p. 109.

20. Ibid., p. 110.

21. Ibid., p. 171.

22. William Gellerman, *The American Legion as Educator* (New York: Teachers College, Columbia University, 1938), p. 93.

23. Gellerman, p. 122; Harold Hyman, *To Try Men's Souls: Loyalty Tests in American History* (Berkeley and Los Angeles: University of California Press, 1959), pp. 323–326; Edward A. Krug, *The Shaping of the American High School, 1920–1941* (Madison: University of Wisconsin Press, 1972), pp. 231–232.

24. C. A. Bowers, *The Progressive Educator and the Depression: The Radical Years* (New York: Random House, 1969), p. 15.

25. Russell Cook, "American Legion," *Proceedings of the National Education Association, 1934*, vol. 72 (Washington, DC: NEA, 1934), pp. 111–116.

26. As quoted in Mary Anne Raywid, *The Ax-Grinders: Critics of Our Public Schools* (New York: Macmillan, 1963), p. 51.

27. Augustin G. Rudd, *Bending the Twig: The Revolution in Education and Its Effect on Our Children* (New York: New York Chapter of the Sons of the American Revolution, 1957), pp. 26–27.

28. Harold Rugg, *That Men May Understand: An American in the Long Armistice* (New York: Doubleday, Dome, 1941), pp. 36–44.

29. Reprinted in Ibid., pp. 54–69.

30. Ibid., pp. 10–11.

31. Ibid., p. 25.

32. Ibid., pp. 29–30.

33. Quoted by Stephen Fox, *The Mirror Makers: A History of American Advertising & Its Creators* (Urbana: University of Illinois Press, 1997), p. 123.

34. Ibid., pp. 123–124.

35. Quoted by Gary Cross, *An All-Consuming Century: Why Commercialism Won in Modern America* (New York: Columbia University Press, 2000), p. 135.

36. Ibid., p. 135.

37. Rudd, p. 85.

38. "Advertising Groups Pursuing Professor Rugg's Books," *Publishers Weekly*, vol. 138 (September 28, 1940), pp. 1322–1323.

39. Ibid., p. 1323.

40. Rudd, p. 65.

41. "Book Burnings: Rugg Texts," *Time*, vol. 36 (September 9, 1940), pp. 64–65.

42. Rugg, p. 3.

43. Ibid., p. 4.

44. Ibid., p. 12.

45. William Carr, "An Educator Bids for Partners," *Nation's Business* (March 1941), pp. 19–20, 96–97.

46. Walter Fuller, "Industry and the War," *Proceedings of the NEA, 1942*, pp. 111–114.

47. John Studebaker, "Our Country's Training Program," *Proceedings of the National Education Association, 1941*, Vol. 79 (Washington, DC: NEA, 1941), pp. 115–122.

48. As quoted by Elaine Tyler May, *Homeward Bound: American Families in the Cold War Era* (New York: Basic Books, 1999), p. 11.

49. Elaine Tyler May, "The Commodity Gap: Consumerism and the Modern House," in *Consumer Society in American History: A Reader* edited by Lawrence Glickman (Ithaca: Cornell University Press, 1999), pp. 298–299.

50. Ibid., p. 302.

51. Mary Anne Raywid, *The Axe Grinders: Critics of Our Public Schools* (New York: Macmillan, 1963), pp. 35–51.

52. Ibid.

53. Ibid., pp. 59–63.

54. Jack Nelson and Gene Roberts, Jr., *The Censors and the Schools* (Westport, CT: Greenwood Press, 1963), pp. 99–100.

55. Ibid., p. 109.

56. Ibid., pp. 109–110.

57. Joel Spring, *The Sorting Machine Revisited: National Educational Policy Since 1945* (White Plains, NY: Longman, 1989), p. 9.

58. Ibid.

59. Ibid.

60. Kelly Schrum, "Teena Means Business: Teenage Girls' Culture and 'Seventeen Magazine', 1944–1950," in *Delinquents & Debutantes: Twentieth-Century American Girls' Cultures* (New York: New York University Press, 1998), p. 149.

61. Ibid., p. 149.

62. Ibid., p. 156.

63. Ibid., p. 136.

64. Ad reproduced Ibid., p. 143.

65. Ad is reproduced in Juliann Sivulka's *Soap, Sex, and Cigarettes: A Cultural History of American Advertising* (Belmont, CA: Wadsworth Publishing Company, 1998), p. 262.

66. Reproduced in Schrum, p. 148.

67. Ibid., p. 142.

68. Erik Barnouw, *The Golden Web: A History of Broadcasting in the United States, 1933–1953* (New York: Oxford University Press, 1968), pp. 295–296.

69. The code can be found in *Documents of American Broadcasting*, ed. Frank Kahn (Englewood Cliffs, New Jersey: Prentice-Hall, 1973), pp. 340–355.

70. As quoted by Ben Bagdikian, *The Media Monopoly, Second Edition* (Boston: Beacon Press, 1987), p. 137.

71. As quoted in Barnouw, p. 257 (capitalization in original).

72. Ibid., pp. 253–257, 265.

73. As quoted in Ibid., p. 273.

74. Ibid., pp. 273–274.

75. Ibid., p. 88.

76. Ibid., p. 92.

77. Ibid., pp. 168–169.

78. "Comic Book Publishers Promise Reforms," *Christian Century*, vol. 71 (November 10, 1954), p. 1357.

79. *Comic Books and Juvenile Delinquency: A Part of the Investigation of Juvenile Delinquency in the United States: Interim Report of the Subcommittee to investigate Juvenile Delinquency to the Committee on the Judiciary Pursuant to S. Res. 89 and S. Res. 190* (Washington, DC: U.S. Government Printing Office, 1955), p. 3.

80. "Senate Sub-Committee Holds Hearings on 'Comics'," *Publishers Weekly*, vol. 165 (May 1, 1954), p. 1903.

81. *Comic Books and Juvenile Delinquency . . .* , pp. 8–9.

82. "Purified Comics," *Newsweek*, vol. 32 (July 12, 1948), p. 56; "Better Than Censorship," *Christian Century*, vol. 65 (July 28, 1948), p. 750; *Comic Books and Juvenile Delinquency . . .* , p. 31.

83. "Comics' Publishers Institute Code, Appoint 'Czar'," *Publishers' Weekly*, vol. 166 (September 25, 1954), p. 1386; "Progress in Comic Book Cleanup," *America* (October 30, 1954), pp. 1–14; "Code for Comics," *Time* (November 8, 1954), p. 60.

84. "First 'Seal of Approval' Comics Out This Month," *Publishers' Weekly*, vol. 167 (January 15, 1955), p. 211.

85. "Comics' Publishers Institute Code," p. 1386; "Correspondence: Comic-Book Code," *America* (November 13, 1954), p. 196.

86. May, p. 148.

87. Abraham Tannenbaum, "Family Living in Textbook Town," *Progressive Education*, March 1954. Reprinted in *Hearings Before the Ad Hoc Subcommittee on De Facto School Segregation, Committee on Education and Labor, House of Representatives, 89th Congress, 2nd Session, on Books for Schools and the Treatment of Minorities, August 23, 24, 30, 31, and September 1, 1966* (Washington, DC: U.S. Government Printing Office, 1966), pp. 806–816.

88. Ibid., pp. 813–814.

89. Wini Breines, "The Other Fifties: Beats and Bad Girls," in *Not June Cleaver: Women and Gender in Postwar America, 1945–1960* edited by Joanne Meyerowitz (Philadelphia: Temple University Press, 1994), p. 385.

90. As reported by Ronald L. Doris, *Duke: The Life and Image of John Wayne* (Norman: University of Oklahoma Press, 1998), p. xi.

91. Ibid., pp. 15–96.

92. See Clayton R. Koppes and Gregory D. Black, *Hollywood Goes to War: How Politics, Profits and Propaganda Shaped World War II Movies* (Berkeley: University of California Press, 1987).

93. Doris, p. 279.

94. Ibid., p. 119.

95. Larry Ceplair and Steven Englund, *The Inquisition in Hollywood: Politics in the Film Community, 1930–1960* (Berkeley and Los Angeles: University of California Press, 1983), p. 211.

96. John Cogley, *Report on Blacklisting* (Fund for the Republic, 1956), p. 11.

97. Quoted by Doris, p. 118.

98. Quoted by Doris, p. 12.

99. Ibid., p. 5.

100. Ibid., p. 8.

101. Sivulka, p. 279.

102. Molly Haskell, *From Reverence to Rape: The Treatment of Women in the Movies Second Edition* (Chicago: University of Chicago Press, 1987), p. 254.

103. Ibid., p. 243.

104. Ibid., p. 253.

105. Breines, pp. 390–396.

106. Ibid., p. 398.

107. The ad is reproduced in Lynn Spigel's *Make Room for TV: Television and the Family Ideal in Postwar America* (Chicago: The University of Chicago Press, 1992), p. 87.

108. Ibid., p. 83.

109. Ibid., p. 83.

110. Reproduced in Ibid., p. 93.

CHAPTER 6

1. "The Negro in American History Textbooks: A Report of a Study of the Treatment of Negroes in American History Textbooks Used in Grades Five and Eight and in the High Schools of California's Public Schools" (Sacramento: California State Department of Education, 1964), p. 2.

2. "The Negro in American History Textbooks," reprinted in *Hearings Before the Ad Hoc Subcommittee on De Facto School Segregation,* of the Committee on Education and Labor, House of Representatives, 89th Congress, 2nd Session, on Books for Schools and the Treatment of Minorities, August 23, 24, 30, 31, and September 1, 1966 (Washington, DC: U.S. Government Printing Office, 1966).

3. Erik Barnouw, *The Golden Web: A History of Broadcasting in the United States, 1933–1953* (New York: Oxford University Press, 1968), p. 297.

4. "The Negro in American History Textbooks . . . ," p. 770.

5. Ibid., pp. 770–771.

6. Ibid., p. 772.

7. Roy Wilkins, "Books for Schools and Treatment of Minorities: Introduction" (National Association for the Advancement of Colored People, 1966), p. 1.

8. "Statement of Lerone Bennett," *Hearings Before the Ad Hoc Subcommittee . . . ,* pp. 214–215.

9. Ibid., pp. 213–214.

10. "Statement of Austin J. McCaffrey, Executive Director, American Textbook Publishers Institute," Hearings Before the Ad Hoc Subcommittee on De Facto School Segregation, of the Committee on Education and Labor, House of Representatives, 89th Congress, 2nd Session, on Books for Schools and the Treatment of Minorities, August 23, 24, 30, 31, and September 1, 1966 (Washington, DC: U.S. Government Printing Office, 1966), p. 107.

11. Joel Roth, "Dick and Jane Make Some New Friends," *Book Production Industry,* June 1965, reprinted in *Hearings Before the Ad Hoc Subcommittee on De Facto School Segregation . . .* , p. 816.

12. "Statement of Austin McCaffrey . . . ," p. 114.

13. "Statement of Robert W. Locke, Senior Vice President, McGraw-Hill Book Co.; Accompanied by Dr. Richard Smith, Senior Editor, Text-Film Division, McGraw-Hill Book Co., *Hearings Before the Ad Hoc Subcommittee on De Facto Segregation . . .* ," p. 191.

14. "Statement of Darrel E. Peterson, President, Scott, Foresman & Co.," *Hearings Before the Ad Hoc Subcommittee on De Facto Segregation . . .* , pp. 122–123.

15. "Integrating the Texts," *Newsweek,* March 7, 1966, reprinted in *Hearings Before the Ad Hoc Subcommittee on De Facto Segregation . . .* , pp. 826–827.

16. A. Kent MacDougall, "Integrated Books-School Texts Stressing Negroes' Role in United States Arouse the South's Pre-Primers Show Mixed Scenes, Some Publishers Turn Out Special Editions for Dixie," *Wall Street Journal,* March 24, 1966, reprinted in *Hearings Before the Ad Hoc Subcommittee on De Facto School Segregation . . .* , p. 804.

17. "Statement of Darrel E. Peterson . . . ," p. 122.

18. Ibid., pp. 124–125.

19. "Statement of Ross Sackett, Executive Vice President, Holt Rinehart & Winston, Inc.," *Hearings Before the Ad Hoc Subcommittee on De Facto Segregation . . .* , pp. 217–273.

20. "Statement of Craig T. Senft, President, Silver Burdett Co., a Division of General Learning Corporation," *Hearings Before the Ad Hoc Subcommittee on De Facto School Segregation . . .* , pp. 115–117.

21. Statement of Robert W. Locke, Senior Vice President, McGraw-Hill Book Co.; Accompanied by Dr. Richard Smith, Senior Editor, Text-Film Division, McGraw-Hill Book Co., *"Hearings Before the Ad Hoc Subcommittee on De Facto Segregation . . .* , p. 191.

22. "Statement of G.M. Fenollosa, Vice President and Director, Houghton Mifflin Co., Boston, Mass.," *Hearings Before the Ad Hoc Subcommittee on De Facto School Segregation . . .* , p. 129.

23. Robert E. Weems, Jr., "Consumerism and the Construction of Black Female Identity in Twentieth-Century America," in *The Gender and Consumer Culture Reader* edited by Jennifer Scanlon (New York: New York University Press, 2000), p. 167.

24. Ibid., p. 171.

25. Ibid., pp. 171–172.

26. Ibid., p. 173.

27. Ibid., p. 173.

28. Ibid., p. 175.

29. Ibid., p. 175.

30. The ad is reproduced in Juliann Sivulka, *Soap, Sex, and Cigarettes: A Cultural History of American Advertising* (Belmont, CA: Wadsworth Publishing Company, 1998), p. 293.

31. Ibid., p. 264. See Stephen Fox's *The Mirror Makers: A History of American Advertising and Its Creators* (Urbana: University of Illinois Press, 1997), pp. 272–314 on the racial integration of advertising agencies and ad content.

32. Bernice Kanner, *The 100 Best TV Commercials . . . and Why They Worked* (New York: Random House, 1999), p. 137.

33. Ibid., p. 137.

34. Ibid., p. 139.

35. Ibid., p. 139.

36. Ibid., p. 141.

37. Elissa Moses, *The $100 Billion Allowance: Accessing the Global Teen Market* (New York: John Wiley & Sons, Inc. 2000), p. 10.
38. Ibid., p. 36.
39. Leslie Savan, *The Sponsored Life: Ads, TV, and American Culture* (Philadelphia: Temple University Press, 1994), p. 55.
40. Gail Bedesman, *Manliness & Civilization: A Cultural History of Gender and Race in the United States, 1880–1917* (Chicago: University of Chicago Press, 1995), p. 3.
41. Quoted by Kenon Breazeale, "In Spite of Women: Esquire and the Male Consumer," *The Gender and Consumer Culture Reader . . .* , p. 229.
42. Ibid., p. 233.
43. Ibid., p. 235.
44. Ibid., p. 235.
45. Ibid., p. 239.
46. "National Organization for Women's 1966 Statement of Purpose" (Adopted at the Organizing Conference in Washington, DC, October 29, 1966), http://www.now.org.
47. For a survey of accomplishments in changing female images in public schools see "Opening Doors in Education," http://www.feminist.org.
48. Savan, p. 225.
49. Ibid., pp. 226–227.
50. Sivulka, p. 303.
51. Reproduced in Ibid., p. 374.
52. Reproduced in Savan, p. 205.
53. Ibid., p. 205.
54. Ibid., p. 198.
55. Ibid., p. 198.
56. Ibid., p. 199.
57. Kanner, p. 41.
58. Eric Johnston, *America Unlimited: The Case for a People's Capitalism* (Garden City, NY: Doubleday, Doran, 1944), p. 13.
59. Ibid., p. 6.
60. Ibid., p. 343.
61. Eric Johnston, *Intolerance* (New York: U.S. Chamber of Commerce, 1945), pp. 3–7.
62. Edward De Grazia and Roger Newman, *Banned Films: Movies, Censors & The First Amendment* (New York: Bowker, 1982), pp. 70–71.
63. Ibid.
64. Ibid., pp. 230–231.
65. Ibid., pp. 238–240.
66. William S. Paley, *As It Happened: A Memoir* (Garden City, NY: Doubleday, 1979), p. 232.
67. Thomas Cripps, "Amos 'n' Andy and the Debate over American Racial Integration," in *American History/American Television: Interpreting the Video Past*, ed. John E. O'Conner (New York: Frederick Ungar, 1983), pp. 33–54.
68. Ibid., p. 41.
69. Ibid., p. 49.
70. J. Fred MacDonald, *Blacks and White TV: Afro-Americans in Television since 1948* (Chicago: Nelson-Hall, 1983), pp. 68–69, 72–73.
71. As quoted in Ibid., p. 16.

72. Ibid., pp. 81–82; quote from p. 101.

73. Ibid., pp. 93–95.

74. *Office of Communication of the United Church of Christ v. Federal Communications Commission*, reprinted in *Documents of American Broadcasting*, ed. Frank J. Kahn (Englewood Cliffs, NJ: Prentice-Hall, 1973), pp. 639–681.

75. As quoted in Kathryn C. Montgomery, *Target: Prime Time Advocacy Groups and the Struggle over Entertainment Television* (New York: Oxford University Press, 1989), pp. 23–24.

76. Ibid., pp. 24–26.

77. Ibid., p. 58.

78. Ibid., pp. 51–58.

79. Ibid., p. 73.

80. Ibid., pp. 75–80.

81. Ibid., pp. 28–30.

82. MacDonald, pp. 108–111.

83. Angela M. S. Nelson, "Black Situation Comedies and the Politics of Television Art," in *Cultural Diversity and the U.S. Media* edited by Yahya R. Kamalipour and Theresa Carilli (Albany: State University of New York Press, 1998), p. 80.

84. Ibid., pp. 81–86.

85. See Richard Morris and Mary E. Stuckey, "Destroying the Past to Save the Present: Pastoral Voice and Native Identity," in *Cultural Diversity and the U.S. Media . . .* , pp. 137–147.

86. Kanner, p. 222.

87. Ibid., p. 223.

88. Ibid., p. 222.

89. Ellen Condliffe Lagemann, *The Politics of Knowledge: The Carnegie Corporation, Philanthropy, and Public Policy* (Middletown, CT: Wesleyan University Press, 1989), pp. 222–223.

90. As quoted in James L. Baughman, *Television's Guardians: The FCC and the Politics of Programming, 1958–1967* (Knoxville: University of Tennessee Press, 1985), pp. 34–35.

91. Ibid., p. 33.

92. Ibid., p. 33.

93. As quoted in Lagemann, p. 220.

94. Alan Pifer, "When Fashionable Rhetoric Fails," *Education Week*, vol. 23 (February 1983), p. 24.

95. Carnegie Commission on Educational Television, *Public Television: A Program for Action* (New York: Harper & Row, 1967), p. 95.

96. Ibid., p. 95.

97. Lloyd Morrisett, "Introduction" in Gerald S. Lesser, *Children and Television: Lessons from "Sesame Street"* (New York: Vintage, 1975), p. xxi.

98. Ibid., p. xxvi.

99. Lesser, p. 7.

100. Ibid., pp. 8–9.

101. Ibid., p. 23.

102. Ibid., pp. 24–25.

103. Ibid., pp. 254–255.

104. Ibid., p. 95.

105. Ibid., p. 200.

106. Ibid., p. 80.

107. Ibid., pp. 80–81.

108. Ibid., p. 47.

109. Ibid., p. 204.

110. Ibid., pp. 208–211.

111. "PBSKids: Sesame Street-Caregivers," *http://pbskids.org/sesame/caregivers/index.html.*

112. Ibid.

113. I found these product names and associated icons on the Amazon Web site, *www. amazon.com.*

114. Ibid.

CHAPTER 7

1. Anzia Yezierska, *Salome of the Tenements* (Urbana: University of Illinois Press, 1995), p. 27.

2. Amy L. Best, *Prom Night: Youth, Schools, and Popular Culture* (New York: Routledge, 2000), p. 46.

3. Kurt M. Landgraf, "Testing, Accountability, and Funding: Key to Education Reform," Paid advertisement in *The New York Times* (June 25, 2001), p. A9.

4. Ibid.

5. Alex Molnar, *Giving Kids the Business: The Commercialization of America's Schools* (Boulder: Westview Press, 1996).

6. Constance L. Hays, "New Report Examines Commercialism in U.S. Schools," *New York Times on the Web* (September 14, 2000).

7. Ibid.

8. Lynne Schrum, "Education and Commercialization: Raising Awareness and Making Decisions" (Athens: University of Georgia, College of Education, 2002), p. 5.

9. Alexandra Stille, "Textbook Publishers Learn to Avoid Messing with Texas," *The New York Times on the Web* (June 29, 2002).

10. Ibid.

11. Ibid.

12. Ibid.

13. Ibid.

14. Coby B. Simerly, Penny A. Ralston, Lydia Harriman, and Barbara Taylor, "The Scottsdale Initiative: Positioning the Progression for the 21st Century" in *Themes in Family and Consumer Sciences: A Book of Readings 2001, Volume Two* edited by Coby B. Simerly, Sharon Y. Nickols, and Jan M. Shane (Alexandria, VA: American Association of Family and Consumer Sciences, 2001), p. 15.

15. "Our Mission," *www.cwu.edu/~fandcs/fcsea.*

16. Marilyn R. DeLong, "Apparel Shopping on the Web," in *Themes in Family and Consumer Sciences . . .* , pp. 109–113.

17. "AACS: Who We Are," *www.aafcs.org.*

18. Ibid.

19. "About FCSEA," *www.cwu.edu/~fandcs/fcsea.*

20. "National Standards for Family and Consumer Sciences Education," *www.isbe.net/ secondaryed/FCS/fcs.htm.*

21. Ibid.

22. Ibid.

23. Ibid.

24. Ibid.

25. Elissa Moses, *The $100 Billion Allowance: Accessing the Global Teen Market* (New York: John Wiley & Sons, Inc. 2000), pp. 4, 10–11.

26. Moses, Back cover copy.

27. Back cover copy, Ibid.

28. Back cover copy, Ibid.

29. Ibid., pp. 35–60.

30. Ibid., pp. 168–170.

31. Ibid., pp. 86–87.

32. Ibid., p. 90.

33. Ibid., p. 91.

34. Juliann Sivulka, *Soap, Sex, and Cigarettes: A Cultural History of American Advertising* (Belmont, CA: Wadsworth Publishing Company, 1998), p. 421.

35. Ibid., p. 421.

36. Moses, p. 84.

37. Ibid., p. 86.

38. Ibid., p. 98.

39. Moses, p. 101.

40. Ibid., p. 82.

41. Ibid., p. 155.

42. Ibid., p. 120.

43. Quoted by Ellen Gruber Harvey, *The Adman in the Parlor: Magazines and the Gendering of Consumer Culture, 1880s to 1910s* (New York: Oxford University Press, 1996), p. 54.

44. Ad reproduced in Ibid., p. 63.

45. Ad reproduced in Ibid., p. 56.

46. Susan Strasser, *Satisfaction Guaranteed: The Making of the American Mass Market* (Washington, DC: Smithsonian Institution Press, 1989), pp. 115–119.

47. For a chronological list of Walt Disney's films see Leonard Mosley, *Disney's World* (Lanham, MD: Scarborough House, 1990), pp. 309–315.

48. Quoted by Bob Thomas in *Building A Company: Roy O. Disney and the Creation of an Entertainment Empire* (Hew York: Hyperion, 1998), pp. 67–68.

49. Ibid., p. 68.

50. Quoted in Ibid., p. 69.

51. Quoted in Ibid., p. 70.

52. Ibid., p. 198.

53. Ibid., pp. 187–188, 198.

54. http://www.sixflags.com/intl/intl_movieworldgermany.html.

55. Bob Thomas, *An American Original: Walt Disney* (New York: Disney Editions, 1994), p. 11.

56. Thomas, *Building A Company . . .* , p. 197.

57. http://disneyland.disney.go.com/disneylandresort/ResortInfo/Tickets/TicketPrices/index?id=6072&Grouping=TG.

58. Http://dlr.reservations.disney.go.com.

59. Thomas, *An American Original . . .* , pp. 251–262.

60. Ibid., p. 251.

61. Http://disneyland.disney.go.com.

62. Ibid.

63. Ibid.

64. Ibid.

65. Gottdiener, p. 127.

66. Http:dollywood.com.

67. Http://www.wholesaleeverday.com.

68. Henry A. Giroux, *The Mouse that Roared: Disney and the End of Innocence* (New York: Rowman & Littlefield Publishers, Inc., 1999).

69. Eric Schlosser, *Fast Food Nation: The Dark Side of the All-American Meal* (Boston: Houghton Mifflin Company, 2001), p. 48.

70. "McDonald's USA–Happy Meal Featuring the Many Adventures of Winnie the Pooh," *http://www.mcdonalds.com.*

71. Schlosser, p. 41.

72. Ibid., p. 48.

73. Ibid., p. 47.

74. "Little Known Black History Facts," *http://www.mcdonalds.com.*

75. "Little Known Black History Facts: Scope and Sequence," *http://www.mcdonalds.com*, Ibid., p. 1.

76. Ibid., pp. 2–3.

77. Schlosser, p. 22.

78. "Burger King Big Kids," http://www.burgerking.com.

79. "BK Academies," http:www.burgerking.com.

80. Ibid.

81. "BKScholars," http:www.burgerking.com.

82. "Welfare Reform," http:www.burgerking.com.

83. "Welcome to yum!," http://www.yum.com/home.asp.

84. "America's Original Fast Food Chain" and "History," *http://www.a-wroobeer.com.*

85. "Long John Silver's," *http://www.ljsilvers.com/about/history.htm.*

86. "The Pizza Hut Story," *http://www.pizzahut.com*, p. 6.

87. "Taco Bell History," http://www.tacobell.com.

88. "Discovery Science Center," *http://www.discoverycube.org.*

89. "TEEN SUPREME," http://www.teensupreme.org/main.html.

90. "Pizza Hut Story . . . ," p. 4.

91. Ibid., p. 3.

92. "Pizza Hut News: Facts about Book It and Book It! Beginners," *http://www.pizzahut.com.*

93. "About KFC: The Story of Colonel Harland Sanders," http://www.kfc.com.

94. "Nation's First Colonel's Kids Child Care Center Opens August 4, 2001!," http://www.colonelskids.com.

95. "Colonel's Kids charity–The Child Care Issue," http://www.colonelskids.com.

96. Schlosser . . . , pp. 52–53.

97. Ibid., p. 53.

98. Ibid., p. 53.

99. Ibid., p. 57.

Author Index

Numbers in parentheses are footnote numbers and indicate that an author's work is referred to, although his or her name may not be cited in the text. Numbers in italic show the page where the complete reference is given.

Peterson, L. M., 66(22, 23, 24), 67(25),
    109(57, 58, 59), *217, 223*
Peterson, R. C., 107(48), *223*
Pierce, B. L., 84(104, 105), *220*
Pifer, A., 175(94), *232*
Pinar, W., 91(126), *220*
Pole, J. R., 9(15, 16, 17, 19, 20), *210*
Prucha, F. P., 8(12), *209*
Purdy, M., 1(2), *209*

Q

Quigley, M., 111(66), *223*

R

Rachman, S., 11(26), *210*
Ralston, P. A., 186(14), *233*
Randall, R., 98(13), 105(36), *221*
Raywid, M. A., 131(26), 137(51, 52),
    138(53), *226, 227*
Register, W., 25(84, 85, 86, 87, 88, 89), *212*
Renshaw, S., 107(48), *223*
Roberts, G., Jr., 138(54, 55, 56), *227*
Rosen, P. T., 115(75), *224*
Roth, J., 156(11), *230*
Rotundo, E. A., 72(46, 47), 73(48), *218*
Ruckmick, C., 107(48), *223*
Rudd, A. G., 131(27), 133(37), 134(40),
    226
Rugg, H., 132(28, 29, 30, 31, 32), 134(42),
    135(43, 44), *226*

S

Saunders, A. H., 102(24), *222*
Savan, L., 162(39), 165(48, 49, 52, 53),
    166(54, 55, 56), *231*
Scanlon, J., 45(74), *215*
Schlosser, E., 1(1), 200(69), 201(71, 72, 73),
    202(77), 207(96, 97, 98, 99), *209, 234*
Schrum, K., 79(80), 139(60, 61, 62, 63,
    64), 140(66, 67), *219, 227*
Schrum, L., 184(8), *233*
Shane, J. M., 186(14), *233*
Shapiro, L., 30(7), 31(9, 10), 32(16),
    33(17, 19, 20, 21), 34(22, 23, 24,

26), 35(27, 28), 36(29), 37(32),
    43(60, 61), 44(66, 67), *213*
Sheldon, E. M., 13(33, 34, 35, 36, 37, 38),
    14(39), *210*
Shuttleworth, F., 107(48), *223*
Simerly, C. B., 186(14), *233*
Sivulka, J., 18(54), 21(68), 30(4), 48(89,
    90, 91, 92, 93), 49(97, 98), 52(112),
    53(113, 115), 57(129), 65(16, 17),
    87(116, 117), 88(121), 89(122),
    114(72), 140(65), 149(101), 161(30,
    31), 165(50, 51), 190(34, 35), *224,
    227, 230, 234*
Spigel, L., 151(107, 108, 109, 110), *229*
Spring, J., 5(8), 64(8), 138(57), 139(58,
    59), *209, 217, 227*
Stage, S., 32(13, 14), 33(18), *213*
Stedman, R., 119(90, 91, 92), *224*
Steele, J., 50(99), *215*
Stille, A., 185(9, 10, 11, 12, 13), *233*
Strasser, S., 29(2), 30(5), 44(65, 67),
    88(118, 119, 120), 194(46), *212,
    220, 234*
Stuckey, M. E., 173(85), *232*
Studebaker, J., 136(47), *227*
Sugde, J., 8(13, 14), *209*
Swiencicki, M. A., 64(9, 11), *217*

T

Tannenbaum, A., 147(87, 88), *228*
Taylor, B., 186(14), *233*
Thomas, B., 194(48, 49, 50), 195(51, 52,
    53), 196(55, 56), 197(59, 60), *234*
Thompson, J. W., 50(100, 101, 102, 103),
    215
Thrasher, F., 107(48), *223*
Thurstone, L. L., 107(48), *223*
Tyack, D., 10(23), *210*

V

Vicenti, V. B., 32(15), 34(25), *213*

W

Walker, A., 91(127), 92(128, 129, 130, 131,
    132), 93(133, 134), 94(135), *221*
Warfel, H., 9(18), *210*

Subject Index